YOUR TOWNS & CIT

TYNEMOUTH AND WALLSEND
AT WAR 1939–45

YOUR TOWNS & CITIES IN WORLD WAR TWO

TYNEMOUTH AND WALLSEND
AT WAR 1939–45

CRAIG ARMSTRONG

Pen & Sword
MILITARY

First published in Great Britain in 2018
by Pen & Sword Military
An imprint of Pen & Sword Books Limited
47 Church Street
Barnsley
South Yorkshire
S70 2AS

Copyright © Craig Armstrong 2018

ISBN 978 1 47386 754 3

The right of Craig Armstrong to be identified as Author of this Work has been asserted by him in accordance with the Copyright, Designs and Patents Act 1988.

A CIP catalogue record for this book is available from the British Library.

All rights reserved. No part of this book may be reproduced or transmitted in any form or by any means, electronic or mechanical including photocopying, recording or by any information storage and retrieval system, without permission from the Publisher in writing.

Typeset in Times New Roman by Mac Style

Printed and bound in the UK
by CPI Group (UK) Ltd, Croydon, CR0 4YY

Pen & Sword Books Limited incorporates the imprints of Atlas, Archaeology, Aviation, Discovery, Family History, Fiction, History, Maritime, Military, Military Classics, Politics, Select, Transport, True Crime, Air World, Frontline Publishing, Leo Cooper, Remember When, Seaforth Publishing, The Praetorian Press, Wharncliffe Local History, Wharncliffe Transport, Wharncliffe True Crime and White Owl.

For a complete list of Pen & Sword titles please contact
PEN & SWORD BOOKS LIMITED
47 Church Street, Barnsley, South Yorkshire, S70 2AS, England
E-mail: enquiries@pen-and-sword.co.uk
Website: www.pen-and-sword.co.uk

Contents

Introduction		vi
Chapter 1:	1939: The Clouds Gather	1
Chapter 2:	1940: The Longest Year	20
Chapter 3:	1941: The Continuing Crisis	48
Chapter 4:	1942: The End of the Beginning	75
Chapter 5:	1943: A Year of Victories and Attrition	109
Chapter 6:	1944: The Beginning of the End?	141
Chapter 7:	1945: Victories	182
Conclusion		213
Index		215

Introduction

Tynemouth and Wallsend had, like many areas of the North-East, suffered badly during the inter-war years. The temporary and artificial boom which had propelled industries during the First World War quickly came to an end in peacetime, and traditional heavy industries along the banks of the Tyne found themselves pitted against more advanced overseas rivals competing for a far smaller market. As a result of this, several large and important shipyards and other engineering concerns went out of business altogether, whilst others reduced their workforces and attempted to struggle on.

Unemployment during the inter-war years was a very severe problem in Tynemouth and Wallsend. Although the town of Tynemouth itself largely escaped the more troublesome problems because of its relative wealth and reliance on the service sector, neighbouring North Shields was severely affected and the poverty which went hand-in-hand with unemployment grew worse, with slum conditions affecting many. The series of slum clearances in the 1930s, especially the building of the Ridges Estate,[1] were intended to alleviate this problem, but such was the poverty in the town that the problems of poor living conditions continued to affect many residents.

In Wallsend similar conditions prevailed, largely due to the fact that so many of the residents were reliant upon employment in the shipbuilding, engineering and associated industries. Once again, living conditions in the closely crowded houses were poor, which led to both illness and crime being a concern for the local authority.

The later 1930s, however, saw a resurgence in some of the industries on the Tyne with the rearmaments programme that was being backed by the government in the knowledge of Germany's own rearmament providing much-needed work for the beleaguered shipyards and engineering firms on the Tyne. By 1939, it was increasingly clear to the residents of the area that another war with Germany was coming, and the industries prepared themselves for the conflict. The area also had a well-established reputation for the numbers of men who served in the armed forces, and it was obvious that many of the young men of the area would once again be called upon to fight for their country.

Note
1. Now renamed the Meadowell Estate.

CHAPTER ONE

1939: The Clouds Gather

Due to the geographical location of Tynemouth and Wallsend, the area was key to a large export/import industry, for which the Tyne was the driving force, this industry being dominated by coal and engineering exports and agricultural and timber imports. With the regional capital, Newcastle, just a few miles upriver, the area was also the entry point to a large distribution network and by 1939 more than 51,000 people were employed in the transport and distributive trades on Tyneside. North Shields was also home to a substantial fishing fleet and the businesses which the fishing industry supported (including a guano/fish meal fertilizer factory). Many of the trawlermen who called the port of North Shields home were also members of the Royal Naval Reserve (RNR) and were called up at the start of the war.

North Shields and particularly Wallsend were dominated by engineering and shipbuilding giants such as Swan Hunters, but the war came at a time when the yards were still suffering from some of the effects of the slump which followed the decades after the First World War. The latter part of the Thirties had seen some improvement as military orders started to flow in as a result of the rearmament policy which the government instituted. However, the higher demands from home came at a time of slack orders from abroad and the miniature boom was an artificial and ultimately unsustainable one.

Not that many of the masses of unemployed on Tyneside cared about such causes, and when the first year of the war resulted in an increase in engineering jobs of over 20,000 there were no complaints. The expansion of Vickers Armstrong in Newcastle was responsible for many, but there were also vacancies filled in various other shipbuilding yards and engineering concerns in Tynemouth and Wallsend. Unfortunately, many of the engineering magnates of the area let themselves be seduced by the immediate wartime boom and ignored the fact that in preparations for the future they would have to plan for a swift decrease in orders once the war ended.

Wallsend was a largely working-class urban area which was dominated by shipbuilding and heavy engineering, although there were also a number of other concerns, ranging from T.W. Clark & Sons – who owned the Mid-Tyne Pickle Works on Birket Street – to the dyers Johnson Bros Ltd. Other large industrial concerns included: W.R. Dixon & Co. Ltd, steel packing manufacturers; R.N. Dodds & Son, iron workers; Duit Engineering Co. Ltd; Robert Dickie Lambie, boat builders; the car manufacturer Lanchester Motor Co. Ltd.; McVickers & Co. Ltd, printers; Monitor Patent Safety Devices Ltd; North Eastern Marine Engineering Co. Ltd; Ogle & Wordsworth, sheet metal workers; Parsons Marine Steam Turbine Co. Ltd; T.B. Pearson & Sons, engineers; the Seaton Burn Coal Co. Ltd; the Singer Sewing Machine Co. Ltd; Swan Hunter & Wigham Richardson Ltd; W.M. Swinburne & Sons Ltd, brassfounders; the Thermal Syndicate Ltd, manufacturers of silica, magnesia and alumina; Wallsend & Hebburn Coal Co. Ltd; Wallsend Slipway & Engineering Co. Ltd (a subsidiary of Swan Hunter's); and Watson-Norie Ltd, electrical engineers. All of these companies became involved in the manufacture of military equipment in addition to and sometimes in place of their regular product lines.

Although shipbuilding and marine engineering dominated the engineering scene in the town, even this area of industry was remarkably varied. One of the most important alternative engineering concerns was the firm of Charles Crofton & Co. Ltd. From its beginning in 1929 at Newcastle, the firm had built up its lines of electric rotary drills, flameproof plugs and sockets and miscellaneous equipment for the coalmining industry. By 1931, the firm had taken out patents on its new designs of electric rotary drills, which it named 'Victor'. The increasing use of machinery in the mines meant that the company thrived throughout the 1930s, with a breakthrough being the production of the revolutionary 'Ardeloy' drill bit which sold in the millions and allowed the company to relocate to Wallsend.

At nearby Howdon (Willington Quay), there were several other large industrial concerns which would make a contribution to the war effort and which would probably be targets for the Luftwaffe. One of the main sites was the Befola oil works of George Catcheside Ltd.

Tynemouth Borough, and especially North Shields, was also home to major industrial concerns. There was the large oil depot of the Anglo-American Oil Co. Ltd at Tynemouth Road, which would have been a prime target and appeared on Luftwaffe bombing maps found after the war. There were a large and varied number of industrial concerns which all played a role in wartime production.

Sample of Industries in North Shields

Company	Type
Fred W. Johnson & Sons Ltd	Electrical & Wireless Engineers
Ringtons Ltd	Tea Merchants
William Russell	Motor Engineers
Albert Edward Dock Sawmills Ltd	Sawmills & Timber Merchant
Robert A. Anderson Ltd	Salters
Armstrong, Addison & Co	Timber Merchants
Backworth Colliery Co. Ltd	Coal Merchants
Baird Bros Ltd	Marine Engineers
Bedford Paper Stores	Paper Manufacturer & Merchant
T.B. Bilton & Sons Ltd	Coppersmiths
Bonham Electrical & Engineering Co. Ltd	Electrical Engineering
J. Bradburn & Co. Ltd	Dyers
British & Argentine Meat Co. Ltd	Meat Importer/Exporter
Brown, Hardy, Tinn & Co. Ltd	Paint Manufacturer
Burton & Son	Dyer
Coast Road Motor Co. Ltd	Motor Engineers & Trader
Cookson Lead & Antimony Co. Ltd	Lead Paint/Products Manufacturer
County Coal Co.	Coal Merchants
Joseph William Dale & Son	Engineers
J. Dampney & Co. Ltd	Paint Manufacturer
Electric Equipments Ltd	Electrical Engineers
Empire Engraving Co.	Maritime Engravers
Empire Tea & Butter Stores	Tea & Butter Merchant

Company	Type
Evans, Reid, Teasdale, Lidstrong Ltd	Timber Merchants
George Fleming & Son Ltd	Tarpaulin Manufacturer
Gray Bros	Motor Engineers & Manufacturer
Hartley Main Collieries Ltd	Coal Merchants
James Hogg & Sons Ltd	Brass Founders
Hoover Ltd	Vacuum Cleaner Manufacturer
Percy A. Hudson Ltd	Sawmills & Timber Merchants
Johnson Bros Ltd	Dyers
Karoyl Super Lubricants	Oil Merchants & Stores
Kleen-e-ze Brush Co. Ltd	Brush Manufacturer
L. & C. Rubber Co. Ltd	Rubber Manufacturer
E.M. Martin & Co	Wholesale Sausage Manufacturer
S. Matthews & Co	Firewood Merchant
J. Mayo & Co	Wireless Engineers
North Eastern Rubber Co. Ltd	Rubber Manufacturer
North Shields Fish Guano & Oil Co. Ltd	Fertilizer Manufacturer
Osbeck & Co. Ltd	Timber Merchants
Payne & Hornsby Ltd	Wireless Engineers
Pyman, Bell & Co. Ltd	Timber Merchants
Renown Boxwood Co. Ltd	Box Manufacturers
James Riley & Co.	Timber Merchants
George S. Robinson & Co.	Tinplate Workers
Robson Miller's Sawmills Ltd	Sawmills & Timber Merchant
Stephen L. Robson & Son Ltd	Timber Merchants
Peter A. Scarth & Co.	Timber Merchants
Shell-Mex & BP Ltd	Petroleum Merchants
Shields Coal & Lime Deposits	Coal & Lime Merchants
Singer Sewing Machine Co. Ltd	Sewing Machine Manufacturer
Thirlwell Spring-lock & Engineering Co. Ltd	Engineers
United Yeast Co. Ltd	Yeast Manufacturers & Merchants

1939: THE CLOUDS GATHER

Maritime & Fishing Companies at North Shields

Company	Type
Anchor Line	Steam Tugs
Harold A. Anderson	Tugs
G.S. Ballard & Sons	Fish Curers
James Bell & Sons	Fish Buyers
Isak Clemmetsen	Ships Chandler
Coast Packing Co.	Dry Salters
Joseph Crosthwaite Tugs Ltd	Tugs
Edward J. Fleming	Fish Merchants
Frazer & Co.	Ships Store Merchants
William Freestone	Fish Curer & Buyer
Alfred John Freeth	Ships Chandler
Sarah Elizabeth Gaer	Ships Chandler
Andreas Geilberg & Co. Ltd	Fish Merchants
Gourock Ropework Co. Ltd	Rope Manufacturer & Merchant
W. & A. Grix	Fish Merchants
R. Hood Haggie & Son Ltd	Rope, Twine & Wire Rope Maker
Thomas Hails	Fish Curer
Harrison, Robinson & Otto Ltd	Ships Chandler
Robert Hastie & Sons Ltd	Trawler Owners & Fish Sellers
Hastings & Stewart	Fish Merchants
Henry Horn & Sons	Fish Curers
George Hunter	Fish Merchants
Hurst & Duff	Fish Merchants
R. Irvin & Sons Ltd	Trawler Owners & Fish Sellers
Sam Larkin	Fish Buyer
George Lauder	Fish Merchant
Thomas Lawson & Co.	Basket Makers
B. & C. Lidgard	Fish Merchants
John Lilley & Sons Ltd	Compass Manufacturers
Linkleters Patent Ship Fittings Co. Ltd	Ships Fittings & Chandler
Marshall & Co.	Shipbuilding Suppliers

Company	Type
James Miller & Sons	Fish Curers
John Miller	Fish Curer
Morrison & Co. Ltd	Ships Stores Dealer
Newtons' Ltd	Fish Curers
Ogilvie & Son	Salt Merchants
Robert Oliver	Fish Curer
F.H. Phillips & Co.	Fish Merchants
N.V. Polites & Co	Ships Stores Merchants
G.R. Purdy Trawlers Ltd	Trawler Owners & Fish Sellers
William Rayner	Fish Buyer
Reed, Phillips & Co. Ltd	Fish Merchants
Joseph Robinson & Sons	Ship Owners
Robson & Matthews	Ships Chandlers
Rutherford Bros	Trawler Owners
J. Sampson & Son	Fish Curers
Robert Saunders	Fish Merchants
Shields Engineering & Dry Dock Co. Ltd	Ship Repairers
Shields Ice & Cold Storage Co. Ltd	Ice & Canned Fish Manufacturers
J. & H. Smart	Fish Merchants
Smith's Dock Co. Ltd	Ship Repairers
Stag Line Ltd	Ship Owners
Ronald Sutton	Fish Merchant
Nicholas Tripovitch	Seamen's Outfitter
Tyne Fisheries Ltd	Fish Merchants
Union Anti-Fouling Composition Co. Ltd	Anti-Fouling Paint Manufacturer
E.H. Vyse & Co.	Fish Merchants
Samuel H. Walker	Fish Merchants
William Wight Ltd[1]	Ships Chandler
J. Willits & Sons	Fish Merchants
William Wilson	Fish Merchants & Curers
Matthew Wood	Fish Merchant

The many important shipyards in the area not only made the area a key target for the Luftwaffe, but also an important part of the national war effort. With the rearmaments programme in full swing, many of the yards already had work on hand for the Admiralty. One of the earliest vessels to be completed during the war was the 13,175-ton Town Class light cruiser HMS *Edinburgh*, which had been launched by Swan Hunter in 1938 and was completed in July 1939.[1] In the same year,

HMS *Kashmir, which was HMS* Khartoum's *almost identical sister ship.* (Public Domain)

HMS *Edinburgh, completed by Swan Hunter in 1939 and scuttled in 1942.* (Public Domain)

HMS Tartar, *launched at Swan Hunter in 1939, led a charmed life and had an eventful wartime career.* (Public Domain)

Swan Hunter completed three further naval vessels (all destroyers): HMS *Janus*, HMS *Khartoum* and HMS *Tartar*.[2]

The introduction of the blackout caused significant problems in the licensed trade. The conditions of the blackout forced many local authorities to curtail late-night tram and bus services, and this had a knock-on effect on the licensed trade. In December 1939, Tynemouth Borough Council wrote to the Licensed Trade Association informing them that public transport services would cease at 10.00 pm due to the restrictions on street lighting. This resulted in a succession of meetings to discuss the possible responses to this predicament. Proposals included the early opening and closing of pubs, but this would require the permission of the Brewery Sessions, whilst early closing was disagreeable because it would mean that public houses would lose custom to clubs which did not close early.[3] The majority of local breweries decided to have their pubs stop serving at 9.30 pm so that customers and staff could use public transport to get home.

The initial formation of ARP services in some parts of the area seems to have been ponderously slow and marked by petty officialdom, which slowed its progress even further. By the time of the Munich Crisis, there were only eighteen enrolled and trained wardens in the Whitley Bay Urban District area. This in turn led to problems with the training of other warden volunteers. Throughout 1938, recruitment meetings were widely held in the area and although attendances were always reportedly high, this failed to be converted into large numbers of completed application forms. In Whitley Bay, the number of completed forms was only 5 per cent of those distributed at meetings.[4]

By early 1939, with war looking increasingly likely, the local authorities were distinctly worried by the manpower shortages in the proposed ARP schemes and resorted to a large-scale publicity campaign, with posters and advertisements at cinema shows and sports meetings. During this period, it would seem that many women volunteered for duty in the ARP services, with a large ratio of public shelter wardens in the area being women who were well known in the local community.

Training of wardens, however, remained problematic, with the authorities being unaware of exactly what would be expected of the service in the event of aerial bombardment. Many early classes throughout 1939 focused largely on anti-gas measures, highlighting the fears of this type of attack taking place. Another focus was in the methodology of enforcing the widely disliked blackout, a reason many overly zealous wardens became instantly unpopular before large-scale attacks took place. Much of the training was led by those few wardens who were already fully trained, but as the year went on the scheme became more organized. Local and regional exercises and simulations of raids became a focus for the training regimen, and these proved beneficial to the newly appointed wardens and other ARP workers as well as allowing the organizations to resolve problems and develop new techniques.

The ARP services would have to work in close cooperation with the first aid parties who could be called to respond to an incident by the area controller. The first aid parties were based at the established first aid posts in every sector, and the activities of these men and women involved great courage, often under fire. In Tynemouth, the first aid headquarters was at Holmlands beside Preston Hospital, home to a number of first aid parties, whilst others were scattered throughout the borough. At Whitley Bay, there were two first aid posts (at the Garden Cafe and West Monkseaton High School) which were home to nine first aid parties and eleven ambulances. These roles demanded a high degree of commitment, as the posts had to be manned for twenty-four hours a day and the first aid parties were expected to respond to incidents even when heavy raids were still taking place and there were a number of casualties suffered as a result.

With incendiary bombs expected to start widespread fires, it was also recognized that the regular fire brigade would likely be quickly overwhelmed, so men were sought to form the Auxiliary Fire Service (AFS), which would respond to the same incidents as regular firemen and, although purely voluntary, would be paid the same rate as regulars (a fact which caused some resentment amongst regular firemen). The men of the AFS were initially woefully inexperienced and, for many of them, their first incident response would be their first experience of fighting a fire. AFS men served forty-eight hours on and twenty-four hours off, and the force consisted of roughly 40 per cent full-time members and 60 per cent part-time.

The AFS was at first not only inexperienced, but suffered from horrendous equipment shortages, with many crews using private cars to attend incidents and even uniforms initially being a problem. Typical of the poor equipment possessed by the AFS was the Whitley Bay branch, which had only two fire engines and relied upon its eighteen trailer pumps. The trailer pumps, many of which were manufactured locally, were vital to all of the area's AFS units, and the equipping of AFS (and regular) fire units with the Sigmund pump would prove of great value in the heavy raids of 1941. The ubiquitous item of equipment which became so familiar to AFS men, however, was the stirrup pump, which could be used to extinguish minor blazes such as small single incendiary bombs.

Possibly the greatest physical demand fell on the men of the rescue squads (which were divided into heavy and light categories), who were expected to shift debris and remove obstacles to rescue those trapped in bombed buildings. Many of the men were council employees and physical fitness was a prerequisite for the role. However, there was also some degree of technical know-how required, as the safe extraction of trapped persons required some knowledge of construction and, in some cases, of mining techniques required to shore up debris to prevent further collapses. The men of the rescue squads in the area seem to have attracted the reputation of being the leading rumour-mongers in the ARP services, possibly because they spent some time refreshing themselves, after their labours, in ARP canteens.

Like many other ARP services, the men of the rescue squads also filled in in other roles. Many rescue squads (and their vehicles) were used to help the established salvage and storage squads to transport salvaged goods from bombed premises to secure sites.

Before the war even began, the government was planning for the evacuation of children and the vulnerable from areas in which aerial bombardment might be expected. This covered much of the North-East, with its valuable industries, ports and geographical position. However, there seems to have been some initial muddle over the process, and concerns were voiced in March over the splitting of the evacuation areas along artificial local authority boundaries. The community of Wallsend was particularly concerned because, as things stood, whilst children from Newcastle would be immediately evacuated, those in Wallsend, which bordered Newcastle and in many areas was largely indistinguishable, would not be evacuated. This was obviously unacceptable and the local press highlighted the issues, repeatedly stating that the scheme had been put together hurriedly and without expert local knowledge or consultation. The local authorities were also concerned over the scheme and had petitioned the Minister of Health over the matter. This resulted in a conference being held, including representatives of the Ministry of Health and several local authorities, including both Wallsend and Tynemouth. The local press praised this, saying that it would allow the Whitehall representatives to see that there were 'other crowded areas on Tyneside besides Newcastle and Gateshead'.[5]

At the end of June, it was announced that many Tynemouth parents had told the authorities that they would refuse to be parted from their children in the event of war and wanted no part in the evacuation scheme. One teacher asked her pupils what their parents had decided, and a typical answer was supplied by one young girl who answered that her parents would not send her away, stating 'if the worst happens, we will all go together'. An editorial in a local newspaper criticized these results and put the blame on the authorities for not informing people just how deadly a bombing campaign could be, declaring that not enough had been done 'to give them a true picture of how hideous and brutal the next war will be'.[6]

The day after war was declared, attention quickly focussed on necessary wartime measures. The pre-prepared evacuation scheme quickly swung into action, with schoolchildren in both Tynemouth and Wallsend being told to report to their schools on the afternoon of Monday, 4 September, when their gas masks and other evacuation kit would be inspected whilst teachers, who were to be evacuated with their charges, were told to report to their schools at 9.00 am in order to finalize the organization of the evacuation. In both areas, the plan was to evacuate schoolchildren and teachers on Wednesday, 6 September, followed by other eligible people including children under school age (with their mothers), pregnant women and certain other adults such as the blind on the following day. In all other respects, normal schooling was suspended in evacuation areas for at least a week.

Amidst bright, sunny conditions the children from Tynemouth and Wallsend were evacuated on schedule, with groups of classmates being escorted by teachers and volunteer marshals who accompanied them on the buses and trains which took them to their rural destinations. From Tynemouth, an estimated 2,000 children were evacuated on 6 September to seven rural Northumberland destinations. The Tynemouth children assembled with their teachers and volunteer helpers at North Shields station, from where they were taken by train to their destination district. The only exception were the children from Percy Main, who left from Percy Main station. At both stations there were large crowds assembled to see the children off, despite government warnings not to gather in large numbers.

Children at Christ Church School, North Shields, having their gas masks inspected prior to evacuation. (Shields Daily News)

1939: THE CLOUDS GATHER

Destinations of Tynemouth Schoolchildren Evacuees, September 1939

Location	Number of Children
Rothbury	479
Bellingham	Approx. 300
Morpeth	444
Wooler	366
Norham	88
Belford	255
Hexham	70

From Wallsend, 350 schoolchildren along with forty-two teachers and eight volunteers left the town by bus or car to their appointed billeting area in and around Haltwhistle in the Tyne Valley. The evacuees met with an enthusiastic welcome in Haltwhistle, where sandwiches and soup were immediately provided. A further contingent left by train for Morpeth, where they were to be billeted in the surrounding rural areas.

Of course, some children had already been evacuated prior to this, and a journalist from the *Evening Chronicle* was able to report on 6 September that whilst touring the Morpeth area he had found the majority of evacuees settling in gradually and coming to terms with their unfamiliar rural surroundings. The reporter also found that some in the rural areas were taking great delight in assisting in farm tasks, including haymaking. However, the children he interviewed who were involved on this particular farm also demonstrated some of the inevitable dislocation that evacuation caused. Sharing a farmhouse tea, the reporter took the opportunity to interview the farmwife who was caring for the evacuees. She told him that one of the children had asked her what she was putting in his tea, and when she told him it was milk from the cows on the farm he replied that 'they always got it out

A marshal leads a group of Wallsend evacuees to the train station. (Evening Chronicle)

Richardson Dees School, Wallsend, being evacuated. (*Evening Chronicle*)

of [a] tin!'. The journalist was also able to reassure anxious parents that children in the areas of Longhorsley, Pegswood and Lynemouth had met with enthusiastic welcomes, with families (many of whom already had children) clamouring for children to be billeted with them, and that the children in these areas were being well looked after, being 'as happy as anywhere'.[7]

The completion of Tynemouth's evacuation scheme followed the day after the 2,000 schoolchildren had been sent off. Consisting of mothers and young children, pregnant women and the disabled, there were fewer people than expected. The first batch left North Shields at 9.30 am, bound for the Rothbury and Bellingham areas, and was 200 people short of estimates. The next group left for Tweedsmouth, Belford and Wooler shortly after midday, and was again understrength. This was repeated throughout the day, with reports of empty and partially empty train carriages as people had last-minute changes of mind, and officials were forced to admit that 'the number [which] left was far below that catered for'. The second batch had left from Queen Victoria School in North Shields and was led most of the way by a black cat, which many took to be a lucky omen. One young lad, Tommy, was left sorely disappointed when his mother refused to let them take the cat with them, despite his protestations that it would be safer in the countryside.

In all cases the evacuees were aided by large numbers of volunteers, including many fathers who were in uniform, who gave unstinting service for which they were subsequently praised by the authorities. The local press reported that when the youngsters and women departed, the men left behind wore expressions of relief and were 'obviously happy in the knowledge that their loved ones were hastening to havens of safety'. One middle-aged lance-corporal, interviewed by a journalist, commented: 'It means a lot to know they're safe.'[8]

The final group to leave, consisting of the disabled and some others, was consistent with expectations in terms of numbers, and there were sad scenes as they left the station, waving goodbye to friends and family. A local commented on two particular scenes when a 'legless man helped a blind evacuee to find a seat whilst nearby another cripple held a mother's child as she searched for its bottle of milk'.[9]

The evacuation scheme was not a great success in Tynemouth or Wallsend, despite widespread popularity (if not enthusiasm) in other areas of Tyneside. There would certainly seem to be evidence that the more working-class districts were the most reluctant to send their children away, even though these were the areas likely to be hit hardest due to their proximity to important industries and the overcrowded housing conditions. In the first wave of evacuations, only 29 per cent of eligible children from Tynemouth and Wallsend took up the opportunity (compared with 57 per cent from Newcastle, 28 per cent from Jarrow and just 26 per cent from South Shields).[10] These figures, however, are only for those who signed up to the official evacuation scheme. Others, especially in the more middle-class areas of Tynemouth, made their own arrangements for evacuation. However, it was not only the middle-classes who took this option: there is evidence that some working-class families also evacuated their children (often accompanied by one of their parents or other relatives).[11] Interestingly, it would seem that fairly large numbers took this route, as the Mayor of Tynemouth, Councillor Harry Gee, gave figures (which included all of those who had been evacuated) which imply that an additional 10 per cent in Tynemouth Borough had been evacuated unofficially (the figures given were 1,782 evacuees out of a total of 4,672 who were eligible).[12]

Because of the somewhat disappointing response to the official evacuation scheme, it was agreed that a second wave of evacuation would be offered in Tynemouth in mid-September. This also failed, with only 150 enrolments taking place as a mood of apathy was detected in the wake of the lack of immediate bombing. The Mayor of Tynemouth was at a loss to explain this apathy, as he had expected a substantial response. Admitting to a reporter that he could not explain the lack of enthusiasm, he said that 'apathy towards evacuation appears to be pretty general', with a lot of people preferring their families to remain together, although he added that 'if there is an air raid, I am afraid it will alter a lot of their opinions'. Councillor Gee also believed the evacuation should have taken place earlier in the year, as people may have been more receptive. His rather flimsy evidence for this is that he thought some people did not want to spend a winter in the countryside.[13]

For many, the beginning of the war meant reporting for assigned wartime duties. This obviously included members of organizations such as the Territorial Army, Royal Naval Reserve (RNR), Royal Naval Volunteer Reserve (RNVR) and Royal Air Force Volunteer Reserve (RAFVR), but others to be called up immediately included those who were on the civil nursing reserve register, who were ordered to report to their wartime hospital posts immediately.

Even for those not affected immediately by call-ups, the war meant an immediate disruption to routine. The government issued immediate guidelines which urged people not to crowd together, to keep the streets as quiet as possible and to carry their gas masks continually. In order to facilitate the order to avoid crowding of public areas, many places of entertainment were immediately closed, including theatres and cinemas. The government said that if bombing did not immediately develop, there was a possibility that these places would be reopened in less vulnerable areas. Many sporting events were also suspended until further notice, but churches and other places of worship were allowed to remain open in order to allow the public to seek religious solace and reassurance.

Amongst the services which became more restrictive was the opening hours of banks in the district. In the first week of the war, Tynemouth Savings Bank announced that its branches would only be open from 10.00 am until 2.00 pm Monday to Saturday, with no evening opening hours due to the blackout. Meanwhile, Lloyds,

Barclays and Midlands Bank also announced that their local branches would be restricting their hours in a similar fashion (although they would shut an hour earlier on Saturdays), whilst the Lloyds branch on Bedford Street was to close at 12.30 pm on Saturdays and the Fish Quay branch would close for the duration of the war.

Whilst the first meeting of the Tynemouth Food Control Committee took place in the first week of the war, many local business owners were discussing the likelihood of opening hours for shops being restricted due to supply issues and the blackout restrictions. With the support of North Shields Chamber of Trade, Councillor Gee urged all businesses to consider closing earlier during the war. The butchers of Tynemouth Borough had already acted, restricting their hours to 6.00 pm on Monday, Tuesday and Thursday and 7.00 pm on Friday and Saturday (Wednesday was early closing day anyway). By the end of the first week of the war, these recommendations had been agreed upon and all grocery and provisions stores in the Tynemouth, Wallsend, Monkseaton and Whitley Bay area would close at 6.00 pm on Monday, Tuesday and Thursday (they closed at 1.00 pm on Wednesday), 7.00 pm on Friday and 8.00 pm on Saturday, although it was also agreed that these hours would be flexible according to season and local conditions.

For many in the Wallsend area, one of the most noticeable early signs of the war impinging on civilian routine was the absence of the noise of hooters, klaxons and sirens which had been part of working life next to the extensive shipyards of the area. Their sounding was forbidden as it could be confused with the sound of air raid warning sirens.

With the rationing of fuel supplies through a coupon system, it was clear that hauliers would be badly affected, so a registration system was quickly brought in to categorize haulage vehicles and enable operators to obtain a supply of fuel so as to go about their business. At North Shields, a sub-district office covering Tynemouth and Wallsend Boroughs, along with Monkseaton and Seaton Valley Urban Districts, was opened at 17 Northumberland Square. On 7 September, hauliers were told to obtain pamphlets which would explain the situation of classification and to register their vehicles at the office immediately.

As the first wartime Christmas approached, people began planning how to celebrate as traditionally as possible, despite the rationing and other restrictions. At Tynemouth and North Shields, it was reported that the shops did a roaring trade on Christmas Eve, with many people rushing to complete their shopping despite the blackout. Many shopkeepers reported setting new record sales during the period; it would appear that people were determined to celebrate despite the international situation. The restrictions on shopping hours had been suspended for Christmas Eve, but the shops were so busy during the day that most managed to close by 9.00 pm.

The weather at Christmas was unseasonably mild and the day was marked quietly, with family celebrations at home being the main feature. The seafront from Tynemouth to Whitley Bay was busy on both Christmas Day and Boxing Day as people took advantage of the good weather to enjoy a stroll. It was reported that there were far fewer carol singers about on Christmas morning than in recent years, whilst the matinee showings at the cinemas on Christmas Day and Boxing Day were all sold out. Whitley Bay was reportedly very quiet, with very few parties or dances being held to celebrate the festive season, but the cinemas were again very well attended.

Notes
1. HMS *Edinburgh* was scuttled whilst returning to Scapa Flow from Murmansk on 2 May 1942 after being badly damaged by enemy torpedoes. She was carrying a cargo of over 4,500kg of gold from the Soviet government when she sunk (valued today at over £63 million). Most of the gold was recovered between 1981–1986, although five ingots remain unaccounted for.
2. HMS *Janus* was destroyed by German aircraft off Anzio in 1944. HMS *Khartoum* was sunk in the harbour of Perim in the Red Sea following battle with an Italian submarine. A fire spread to the aft magazine of HMS *Khartoum* as she lay partially sunk. HMS *Tartar* had a very eventful career, during which she was partially responsible for the securing of important documents from the German weather ship *Lauenburg*, while during the Allied D-Day landings the ship was part of a destroyer flotilla which successfully intercepted a German destroyer group attempting to attack the landings. Because of her seemingly charmed life, the ship was christened 'Lucky Tartar' and was one of just four from sixteen Tribal Class destroyers to survive the war.
3. [T]yne & [W]ear [A]rchive [S]ervice: EM/LT/1/1. Licensed Trade Employer's Association (Minute Book), records of general meeting, 29 March 1939.
4. TWAS: MB/WB/27/1 (T135/45). Whitley Bay Urban District Council (ARP Committee).
5. *Shields Daily News*, 8 March 1939, p.4.
6. *Shields Daily News*, 30 June 1939, p.4.

7. *Evening Chronicle*, 6 September 1939, p.5.
8. *Shields Daily News*, 7 September 1939, p.2.
9. *Shields Daily News*, 7 September 1939, p.2.
10. Brown, M., *Evacuees: Evacuation in Wartime Britain 19391945* (Stroud: Sutton Publishing, 2000), p.20.
11. Indeed, the author's father and his siblings evacuated (with their mother) from North Shields (where his father was a trawler skipper now serving as skipper of a minesweeper) to Alston in Cumbria. They remained there, quite cheerfully, until early 1941, when, missing their home, they returned, just in time for the main period of bombing on Tyneside!
12. *Shields Daily News*, 13 September 1939, p.2.
13. *Shields Daily News*, 13 September 1939, p.2.

CHAPTER TWO

1940: The Longest Year

The fall of Norway, tales of the effectiveness of the Germans' use of a fifth column of traitors, the installation of the Quisling government in Oslo, a ferocious press campaign and the likely entry of Italy into the war on the side of the Axis all combined to place pressure on the government to intern greater numbers of foreigners. With public pressure beginning to turn against such aliens, the government acted on 11 May by ordering all police forces to take into custody all registered enemy (i.e German, Austrian, etc) aliens so that they could be assessed for internment. The police raids began on the next morning, a quiet Sunday. By Monday morning, twenty men at Whitley Bay but only two at North Shields and one at Wallsend had been taken into custody and were being sent to internment camps.

The local press were generally in favour of the internment policy, with a regular column in the *Shields Daily News* opining on 16 May that the policy of interning all enemy aliens was an agreeable one given the circumstances, and claiming that all enemy aliens, hostile or friendly, posed 'a risk which we do not intend to run and the proper place for them is a camp out of harm's way'. However, the opinion piece was at pains to discourage some of the virulent anti-foreigner activity which had occurred during the First World War, stating that there was nothing to be gained from throwing stones through shop windows 'like crowds of Italian schoolchildren'. It pointed out that some of the families with German names who lived in North Shields had resided in the town for over 100 years, and many had fought on the side of the Allies during the Great War. The paper also pointed to the fact that not all naturalized Germans were Nazis, adding that the majority wanted no part of fighting for Hitler. The author went on to say that the question of enemy aliens was best left to the authorities and the alien community themselves, adding, in an attempt at reassurance: 'They are just as anxious as those of us who have not a drop of alien blood in us to win our battle.' However, the paper said that if people heard a foreigner making dangerous or pro-Nazi comments, the best course of action was to inform the police.

As the fighting in France intensified through May, there were a number of local casualties. On 27 May, 34-year old Gunner Robert Noble Metcalfe of 296 Battery, Royal Field Artillery, died aboard a hospital ship whilst being transported to England. Gunner Metcalfe was from Laburnum Avenue, North Shields, and left behind a widow and five young children aged from five months to 11 years. Metcalfe, a member of the Territorials for over eight years, was buried with full military honours in his home town at Preston Cemetery.

Gunner Metcalfe, RFA, from North Shields, was wounded during Battle of France and died whilst being evacuated aboard a hospital ship. (Shields Evening News)

Many associate Dunkirk with only the Army and the Royal Navy, and there was indeed some criticism of the RAF by members of the Army especially, but this was unfounded. RAF Fighter Command was in action daily against large numbers of Luftwaffe fighters and bombers. The RAF fighters were not often seen over the beaches, as they were generally fighting further inland in an attempt to prevent the Luftwaffe from bombing and strafing the masses of British (and French) troops who were gathered on the beaches and to stop bombers from launching attacks against the massed ships which were attempting to rescue the troops. One of those in action was Flight Lieutenant Denys Gillam from Tynemouth. Serving with 616 Squadron, flying Spitfires, Gillam claimed a *JU88* as destroyed on 1 June.

We have already heard something of the Wallsend-based engineering firm Charles Crofton & Co. Ltd. Whilst the mining products which the firm constructed were seen as vital to the war effort, there were other items which, the government decided, were more important. Therefore, 60 per cent of the firm's wartime production was turned over to military items of equipment, including fuel tanks and petrol pumps for Wellington bombers, tank tracks, shell discs, valves for naval vessels, glider release devices and a host of other components. The firm was quick to embrace the necessity of employing far greater numbers of female workers, leading the way in this. Indeed, the firm was innovative in many ways. It was reportedly the first nationally and certainly the first in the North-East to create a Works Committee to oversee closer relations between management and employees. The firm also put in place a suggestion scheme which allowed employees to offer ideas aimed at improving products and increasing productivity and efficiency, with rewards being given to employees who made useful suggestions.

The medical services at Whitley Bay had their first test early in the summer when four bodies, two British seamen and two German airmen, were washed ashore. This early experience allowed the mortuary and its staff to test procedures for identifying and arranging for the burial of those killed by enemy action.

The training of the ARP services continued throughout 1940, with a number of exercises being organized during the early months of the year. In the early spring a simulated attack exercise revealed some confusion and lack of efficiency in the messaging service, which was vital to the functioning of the ARP and emergency services during an air raid or attack. As a result of this, a further exercise was held at the end of May which focussed on the messaging service. This determined that there were too many formats for messages, which resulted in confusion and delay. The format of messages was therefore slimmed down and several types of message were discontinued. This resulted in a far more efficient service, which in turn improved the overall effectiveness of the local ARP scheme. The results of these exercises were shared between neighbouring authorities, and were used to improve the effectiveness of nearby ARP services and to enable greater coordination between areas; something which was very useful as localized raids made local assistance from neighbouring authorities vital. Other training methods employed locally included visiting lecturers from across the country who spoke on a variety of topics which would be of use to the ARP services.

Although, as we have seen, the ARP services were willing, and even keen, to learn from neighbouring areas, there were still teething problems in the period before heavy raids began. Local authorities tended to initially create schemes which were far too complicated and, as a result, were inefficient and prone to breakdown in the event of an emergency. Whitley Bay was a typical example of this. When initiated, the Whitley Bay area (consisting of approximately 50,000 residents) was comprised of fifty-two sectors, each with its own warden post. As the experiences of bombing in other parts of the country and early incidents in the North-East were absorbed, it became clear that this system was far too cumbersome and the number of sectors was reduced to fifteen.

Warden posts were manned by a number of wardens under the command of a head warden. It was the responsibility of wardens to react to incidents in their sector and report the facts back so that the Area Controller in the control post could have an overview of events and allocate units in an efficient manner. Wardens were generally locals in their sector and were expected to be the first to respond to any incident. They thus had great responsibility placed upon them and were expected to deal with scenes which many of them would never have encountered before. Wardens developed relationships with the residents in their sector, and in many cases this was a positive development which bolstered morale, but where a warden was disliked (often because he or she was seen as overly zealous or interfering) morale in a sector could sag. Wardens had a large amount of power, which often went beyond the scope of their role as a warden: many wardens in the area developed their own schemes of volunteer fire watchers or fire fighters equipped with stirrup pumps.

There were still severe problems in some areas of the ARP scheme, with many of those who had been enrolled and trained in Tynemouth failing to report for duty. By May, the mayor was issuing calls for all such people to report to their stations as their services were now urgently needed. The mayor also appealed for all of those who wished to serve in any ARP capacity to register their interest at the ARP headquarters in Cleveland Road, North Shields. The events in Europe had led a new impetus to ARP recruitment, and the mayor agreeing with the Regional Controller, Sir Arthur Lambert, who had issued a similar appeal urged every able-bodied adult of the correct age to register as they would forever regret not doing their part, just a few hours a week, if Britain was attacked by Germany.

The ARP services consisted of a variety of groups with different responsibilities and specialisms. Amongst these were the men of the Gas and Decontamination Squads, who were often chemists, who would be responsible for reacting to any chemical attack launched by the enemy. Throughout 1940 this remained a real possibility, and although no such attack developed the men of the area's squads still found themselves called upon. Often they would attend the same incidents as their ARP colleagues and would do their bit in assisting wardens and rescue squads. There were also several false alarms when concerned citizens believed they could smell gas; each incident had to be responded to as if it was the real thing. A typical example of this occurred in September, when the Whitley Bay decontamination and gas squad responded to a call that phosgene gas could be smelled. Responding quickly and taking full precautions, the squad investigated before establishing that the cause of the aroma was in fact a bed of geraniums in a neighbouring garden!

Sir Arthur Lambert also proposed that Sunday, 9 June should be a Civil Defence Sunday throughout the area, with all ARP volunteers attending civil parades and church services. Whilst many areas complied with this, in Tynemouth the suggestion was met with a more sceptical response. The mayor eventually decided that the suggestion would not be taken up in the borough as, with the present state of affairs in Europe, he believed that gathering all of the borough's ARP forces in one place would be risky if an incident requiring their response occurred.

With the rush of volunteers in a wide variety of organizations, there were questions raised over the physical fitness of some. In response to this, instructors provided by the Football Association and the armed forces organized a nationwide scheme of fitness training for ARP personnel and those who had signed up for the forces but were awaiting call-up. In Tynemouth Borough, training took place at the home of North Shields FC, Appleby Park, and by mid-July 100 men were attending sessions four days a week. The local ARP Controller, Councillor Harry Gee, was enthusiastic and got in touch with the organizer of the local scheme, Mr Stan Shotton, who informed him that ARP personnel would be especially welcome and assured him that he had sufficient instructors for another 200300 participants. Mr Shotton proposed moving the Saturday afternoon session to a Sunday morning so that those employed in the retail trades could participate. Mr Shotton also appealed for facilities to be made available for training indoors in inclement weather, and was enthusiastic that once the men had been trained physically and in drill, the scheme could be expanded to include firearms training.

Alongside the ARP services, it was recognized that facilities would have to be provided for the number of people who would be made homeless due to blast or fire damage to their homes in air raids. This was reinforced by the early experiences of bombing, which showed far fewer fatalities than had been feared but far greater numbers of those rendered permanently or temporarily homeless. To provide for these unfortunates, a number of rest centres were created. The rest centres were manned by volunteers and voluntary organizations such as the WVS. The large numbers of schools that had been closed for the duration were quickly commandeered and designated as either rest or feeding centres. Schools were popular choices, simply because most had catering facilities. Wallsend, for example, possessed ten centres, of which four were combined rest and feeding centres whilst the other six were purely rest centres.[1] The other reason for schools being popular choices was that they were often owned by the local authority and many had already been closed for the duration of the war when children were evacuated.

When local authorities approached private businesses to become rest or feeding centres there were more problems, especially during the 'phoney war' period until May 1940, with many (mainly restaurant and cafe) owners feeling that becoming a centre would have a detrimental effect on their profits. In Whitley Bay, some business owners not only resisted becoming rest or feeding centres but also refused to provide food for ARP workers.[2] Obviously, schools could not house all of the centres and local authorities searched a variety of locations, including cinemas and churches, but also properties with catering facilities (these were difficult to find, as many were in industrial premises which would likely be targeted).

As the effects of bombing became more widely understood, the system was refined and the centres were organized into three categories: first line centres that could provide food and shelter and were fully equipped; additional centres which provided sleeping accommodation but no feeding facilities, and which were opened only in the event of the first line centres being overwhelmed; finally shadow centres were created, which only opened in extremely serious circumstances such as heavy and sustained bombing, such as that which was being experienced by London.

In Tynemouth Borough, the Public Assistance Officer was in charge of the centres from a central location in Northumberland Square, North Shields. There were eight shelters in this area and each had a council-appointed officer in charge, along with a group of voluntary helpers. It was policy to provide at least one hot meal per day and ensure that there were games and toys in order to keep children fully occupied. Bathing was also arranged at nearby cleansing stations, with a noticeboard and common room developed in each centre to engender a community spirit and keep homeless people informed of events.[3]

Recognition of the courage of the civilian members of the ARP services became common as the blitz continued. Amongst the first recipients of the newly established George Medal, granted for acts of great bravery usually by civilians at the end of September was a Shiremoor man. Patrick King was an air raid warden at Seaton Delaval when, during the raid of 26 August 1940, he heard a bomb explode nearby and raced to the scene to find two houses which had suffered severe damage and were in imminent danger of collapse. Mr King entered the first house and ascertained that there was no-one in, but on entering the second he found that the occupant, a blind woman, Miss Hannah Wilson, had taken shelter under the stairs and was now trapped by rubble. Although the house was collapsing, Mr King managed to free Miss Wilson using an axe.

On the night of 24/25 August, the Luftwaffe were active over Tynemouth and Wallsend, with the majority of residents spending much of the night in air raid shelters as the alarm sounded shortly before 2.00 am, with the all-clear not sounding until 5.00 am. Although Luftwaffe records showed that thirty bombs were dropped on Tynemouth, the local ARP records show only two incidents. One bomb exploded just out to sea off Long Sands and blew out a large number of windows at the Galaland complex. Another bomb fell on the North End Foreshore and caused slight property damage. A further bomb fell on

Wallsend in the grounds of the Neptune Hotel. It was thought that the bomb had failed to explode and nearby properties were evacuated until bomb disposal experts found that it had in fact exploded, but not with much force.

On the next night there was considerable aerial activity over the north-east of England and another sleepless night for the residents of Tynemouth Borough. Enemy aircraft were particularly active over Northumberland and Tyneside, with the residents of Tynemouth Borough repeatedly hearing the unmistakable sound of unsynchronised German engines overhead and bursts of machine-gun and anti-aircraft fire. Shortly after midnight, ten bombs were dropped in agricultural fields in the vicinity of the village of New York, causing damage to crops but no property damage or injuries. At approximately the same time, the nearby village of Shiremoor also came under attack when seventeen bombs were dropped in the area. Three of these fell in fields beside Shiremoor Modern School, one bomb was described by the Chief Warden as being 'of very heavy calibre',[4] whilst others fell in gardens next to 6 and 10 Whitley Road and 4 James Avenue. The attack seems to have been aimed at the LNER railway line which ran through the village, and ten bombs detonated in fields to the south and west of Park Lane. One of these bombs destroyed two houses in Grange Avenue (numbers 2 and 4), resulting in two people being slightly injured. The most serious result was the trapping of a woman in the wreckage of one of the properties, but the rescue squad again proved its worth and managed to extricate her safely. It would appear that the air raid alert system may have been caught out by this raid, as it was reported that sirens in the Newcastle area did not sound until shortly before 2.00 am, with the all clear sounding at 3.16 am.

Despite the strain of two raids in two nights, the people of the area seemed to have remained extremely positive and were in good spirits. The Chief Warden for the district praised the civilians and said that 'they remained calm ... and even joked about it'. One man whose house was demolished was asked where he lived, and jokingly pointed to a lump of wood in the middle of the street saying 'that's my door but I don't think it's much good knocking'.[5] Amongst the other incidents on this night were the recovery by rescue squads of several people from wrecked homes. An elderly man was trapped in the ruins of his home for several hours whilst rescue workers attempted to free him, even working whilst the raid was ongoing. They eventually freed him and, suffering from severe leg injuries, he was taken to a local hospital for treatment; shortly after he had been freed the house collapsed. The house next-door was also badly hit and partly demolished; the residents, a family of seven, emerged unscathed from the ruins.

Two nights later the Luftwaffe returned, with bombs being widely scattered over the area. Bombs were dropped in the centre of Monkseaton and in Whitley Bay, resulting in property damage and one fatality at the corner of Algernon Place, Whitley Bay (Doris Elizabeth Burns, aged 29, of Cullercoats). One enemy bomber was brought down by the defences at Hartley.

One night later the Luftwaffe returned, with over 200 bombers attacking in what seems to have been two distinct waves (the air raid sirens wailed out at shortly before 9.30 pm with the all clear sounding at 12.29 am, before the sirens sounded again shortly after 2.00 am and the all clear being given at 3.52 am), which resulted in yet another disturbed sleep for residents of the area. Monkseaton again suffered severely during both attacks when bombs were dropped in the centre of the town, causing extensive damage. At least eleven high explosive bombs were dropped on the town, along with a number of incendiaries. The bombs were very close to where some had dropped on the previous night. At 17 Roseberry Terrace, a direct hit killed two brothers (Robert Brunton, 23, and Richard Strake Brunton, 19). One of the brothers was asleep upstairs, having chosen to ignore the alert, whilst the other was in the kitchen. Other family members had taken shelter in a cupboard under the stairs and survived unhurt but very badly shaken after they had been extricated by the rescue squad.

New York was hit again with at least eight high explosive bombs which caused craters ranging from 12–35ft in diameter. One of these bombs fell within yards of a public trench shelter at Forsyth Street and caused considerable damage to both the trench and nearby properties. Other bombs fell at Jackson's Farm, the Robin Hood public house in nearby Murton, North Farm, Murton and East Farm at Murton village. Alongside the explosive bombs, over 200 incendiary bombs were also dropped in a line extending from High Flatworth Farm, over Chirton estate and on to Moor Park Hospital. One incendiary fell onto a cow byre and started a serious fire which quickly took hold in nearby milking and hay sheds. Despite the efforts of the fire brigade and the AFS, who were quickly on the scene, the three buildings were totally destroyed. However, the actions of the fireman did save the farmhouse, nearby cottages and several hay ricks which were nearby. Throughout this time, the firemen were hampered by damage to water mains in adjacent areas, which resulted in them having to pump water from a reservoir which was almost a mile away.

Another potentially very serious incident occurred when an incendiary bomb penetrated the roof of Moor Park Hospital's diphtheria ward and ignited on the wooden floor. The ward was completely wooden and the resulting fire would have been catastrophic and no doubt would have led to fatalities if it had not been for the brave actions of a patient. Although most patients had taken to the shelters, Able Seaman William G. Furse (who was himself recovering from diphtheria) had elected to stay behind in order to attend to a fellow patient who was in too dangerous a condition to move.[6] Seeing the potential for catastrophe, Furse attempted to pick up the incendiary but could not and instead smothered the device in some bedclothes before throwing it out of the window, where it burned itself out harmlessly. Other incendiary bombs fell in the hospital grounds but were quickly put out by the combined efforts of Home Guard, hospital staff and patient volunteers. The actions of Able Seaman Furse were commended by the Chief Constable of Tynemouth and the Regional Commissioner, and subsequently by Furse's commanding officer aboard HMS *Titania*.

Able Seaman William G. Furse and Matron. Furse's heroic actions saved lives during an incendiary raid. (Evening Chronicle)

Interviewed by the press, the matron of the hospital claimed that the bombing was 'a deliberate attack on a hospital which was unmistakably an institution'. In this she was undoubtedly mistaken, as no night raider could have possibly identified the building from its bombing height; the attack falling on the hospital was most likely an unfortunate coincidence. The matron went on that there 'was no panic and everyone behaved calmly'.

Property damage after this short series of raids was extensive and the repairs demonstrated the levels of cooperation between local authorities, with the work at New York being carried out by men of Whitley Bay Council. The damage would undoubtedly have been even more serious had it not been for the efforts of the police, Home Guard, fire brigades, AFS and volunteers in extinguishing incendiary bombs.

The pattern of minor bombing in August continued into early September but caused relatively little damage, with many of the bombs aimed at Tynemouth falling into the sea or onto the beach at Long Sands. For example, the ARP services recorded a number of bombs being dropped into the sea off the North Pier at Tynemouth and causing no damage. The bombing during early September was scattered and largely ineffectual, although it did of course result in significant stress for the population. A raid on 5/6 September targeted Wallsend and Sunderland but, despite the efforts of the Luftwaffe crews, damage was slight. One noteworthy event on this night was the shooting down of a German Heinkel *HE111* bomber by anti-aircraft guns. The bomber was shot at by guns along the Tyne and was observed by cheering crowds to descend in flames and crash.[7] Typical of the nuisance raids of the period was the night of 7/8 September, when a lone aircraft dropped four bombs in the Howdon area. All of the bombs fell in fields to the side of Brewers Lane and resulted in no casualties, the only damage being to crops in the fields.

Despite the inaccuracy of the Luftwaffe bombing, these small raids could sometimes cause unexpected damage and inconvenience. On the night of 18/19 September, a German aircraft attacked Wallsend Slipway and an oil incendiary bomb and several explosive bombs caused severe damage. The large machine shop, erecting shop and offices were badly damaged, along with a large section of the roof. Production was badly affected: it was not until late December that production got back to normal. Further damage was caused at the North-East Marine Works at Wallsend when three bombs hit the site. The raid involved a large number of incendiaries, and two fire-floats

(*Patrol* and *Salvo*) were used to extinguish fires at various engineering establishments.

The military authorities suspected that there had also been a concerted minelaying effort off the mouth of the Tyne, so the minesweepers based on the river once more set off to open the lanes into this important port. The Luftwaffe recognized the importance of the Tyne as a vital port, and minelaying was constant carried out during the war. On the night of 6/7 September, for example, an enemy aircraft was observed dropping mines into the sea between the mouth of the river and Cullercoats Bay.

The raids continued through October, a heavier one on the night of 7/8 October causing more serious damage to Wallsend. There were a number of unexploded bombs that night, causing severe disruption as properties were evacuated and various establishments cut off due to disruption caused by blocked roads. Property damage was severe, with three houses destroyed, two severely damaged and 318 properties classed as damaged. Dislocation and disruption was considerable, with telephone lines brought down, gas mains damaged and water supplies affected. Surprisingly, the raid resulted in few casualties, with only six civilians receiving minor injuries and a fireman also slightly hurt.

Amongst all the grim news, the local press still managed to highlight the more positive occurrences. In September, the *Shields Daily News* reported on the second birthday party of two girls at 212 Howdon Road, North Shields. The twins, Lillian and Maureen Townsley, had been born along with their late sister, Anne (who died days after birth), at Preston Hospital, and news of the birth of triplets had caused a local sensation. The two girls were described as being healthy and cheerful, and enjoyed the party with several of their young friends.

A further heavy raid hit Tynemouth in the early hours of 24 October, 280 houses in North Shields and Tynemouth being damaged. At least two of the large and deadly parachute mines were dropped during the raid. One fell on the bowling green at Tynemouth Park, whilst the other fell on farmland near the LNER line at Kennersdene Farm; the mines left craters which were measured at 35ft by 15ft and caused substantial damage to the Bowling Club pavilion, Park Cafe, Beaconsfield House Auxiliary Fire Service Station and the Grand Parade First Aid Post in Tynemouth, as well as at the Princes Theatre in Russell Street, North

Shields. The Luftwaffe tried attacking once more with parachute mines the next night, but this time a strong wind blew them to the east and they exploded at sea.

The minelaying efforts continued throughout the winter, the men aboard the minesweepers of the Tyne fighting an increasingly deadly battle to keep the vital sea lanes open. The majority of the minesweepers were converted trawlers, and many of the men crewing these vessels were peacetime trawlermen who were serving in the RNR. Typical of the casualties was the loss of the trawler *Ethel Taylor*, which struck a mine a mile or so off the Tyne piers on 22 November. Thankfully, the crew survived and were successfully taken off the trawler by an Admiralty drifter and the Cullercoats lifeboat. The damaged minesweeper was taken under tow, but sank just off the Tyne. The men of the Cullercoats lifeboat were in action again later that day when they were called out to rescue the crew of the tug *Hercules*, another victim of the mines off the mouth of the Tyne. The tug had been towing a hopper barge at the time and struck the mine just half a mile off the piers, but by the time the lifeboat got there only the barge was still afloat and of the tug's crew there was only one severely injured survivor who was rescued by the barge; the remaining four crewmen were missing and their bodies were never recovered.[8]

December opened with yet another vessel falling victim to the deadly mines off the Tyne. On 1 December, the 6,990 ton tanker SS *British Officer* was coming into the Tyne at the completion of her journey from Sheerness when she struck a mine as she was about to enter the river mouth. As the stern section flooded, five of her crew lost their lives. With the engine room flooded, the tanker was without steam and if she sank she could block the entrance to the river. To prevent this potential catastrophe, the tanker was quickly taken under tow by five tugs, but as they were towing her through the river the tanker's aft section ran aground and her bows lifted out of the water. The tanker was quickly lashed to the south pier to prevent her from blocking the channel.[9]

The Tyne was an extremely busy port, and when the SS *British Officer* struck the mine which crippled it there were several other merchant vessels waiting behind her to enter the river. One of these was a Norwegian vessel, the 18,673 ton SS *Oslofjord*, and whilst the tugs were dealing with the stricken tanker the *Oslofjord* was ordered to stand off and await instructions. Whilst the massive ship altered course to take up its new position, she too struck a mine, killing one of her crew. The SS *Oslofjord* sank slowly off the south pier, allowing the remaining 203 men aboard to be saved.[10]

Just one day after the sinking of the *Oslofjord*, the mines claimed another victim. The 483 ton Admiralty vessel MV *Jolly Girls* was sailing from London to Rosyth with a cargo of ammunition and submarine cables when she too hit a mine just off the mouth of the river. The hard-working men of the Cullercoats lifeboat were once again tasked with rescuing survivors. Upon arriving at the scene, the lifeboatmen became aware that the ten-man crew had been saved by an examination cutter which had taken the MV *Jolly Girls* under tow, but the damage caused by the mine was too severe and she sank.

Weather conditions were extremely poor during this period, with gale force winds and rain. Because of the strength of the wind, it was necessary for three tugs to take it in turns to keep the bows of the stricken SS *British Officer* in the correct position. On 13 December, the tug *Plover* was keeping the tanker in position when the ship broke in half and the tug found itself towing the bow section slowly upriver whilst the stern remained grounded. The *Plover* beached the forward section of the tanker, where it was broken up. The stern was cleared by divers, although the ribs and some of the keel still lay just off the south pier.[11]

With losses such as these being almost everyday incidents, it was increasingly vital for the important Tyneside shipyards to continue at full production. Many of the vessels built at Wallsend were Admiralty contracts for warships, a bewildering variety being constructed at yards such as the huge Swan Hunter's works in Wallsend. Amongst the naval vessels completed by Swan Hunter during the year were: the Crown Class cruiser HMS *Mauritius*, which was commissioned on 4 January but, due to a fault with her internal degaussing system, didn't enter service until 1941; the destroyers HMS *Hambledon*, HMS *Holderness*, HMS *Mendip* and HMS *Meynell*; and the cable ship HMS *Bullfinch*.[12]

For some time there had been many within British society who were demanding a more active role in defending their country against the

HMS Mauritius. (Public Domain)

HMS Hambledon. *(Public Domain)*

HMS Holderness. (Public Domain)

HMS Mendip. (Public Domain)

HMS Meynell. (Public Domain)

HMS Bullfinch. (Public Domain)

threat of an invasion or parachute landings. On 14 May 1940, the British government gave in to these demands and Anthony Eden spoke on the radio (in what was his first speech as Secretary of State for War) to ask for volunteers to form what was initially named the Local Defence Volunteers. During the speech, Eden called for 'large numbers of such men in Great Britain who are British subjects, between the ages of seventeen and 65, to come forward now and offer their services'.[13]

Such men were asked to give their names at local police stations and await the call. Unfortunately, no-one had warned the police and they were completely unprepared for the rush of volunteers. In the spirit of the time, and with invasion looking increasingly likely, it is not surprising that many men, some of whom were veterans of the First World War, wished to serve in the defence of Britain. Such was the enthusiasm that within a day of the announcement, over a quarter of a million men had put their names down.

Tyneside, with its large numbers of veterans and men in reserved occupations, was one of the most active areas, large queues forming at local police stations within 'a remarkably short space of time'.[14] At North Shields, the central police station was overwhelmed and almost 500 men had put their names down by midnight. The following day, the number had increased to over 700 and by 18 May there were 979. This represented a substantial proportion of the eligible population in Tynemouth Borough, and was a sign not only of the enthusiasm of the men but also of the seriousness of the situation. Indeed, it was said that it was 'extremely doubtful whether any town of similar size can equal it'.[15] The men were from all walks of life and included retired ex-servicemen, professionals, businessmen, shipyard workers and labourers.

The men coming forward to join the LDV had many reasons for volunteering. Patriotism certainly played a major role, as did the active nature of the LDV when compared to the passive role of the ARP services. Many would have thought the armed nature of the LDV preferable and more 'manly' than the unarmed ARP services. The traditional masculine emphasis that was present in a Britain, which was under perhaps the worst threat in the nation's history, was another encouraging factor. Many local men were of an age where they could have joined the armed forces but were prevented from doing so by the fact that they worked in a reserved occupation, whilst others had already fought in a war and relished the return to the comradeship of their past experiences.

Despite the masculine nature of the LDV (soon renamed the Home Guard) movement, there was a somewhat ambivalent attitude towards women. Many women wished to play a role in the defence of the country and petitioned to be allowed to join the LDV; there was even a parliamentary movement to demand this right. Although historians have until recently argued that the LDV/Home Guard resisted this call for women to participate, there were certainly exceptions; one such was found in Tynemouth.

The 7th (Tynemouth) Battalion of the Northumberland Home Guard had a woman enrolled as an unofficial auxiliary member from its inception. Miss Muriel Venus was the borough's only female Home Guard, offering support services to the battalion from the first, although it took until 1942 for her to be officially recognized as an auxiliary member with permission to wear an arm badge bearing the letters H.G. Although Miss Venus was a member of the organization, she played no part in any combat activity or training, but was instead used to pass messages and prepare meals for the battalion's officers.[16] Despite this, it is clear from the testimonial given to her when the Home Guard was stood down that she was viewed as an essential part of the unit, and was not seen as just a secretary or tea-lady.

There were worries that men undertaking such duties would put the LDV ahead of their work commitments, and many of the large engineering and heavy industrial concerns in the area expressed these concerns. One way around this was for the firms themselves to organize volunteer detachments, which many local firms did. Whilst this was beneficial to the firms concerned (and provided them with a free night watch), it was not without its problems. There were difficulties amalgamating these work units with the main LDV organization, and the police were concerned about the presence of armed groups of civilians patrolling industrial sites. The command difficulties were particularly problematic, and it was not until 1941 that many of the works units were brought under the umbrella of the local Home Guard command structure. In North Shields, the LDV/Home Guard company formed by Smiths Dock Ltd and the Tyne Improvement Commissioners was not amalgamated with the Tynemouth Battalion until September 1941, at which time it formed a new company (D) in that organization and was tasked with guarding the riverside area from North Shields Fish Quay to Howdon.

Despite the haphazard nature of its formation, the LDV in Tynemouth quickly proved itself capable of great organizational swiftness. The local Group Commander, Colonel Stanley Holmes, was appointed within days, and the first company of LDV were appointed and training that weekend. The formation of further small, company-sized units of LDV took place at speed, with the local organization not waiting for the government to let them know when they were needed and arranging their own impromptu patrols and training regimes.

Within days of being appointed, Colonel Holmes launched an appeal through the *Shields Evening News* for motorcycle dispatch riders to come forward for service. In his appeal, Holmes stated that even if motorcyclists were not acquainted with firearms they could be trained by the LDV to act as armed or unarmed dispatch riders. Holmes urged anyone interested to leave their name at their local police station, emphasizing the importance of dispatch riders to the nascent LDV in the event of an emergency.

The announcement of the creation of the LDV was, as we have seen, met with great enthusiasm, with huge numbers of men coming forward to offer their services. The enthusiasm was, however, a double-edged sword, and some of the early volunteers overstepped the bounds of their authority; whilst the voluntary patrols could be obstructive to members of the public and in some cases even deadly, the construction of defensive anti-invasion works by private individuals was an even greater problem. Despite some MPs advising the creation of such defences, claiming that the LDV would not have time to consult with higher authority if 'a thousand German cyclists were riding over the country', Anthony Eden replied that such works could in fact be detrimental to defensive plans which were already being developed and said that he had no such fear of German cyclists.[17] However, Eden did concede that it would be imperative for the LDV to use a degree of initiative.

One of the greatest problems facing the nascent LDV was a lack of equipment and weaponry. Upon its rapid formation, Tynemouth LDV had only one shotgun between its 100 members. Such was the rapidity of the creation of the LDV that the men could not even initially be provided with uniforms, leading to some fears over their legal status in the event of an invasion. This was resolved by providing members with an armlet bearing the initials LDV. The LDV/Home Guard became renowned for its use of initiative, and at Tynemouth there was an early demonstration of this. Colonel Holmes learned that there was a stock of First World War-issue Mills bomb hand-grenades being stored at a Newcastle drill hall. He applied for and was granted permission to requisition a gross (144) of these so that his men would have some means of fighting in the event of an invasion.

As the year progressed, the government began to rearm the LDV (renamed the Home Guard at the instigation of Winston Churchill, who believed that the name Local Defence Volunteers was too passive) with rifles, uniforms and other equipment. This was not without problems, and supply issues persisted throughout the summer. On 18 June, a Tynemouth patrol fired five rounds at a low-flying German bomber, only to be gently reprimanded by their commander that they had just wasted a substantial portion of the battalion's ammunition. One of the main problems of arming the LDV/Home Guard was that at the same time Britain was rebuilding and re-equipping its regular forces after severe losses during the Battle of France and the Dunkirk evacuation.

Training also became more organized, with the Army sending groups of instructors to Tynemouth and Wallsend to provide some training to the Home Guards. At a more local level, training was largely placed in the hands of the local command structure and consisted of regular target practice, annual and weekend training camps, as well as official informative displays and regular exercises. The Tynemouth Battalion quickly established a reputation for its superior training, which was both well organized and efficiently run. Rifle ranges were quickly organized, utilizing farmland and a nearby quarry, and were extensively used. By November, the platoon and section commanders of the battalion were required to attend weekend courses in nearby Newcastle.[18]

The men of Tynemouth Home Guard also played a significant role in the ARP effort and were required to be on duty at all times during air raid alerts. The 7th (Tynemouth) Home Guard established an observation post on top of Billy Mill, a location that offered unparalleled views of the area. The observation post was manned by a special observation section of the Home Guard under the command of a Mr W. Gallilee. During a raid, these men relayed messages to the local police and ARP services, as well as to the regional Commissioner.

The Billy Mill post developed into the 'eyes of the borough' and was a significant aid to the running of the local ARP organization.[19] The fact that the battalion was in the 'unique position of closely co-operating with the Civil Defence authorities from its ideally sited observation post' was a key factor in improving the skills and abilities of the unit.[20]

With the Battle of Britain raging and the threat of invasion, it is perhaps no surprise that Tynemouth Borough's Spitfire Fund was very popular. Launched in mid-August, within a month the fund had reached £5,032. The donations came from across every strata of society, with individuals giving varying sums and local businesses and business owners also contributing. Amongst the donations in early September were those of Mrs C. Irwin of Coniston House, Cleveland Road, North Shields (£50); Messrs Bakers Pure Foods, North Shields (£21); and Mr Gladstone Walker (owner of a North Shields store) (£10.10s).

With the activities of the RAF being extolled so publicly, it is no surprise that the 'aluminium into planes' campaign launched by the Minister of Aircraft Production, Lord Beaverbrook, proved extremely popular. At both Tynemouth and North Shields, housewives came forward to donate pots, pans, kettles and other metal objects. The North Shields depot at Reed Street reported that in only a few days, over 4cwt of aluminium had already been donated. At Tynemouth, the Howard Street headquarters reported large donations, with the leaders of various women's groups coming forward to ask for aid in assembling and collecting aluminium. The Director of Public Cleansing also opened a shop at Percy Park Road, where people could deliver smaller items or arrange for collection of larger amounts. He also reported that one elderly lady went to the shop and said that she did not have any aluminium but that her late husband had been a keen numismatist and she wished to donate a large collection of silver and copper coins which would probably take two men to carry. Unfortunately, the majority of donated aluminium would never be turned into aircraft as it was not of sufficient quality, but the collection of metals did make a contribution to the war effort.

Amongst the men from Tynemouth or Wallsend who found themselves involved in the ferocious air battle over England was Flight Lieutenant Denys Gillam. Still flying with 616 Squadron, he quickly racked up victories in the crowded skies. On 15 August, he destroyed a *JU88*, followed by a *ME109* on the 26th, an *ME110* on the 29th, an *ME109* on the 30th (along with claims of a probably destroyed *ME109* and two damaged) and another *ME109* on the 31st. On the next day he destroyed a *DO17* bomber and claimed another Dornier and an *ME109* probably destroyed, as well as a third *DO17* damaged. On 2 September, Gillam was in action again when he destroyed an *ME110*. During this fight, however, his Spitfire was hit in the engine by another *ME110* and the engine caught fire, forcing Gillam to bail out of his fighter.

Days after this harrowing affair, Gillam was posted as a Flight Commander to 312 (Czech) Squadron based at Speke on Merseyside. The squadron was equipped with Hurricanes and was tasked with providing protection for the port and important industries on Merseyside. On 8 October, a lone enemy bomber was detected heading towards Liverpool and a section of three Hurricanes was scrambled to intercept it. This was the squadron's first action, and with Gillam leading the section the three Hurricanes climbed and just after taking off (and with their wheels still down) intercepted the *JU88*. All three Hurricanes fired on the bomber, but it was Gillam who did the most damage and shot down the raider. This has been generally regarded as the fastest shooting down of an enemy aircraft during the war. Largely as a result of this, Gillam was awarded the DFC, promoted to squadron leader and ordered to take over command of 306 (Polish) Squadron.[21]

Back in the North-East, petty crime continued to be a problem. Cases such as that of North Shields labourer Charles Tunmore (58) were typical of the small thefts to come before the magistrates' bench. Tried at North Shields, it emerged that Mr Tunmore had stolen an unattended sailor's bag, belonging to Thomas Chater, from the bank above Clive Street in North Shields. The bag contained clothing, a clock and other items to the value of over £7. The next day, Chater saw his reefer coat for sale in a second-hand shop in Prudhoe Street and informed the police. The day following, the owner of the shop, Annie Stagg, aided by some passers-by, detained Mr Tunhope when he returned to sell a pair of black shoes. Under questioning, Mr Tunhope said that he had bought the bag from two hawkers for 2s (and had bought them drinks to the value of 2s 3d), believing that it only held the coat and the clock. At the first hearing the magistrates, Mr R. Hastie and Mrs E. Lamble, had given Mr Tunhope a week to find the two hawkers. Tunhope failed to locate the two men and, through his solicitor, said that he could only ask the magistrates to believe him and to take into account that he had not known the bag was stolen and he had never been brought before the bench for larceny before. His solicitor added that Mr Tunhope had not worked for several months but had served in the Army during the Boer War and the First World War. The bench found Tunhope guilty but said that they were being lenient in fining him the sum of £3 and giving him ten weeks to pay.

Wartime laws and restrictions resulted in many otherwise law-abiding people being criminalized. At the end of August, this was highlighted by the case of a Wallsend Special Constable, Joseph R. Alsop (51), who was charged with failing to immobilize his car and failure to place his road fund licence in a waterproof container. The car immobilization laws had been brought in as fears of invasion mounted and it was believed that fifth columnists might use unsecured vehicles to move about the country. Mr Alsop had left his car unlocked, with the windows down and the keys in the ignition, but when cautioned by a police officer he said that he had had the car under observation and that he too knew 'something about the law'. The police officer had then asked him if he could pay the fine, and a clearly annoyed Mr Alsop said that he could but he wouldn't, after which he was told not to be sarcastic; in his annoyance at his treatment by the officer, he did not tell him that he had in fact removed the distributor arm. The bench was not impressed by Mr Alsop's initial attitude towards the fine and ordered him to be kept in custody until he had paid the fine. When told this, Alsop immediately produced £2 to cover the fines.[22]

Throughout the summer of 1940 there were repeated cases of breaches of the blackout regulations. Typical of these was the case of Florence Klein (50) of 33 Lawson Street, North Shields. Klein was accused of leaving a light on with no blackout curtain at the Temperance Hall on Norfolk Street, which she rented out for meetings for three days of the week. Klein insisted that the incident was an accident and that she had not put the lights on before the meeting, and could not therefore be held responsible. The bench disagreed, saying that as she rented the hall the lights were her responsibility. Fining Klein £2 the chairman, Mr Stanley Holmes, stated that carelessness such as this could easily lead not only to the destruction of property but also to many deaths, and would have to stop. At the same sitting, two further cases relating to the blackout were heard. Plumber John Henry Mudditt (25) of 7 Grosvenor Place was found guilty of failing to obscure a light at his home, whilst Alice Yamada (38) of 8 Dahlia Gardens was found guilty of a similar offence, despite sending a letter explaining to the court that she had been putting up the blackout when she fell off a chair and her son turned on the light to see if she was alright. Both were fined the same sum as Klein.

With North Shields' position as an important east-coast port, there were a large number of itinerant foreign sailors and other aliens in the area. Enemy aliens and those who it was thought posed a risk were rounded up and interned, but for friendly aliens, including sailors and refugees, the wartime restrictions and especially the curfew which was imposed upon them could lead to law-breaking. In July, for example, the Tynemouth Borough Police Court heard the cases of two Danish sailors and a Czech refugee. The two sailors, Einar A.W.E. Johansen (25) and Ebbe B. Neilsen (41), were arrested by the police after being seen in North Shields after their shore leave curfews had expired by some hours. The two, through an interpreter, offered no defence and were duly fined £2, plus 5s. for the cost of the interpreter.

The case of the Czech woman, Blanka Weiss, was somewhat more interesting. Miss Weiss was employed as a housekeeper by Dr Susan Isaacs and lived with her in a fourth-floor flat. Under the terms of her curfew restrictions, Miss Weiss was unable to leave the flat between 10.30 pm and 6.00 am. During a recent air raid, Dr Isaacs had told her to accompany her to a nearby culvert to take shelter, and she had been detected by the police and charged with breaking her curfew. The bench could not initially decide on the case and ordered a retrial, at which they were told that because of her curfew, Miss Weiss was placed in an intolerable position of having to remain in a very vulnerable property during air raid alerts and that on the night in question neither Dr Isaacs or Miss Weiss had even considered the curfew rules, being anxious only for their safety. The police response to the offence was somewhat muddled, with a local Inspector informing the bench that Miss Weiss was viewed as a friendly alien but that the Chief Constable had instructed him to reiterate to the bench that there were special reasons for aliens being ordered to remain at home between those hours. After reflecting on the case, the bench decided that the case had been proven but, apparently moved by the plight of Miss Weiss, dismissed it without any further action. This must have left Miss Weiss in a difficult position in future alerts, but perhaps it also sent a message to the police that the bench perhaps thought that they were being overly zealous in this matter.

Other crimes were more consistent with those associated with peacetime and the hard-drinking culture which was commonplace in areas where there were many employed in heavy manual labour. Typical of these was that of ten North Shields men who were accused of behaving in a disorderly manner on the corners of Saville Street and Stephenson Street. The men were Henry Rowley (27) of 75 Tyne Street; William Johnston (37), Thomas Johnston and George Johnston, all of 91 Park Crescent; Robert Davy (28) of 40 Briarwood Avenue; Thomas Brownlee (37) of 121 Church Street; William Smith (25) of 136 Linskill Street; James Churnside of 31 Linskill Street; William Bowden (28) of 1 Lansdowne Terrace West; and William Robertson (33) of 178 Linskill Street. They were all employed as labourers, fishermen or in the building trade. On the night of 7 July 1940, they had been observed shouting, singing and using obscene language, and were told to disperse by a police officer. However, the men had later met up again and were once more found causing a disturbance. Upon being arrested, they refused to give their names and addresses, but did so when taken to the police station. Interestingly, several of the men did not turn up at the court proceedings, whilst Henry Rowley was represented by his mother. Unsurprisingly, despite two of the men (William Johnston and James Churnside) denying that they were behaving in a disorderly manner, the bench found all ten guilty and fined them each 5s. before advising them that this was lenient and they hoped that the men 'would play the game and not stand at street corners late at night frolicking and making a noise at a time like the present'.[23]

Some of the crimes for which otherwise law-abiding folk were prosecuted seem trivial given the wartime situation. The fining of North Shields shopkeeper John Turnbull Holland of 67 Church Way, North Shields, for leaving boxes on the pavement outside his shop (which was a greengrocers and florists) seems to have been one such case. Mr Holland was using the boxes to display his wares when PC Bianchi took exception and cautioned him to move the boxes. Mr Holland was unloading stock at the time and queried why the officer was picking on him when other shops had billboards on the pavement, before telling him that he would not move the flowers (indicating he would move the vegetable and fruit boxes). PC Bianchi said he would report Mr Holland, to which the shopkeeper replied, 'If you are going to be awkward, I will be awkward.' When asked if he would like to give evidence, Mr Holland queried the point of doing so, adding that labour shortages meant deliveries could not be moved inside quickly and that he did not see how he was causing an obstruction when the path was 10ft wide. The police took an obstinate view, with Chief Inspector Radcliffe saying that it did not matter how wide the path was, as it was illegal to display goods on it. The bench found Mr Holland guilty and fined him £1 before stating, somewhat pompously, that the footpath was not to be used as a marketplace as people had the right to walk without hindrance.

Notes
1. TWAS: 359/794 (18). Emergency Shelters/Feeding Centres. See also *After the Raid – Wallsend* (Wallsend Council, official pamphlet, 1940).
2. TWAS: MB/WB/27/1 (T135/45). Whitley Bay Municipal Borough Council ARP Committee. Memo from local ARP Controller, 12 February 1940.
3. TWAS: 359/794 (93). County Borough of Tynemouth – Emergency feeding and shelter scheme. Report of Mr G. Brown, Public Assistance Officer, November 1940.
4. *Shields Evening News*, 26 August 1940, p.4.
5. *Ibid.*
6. Able Seaman William Godfrey Furse was from Abercumbie, Aberdare, South Wales.
7. The aircraft actually crashed at Hendon, Sunderland. Unfortunately, the stricken bomber crashed onto a house and one of the residents was killed and another seriously injured; the four-man German crew were also all killed.
8. The dead crewmen are all commemorated on the Tower Hill Memorial. They were: Master James Robson (66); Engineer Officer Ralph Robson of Dunston, Gateshead (43); Fireman James Henry Young Thomas Clayton (36); and Mate Harold Robson (27).
9. The SS *British Officer* had already suffered through enemy action when she was attacked by German bombers in January 1940 off the coast of Kent.
10. The SS *Oslofjord* had had an interesting career. Built as a liner (she was the largest in the Norwegian fleet) in 1938, she had been used to carry the Crown

Prince and Princess of Norway to New York, USA, in April 1940, but was involved in a collision which caused extensive damage. By November 1940, she had been refitted as a transport ship at Halifax, Nova Scotia, and set sail for Newcastle via Liverpool to join the British merchant fleet.

11. Interestingly, the master of the tug *Plover* was killed, along with his wife, during one of the heavy air raids on South Shields in April 1941.
12. All of these vessels survived the war. Of the four Hunt Class destroyers, HMS *Mendip* eventually saw service with three navies (in the RN during the war, after which she was sold to the Egyptian Navy and saw service in the Suez Crisis, before being captured and then reused by the Israeli Navy as INS *Haifa*; and HMS *Meynell* saw post-war service with the Ecuadorian Navy (she was sold to them in 1954) as the *Presidente Velasco Ibarra*.
13. Eden, A., *Freedom and Order: Selected Speeches 1939–1946*, 2nd ed. (New York, 1971), pp.7173.
14. *The Shields Evening News*, 15 November 1944, p.3.
15. *The Shields Evening News*, 15 November 1944, p.3.
16. *The Shields Evening News*, 21 December 1944, p.3.
17. *The Evening News*, 16 July 1940.
18. *The Shields Evening News*, 5 December 1944, p.6.
19. *The Shields Evening News*, 21 November 1944, p.3.
20. *Ibid*, 15 November 1944, p.3.
21. Denys Edgar Gillam was born at Tynemouth in 1915 and joined the RAF in 1935. After serving with 29 Squadron, he was posted to the Meteorological Flight and whilst there gained distinction, and the award of the Air Force Cross (AFC), after he made two dangerous landings to supply food to Rathlin Island in Northern Ireland, which had been cut off by gales for three weeks. On 18 September 1939 he was posted to 616 Squadron.
22. *Evening Chronicle*, 29 August 1940, p.1.
23. *The Evening News*, 16 July 1940.

CHAPTER THREE

1941: The Continuing Crisis

The severe winter which dominated the early months of 1941 brought many problems. The ARP services suffered as the numbers of those falling ill increased and snow led to a breakdown in the transport network. In February, the Whitley Bay area control room was left isolated when heavy snow brought down priority telephone lines.

Thankfully, Whitley Bay already had some experience in adjusting its messaging system, and volunteer messengers were hastily recruited and employed. The majority of these volunteers were youths aged 16–18 and many were members or former members of organizations such as the Boy Scouts. Although these messengers played a key role, some remained cautious of their use, believing that many of the youths were irresponsible and failed to attend meetings and drill sessions. These suspicions appear to have been confirmed in Whitley Bay when an official report to the authorities accused the volunteer messengers of being recalcitrant in their duties, stating that 'only a very few were really interested in the Service unless there had been an alert … but certain of the neighbouring areas seemed to have a very efficient Messenger Service and interest was very keen'.[1] Obviously, this was not a judgement which could be applied to all and evidence from the Tynemouth area hints that the volunteer messengers in this area were conscientious and took their duties extremely seriously. When youths were brought together in a time of high excitement, youthful spirits could often go too far. During one alert, fifteen messengers from Whitley Bay had grown bored and decided to enliven their duty period. This resulted in the youths being disciplined after they alarmed local residents by parading along the Promenade wearing their anti-gas clothing and steel helmets.

On the night of 15/16 February, the Luftwaffe launched an attack on several communities in south-east Northumberland, including

Tynemouth Borough. There was extensive property damage in the borough, although thankfully no casualties, whilst the large numbers of incendiary bombs were dealt with by volunteer fire watchers and the fire brigades. The greatest dislocation of this raid was caused by the high number of time-delayed and unexploded bombs which fell on Tynemouth, causing the temporary evacuation of several hundred people to emergency centres. This raid was followed the next night by a solitary bomber – what was termed a nuisance raid with bombs dropped in Northumberland Park and at Northumberland Terrace.

The shipbuilding yards continued their frantic efforts to produce new naval vessels and replace naval and merchant vessels which were being lost at a prodigious rate due to Germany's unrestricted submarine warfare. Wallsend Slipway and Engineering Company (a subsidiary of Swan Hunter's) was turned over almost entirely to naval orders during 1941, with many of the vessels being the destroyers and corvettes which played such a vital role in escorting convoys and engaging with U-boats. Reports from the firm confirmed that merchant construction had fallen dramatically, concluding by saying that the yard was 'working solely on Admiralty contracts' by the summer.[2]

Amongst the ships completed in 1941 were seven Hunt Class (I and II Type) destroyers (HMS *Calpe*, *Eridge*, *Exmoor*, *Farndale*, *Heythrop*, *Hursley* and *Lamerton*) and the Dale Class fleet tanker and gantry landing ship RFA *Ennerdale*.[3]

There was yet another maritime loss off Tynemouth on 17 February. This time the vessel, the 2,824 ton SS *Empire Knoll*, was waiting to be loaded off the North Pier before setting off on what would have been her maiden voyage carrying coal to Lisbon. For undetermined reasons, the ship foundered on the remains of the foundations of the old pier. The vessel sank and could not be refloated before the punishing tides battered her to wreckage (her remains still lie off the north wall of the pier). Thankfully, the thirty-two-man crew were all saved.[4]

After a fairly quiet end to March with regard to enemy action over the area, April opened in a similar manner with little sign of the Luftwaffe. Recognizing the vulnerability of some of the key strategic sites on the Tyne, large Haslar smoke generators were fitted around Newcastle; it was almost as if the authorities knew that worse was to come in April.

HMS Calpe. (Public Domain)

HMS Exmoor. (Public Domain)

HMS Farndale. (Public Domain)

HMS Hursley. (Public Domain)

HMS Lamerton. (Public Domain)

HMS Ennerdale. (Public Domain)

HMS Eridge. *(Public Domain)*

On the night of 7/8 April, a small force of German raiders attacked various locations in Northumberland and Durham. One bomber released nine small bombs which fell in a neat row in fields at Close Farm, Preston Village; although damage was done to some windows in the area, there were no casualties. It appears that the raider paid the price for this sortie as minutes later an aircraft was heavily fired on by nearby anti-aircraft batteries and tracer machine-gun fire, and two parachutes were reported out to sea off Cullercoats.

Wallsend was not so fortunate, a cluster of bombs and parachute mines falling in the area around Willington Square. Two of the parachute mines landed near to the old Edward Pit, and when police arrived to investigate they were refused access and told that an RAF pass was required to access the site. This was confirmed by a senior police officer, and the officers at the site reported strange contraptions in some of the fields. These were in fact the prototype 'Z' anti-aircraft rocket projectors which would shortly be trialled at Tynemouth. Despite the detonation of several more parachute mines, the Willington area escaped relatively lightly this time, with the only reported damage being broken windows.[5]

After a relatively peaceful night on the 8th, the Luftwaffe returned the next night, a heavy attack developing which focused on the communities on either side of the mouth of the Tyne, as well as Newcastle. In Tynemouth and Wallsend, the air raid alert first sounded at 11.25 pm and heavy anti-aircraft guns opened fire immediately. In Tynemouth, the raid opened with the Luftwaffe dropping numerous incendiaries over the north and centre of the borough, followed by several explosive bombs. Then, for an hour commencing at 12.30 am, a further wave of bombers began dropping a larger number of mixed incendiaries and explosives before the raid finished after over five hours with a further attack which fell mainly on the timber yards and docks lining the north bank of the river.

Post-raid analysis by the authorities estimated that at least thirty-five very heavy high explosive devices were dropped, including several parachute mines, along with thousands of incendiary bombs, a large number of which were explosive in nature. The large bombs dropped resulted in craters 70–80ft in width, and they were described as having a terrific blast radius which resulted in extensive property damage. The authorities estimated that all but four of the bombs dropped on this night were of this type, but they also stated that the four medium bombs, although leaving smaller craters, had a very large blast radius. Five of the heavy bombs seemed to have been of even greater capacity, leaving craters 120ft across and 35ft deep. Thirty-five people were killed during the course of the raid, with a further 101 injured. Demonstrating the bravery and vulnerability of those people in the services which remained active during raids, two police officers, two first-aid workers and a soldier were among the dead, with eighteen civil defence personnel and nine police officers among the injured.

	Men	*Women*	*Children u-16*
Killed	17	13	5
Seriously Injured	10	4	1
Slightly Injured	62	15	9

Because of the use of heavy blast bombs in conjunction with a large number of incendiaries, there was very extensive property damage in the borough. Preston Hospital (and its first-aid post) and the Public

Assistance Institution were both heavily damaged as a result of direct hits being scored upon them. The x-ray department of the hospital was destroyed and four people were killed (three staff members and a patient). The first-aid headquarters which was established at the hospital (at Holmlands) was also hit and suffered severe damage (two members of staff were killed). This damage was obviously a serious hindrance to ARP and first-aid care during the raid, with many patients having to be moved from the hospital to Linskill School and the first-aid headquarters being rendered inoperable. In addition to this damage, the Royal National Lifeboat Station was destroyed when it suffered a direct hit.

Serious fires took hold during the raid, with the timber storage yards on the banks of the river hit by numerous incendiaries. There were initially five separate fires in the yards, beside Dock Road, Occupation Road and Hayhole Road, but these coalesced and the fire became a major one which raged out of control for a time, extending

The wreckage of Tynemouth Lifeboat Station after a raid in September 1941. (Shields Daily News)

for a mile along the bank of the river. The authorities estimated that over 400 small fires were extinguished during the course of the raid, the majority of incidents being dealt with by the fire brigades, ARP services, police and civilians. The after-raid report declared that the mobile water carriers that had recently been purchased by the authorities in Tynemouth had proven a great success, and that without them the situation would have been far more serious. Although the fire situation had seemed extremely dangerous at 3.00 am, the majority of fires, with the exception of those at the timber yards, were under control an hour later.

The efforts of the firemen, police and ARP services were placed under even greater strain as the communications network failed. By 1.30 am, almost all telephone lines to fire stations and first-aid posts were severed or badly damaged, whilst all police box telephones were also rendered inoperable.

The first-aid and medical services of the borough were also placed under massive strain as the number of incidents increased rapidly during the raid. Once again, aid was sought from neighbouring areas, in this case Whitley Bay. Unfortunately, one of the ambulances from Whitley Bay had just arrived at Holmlands when the first-aid headquarters suffered a direct hit shortly before 3.00 am and two of the Whitley Bay personnel were killed: Mr Edward William Sutton (49) and Miss Doris Ewbank (28). Miss Ewbank was a school teacher who worked at Backworth Infants School and was a volunteer in the Voluntary Aid Detachment (VAD). The bombing of the first-aid headquarters and severe damage suffered by the casualty control service office hindered the efforts, but the system by and large coped well with a very difficult night

Miss Doris Ewbank, schoolteacher and volunteer ambulance driver, was killed in a bombing raid on North Shields in 1941. News of her death was not announced to the public. (Unknown)

and a stern test of the organizations. The very next day, the first-aid headquarters was moved to the Smith's Dock Institute.

Although morale was said to have not suffered as a result of the recent raids, and was described as being positive in all after-raid reports, it is interesting to note that many incidents were not widely reported. Indeed, the news of Miss Ewbank's death could be said to have been covered up, with the press ordered not to reveal the information for fear of female volunteers in the ARP and first-aid services suffering a decline in morale and perhaps refusing to complete their duties (although there was no evidence of such a decline in morale, and the news was widely disseminated throughout the district by word of mouth).

During the course of the raid there were over seventy calls for ambulances or first-aid parties, with forty-eight people passing through first-aid stations (at Holmlands, Balkwell and the Royal Navy Sickbay), whilst sixty-two patients were admitted to hospitals during the raid (of whom fourteen died).

It was also an extremely busy night for the men working in the rescue parties. They were aided in their work by men from the repair services and the decontamination squad, as well as by one squad from Whitley Bay. The men in these services fought to save lives and extricate bodies from the wreckage of many properties. The men worked continuously until the last body was recovered late on the night of 12 April. The rescue teams managed to save the lives of eleven people who had been trapped, whilst they also worked to recover fifteen bodies. The men of these squads witnessed scenes of horror for which many of them would have been completely unprepared.

Shortly after midnight, explosive bombs dropped on properties at Bedford Street and West Percy Street, causing damage to the gas and electricity supplies. Just ten minutes later, Preston Hospital was hit, whilst explosive bombs destroyed properties in Brandling Terrace shortly after, killing four people (Clara Morrison (65), Mary Baird (aka Morrison) (27) and Brian Baird (aka Morrison) (4) at number 3, and Alice Sarah Jane Anderson (74) at number 1) and once again disrupting electricity, gas and water supplies, as well as bringing down telephone lines.

Half an hour later, at 1.30 am, Stanley Street West was badly hit, with seventeen fatalities (the official report lists twelve, so perhaps some died in hospital) and once again the utility supplies being affected. The after-raid report stated that several of these fatalities were amongst families who had been supplied with surface shelters but who had preferred to take shelter in their houses. At least two of those killed had sheltered under a kitchen table, onto which a piano fell, whilst others were buried in powdered plaster from the walls (which had been turned into powder by the effect of concussive blast). The post-raid report highlighted the fact that two nearby surface shelters (each sheltering fifty people), which had suffered very near misses by heavy capacity bombs, had survived intact with no casualties. At the same time, the lifeboat station at the east end of the Fish Quay was also destroyed, with one man being killed.

Casualties at Stanley Street West on 9/10 April 1941

Name	Age	House No.
Doreen Steel	17	15
Mary Ann Steel	58	15
David Swinney	w5	15
Jane Ann Swinney	33	15
Peter Swinney	36	15
Henry Martin Carr	4	27
James Dillon	1	27
Rose Ann Dillon	24	27
William Joseph Dillon	7	27
Rose Ann Thewlis	67	27
Alice Mary Brice	54	28
George Gully Brice	54	28
Joan Brice	18	28
Patricia McKever	8	28
Sidney McKever	24	28
Emmanuel Kelsey Dodds	66	31
Margaret Jane Dodds	65	31

Just five minutes after the incident at West Stanley Street, bombs fell on Biddlestone Crescent. At number 39, three people from the Cavener family (Edward Cavener (51), a firewatcher, his wife Georgina Davy Cavener (50) and their daughter Minnie Cavener (27)) had taken shelter in their Anderson Shelter; all three family members were killed when the Anderson Shelter received a direct hit. Highlighting the capricious nature of blast damage, the adjoining property was totally destroyed but the Anderson Shelter there was undamaged and the family sheltering in it unhurt. At roughly the same time, bombs were dropped at Maple Crescent, at number 3 The Quadrant, where William Henry Matthews (66) was killed, and on Cartington Road, where Arthur John Thompson (50) was killed at number 6.[6]

Meanwhile, a serious fire had broken out in North Shields when three large neighbouring shop premises were set on fire by incendiaries at 3.00 am (the premises were a ladies' outfitters, an outfitters' and drapers' shop and a furniture depository) and the water pressure available to the fire brigades dropped. Whitley Bay responded to a plea for assistance and dispatched nine engines and crews to the area, whilst a fire float, via a system of pumps, helped by pumping water from the river to fight the fires. This fire was brought under control and extinguished by 7.00 am.

When the all-clear sounded at around 5.00 am, the Town Clerk's Office immediately opened as an information centre, catering for those seeking word of missing relatives and friends as well as those requiring help organizing funerals, finding accommodation, making repairs to their homes and property and salvaging damaged or undamaged furniture from bombed homes. The office dealt with over 400 enquiries and remained open in this capacity for a further five days, dealing with an additional 450 enquiries. Once obtained, names of the dead were posted on the doors of the office and at the police station. The mortuary on Church Way was also opened immediately and the honorary mortuary superintendent, Arthur Cragg, worked tirelessly, despite some difficulty in finding relatives to identify bodies. Nineteen bodies were brought to the mortuary, identified and arrangements for funerals made. In twenty-three cases there was no-one able or willing to organize funerals and the responsibility fell to the local authority. In some cases this was because entire families had been wiped out.

Furniture from fifty bomb-damaged properties was salvaged by the local authority and stored in several locations, including Queen

Victoria School, St Andrew's Hall, the Liberal Club and Bishopsgate House.

Whilst the clear-up began, the timber yards' fire was obviously an ongoing and serious concern as the blaze was not only destroying important supplies of timber but would also become a beacon for enemy bombers if they returned the next night. By 10.00 am on 10 April, the fire brigades were beginning to get the blaze under control, but then the winds strengthened and it got out of control again. The Regional Fire Inspector, Mr C. Thomas, arrived on the scene and declared an emergency, calling for assistance from nearby areas. Blyth, Gosforth and Newburn responded by sending a total of six engines, whilst the Army contributed by sending nearby troops to assist in the removal of timber from the path of the blaze.

Over 100 troops were dispatched, with a further 100 used to provide cordons around damaged properties and guard against looting. In the event, there was only one case of looting when a 12-year-old boy was apprehended by a special constable whilst stealing from a bomb-damaged house.

Damage to property was extremely heavy, with over sixty properties destroyed or demolished and more than 600 damaged to some extent, whilst several hundred others had all of their windows blown out.

Property damage (excluding glass-only) in Tynemouth Borough, 9/10 April 1941

Damage Category	No. of Buildings
Demolished	22
Requiring Demolition	41
Seriously Damaged (Repairable)	99
Slight Damage (Not Windows)	513

Due to the high amount of damage to homes and shops in the borough, the raid resulted in a very large number of people rendered homeless (or bombed-out as it was often termed) and in need of emergency housing. Two of the borough's rest centres opened whilst the raid was still ongoing, and between them the Youth Centre rest centre and the Western rest centre catered for approximately 279 people in the days following the raid. Obviously vastly more people were affected, but the majority seem to have found shelter with friends or relatives.

In addition to the severe damage at the timber yards, several other important industrial properties were affected, and the development of firm-specific ARP services proved invaluable at a time when the regular ARP services were in danger of being overwhelmed. At the North Shields Works of the Newcastle & Gateshead Gas Company, an extremely dangerous situation developed after the site was hit by three explosive bombs and over 200 incendiaries. The railway lines leading into the site were badly damaged by blast and several incendiary bombs fell onto the large gas holders. Whilst the company's own ARP detail dealt with the majority of fires, some incendiaries burned through one of the gas holders and a dire situation was only averted when the manager of the works, Mr C.J. Duncan, along with his daughter, Miss L. Duncan, and works foreman Mr J. Callaghan climbed the holder and, despite great danger to themselves, managed to successfully smother the incendiary. For their extraordinary courage, Mr Duncan was awarded the British Empire Medal and Mr Callaghan the George Medal; Miss Duncan received only a commendation.

Joseph Callaghan, who was awarded the George Medal for extinguishing a gas holder. (Newcastle Journal)

Other industrial concerns to be hit were: the Tyne Improvement Commission (which ran the timber yards), which suffered hits by fifteen high explosive bombs which caused severe damage to buildings, railway lines and railway trucks; Messrs Cookson's Lead & Antimony Company Ltd, which was struck by incendiaries which were extinguished by the works' own ARP services; and Smith's Dock Co. Ltd, which was also hit by incendiaries which, once again, were extinguished by the prompt response of their own ARP.

Although the people of Tynemouth Borough had suffered a very heavy raid, they had behaved well, with no signs of panic amongst the general populace and a spirit of determination evident. Many, however, must have feared that the Luftwaffe would follow up the attack with further raids to put the important industries of the Tyne out of action. This did not develop, and the residents had a relatively peaceful period of four nights with little enemy action, although for many it was a time of bereavement and loss, whilst the ARP workers and other services continued the clean-up efforts. On the night of 14/15 April, the sirens sounded once again but the raid that night fell across the river on South Shields, where over 600 incendiaries were dropped.

Press coverage of the raid was somewhat muted, and many local people would have depended upon word of mouth in this tightly knit largely working-class area. The focus of the local press was clearly to help maintain the morale of the civilian population, and it is no surprise that the focus remained on the more positive aspects, especially resistance to the raids, damage to the bombers and the positive reaction of ordinary people and the ARP services. The *Shields Evening News*, for example, highlighted how housewives with stirrup pumps had 'helped to defeat a Nazi fire-raising attempt in a North East coast town'.[7]

In an editorial appearing in the *Shields Evening News* on the night after this attack, perhaps designed to bolster morale after the period of bombing raids, the editor gave a surprisingly realistic account of the current war situation facing Britain. He began by emphasizing that Britain was fighting for its existence and its way of life, explaining that this was not a romantic notion but simply a fact, although he agreed with the words of an unnamed Belgian minister who in addressing American audiences had said that 'the British bear the brunt everywhere'. The editor went on to explain how this situation had come about, with Britain honouring its treaty commitments to various nations and territories such as Greece, Yugoslavia, Egypt and Abyssinia, as well as attempting to keep the idea of liberation alive in Poland, Norway, Denmark, Holland and Czechoslovakia. At the same time, he continued, Britain was having to defend its own skies and shores whilst others such as France, whom the editor accused of collapsing and defaulting 'in the Anglo-French alliance to resist Germany's assault',[8] Turkey and Russia, which had just agreed a deal with Japan which the editor presciently pointed out left Singapore and the Dutch East Indies vulnerable to Japanese aggression in the near future – stood idly by. Recent Easter messages from what the editor described as 'these little nations' which Britain was fighting for reassured the British that they were doing something to be proud of. Such matters, the editor argued, should encourage the British to even greater efforts, but the populace should be under no illusions as to what faced them; there was 'a long road yet to travel before the Nazi menace is defeated'.[9] Coming at a time when the area was experiencing severe attacks, this piece was a realistic though reassuring message of hope and pride intended to bolster morale amongst the civilian population and spur them on to even greater effort and resilience.

On the following night the bombers returned, meaning another long night in the shelters, air raid warnings sounded at 10.45 pm and the all-clear was not sounded until 5.00 am. It was estimated that over 100 bombers were active over the North-East and, once again, the attacks were scattered over a wide area.[10] Once more the bulk of the attack north of the river fell heavily on Tynemouth Borough (although the attack on this night seemed to focus on Tynemouth itself and the north of the borough), but nearby communities such as Whitley Bay were also badly affected and parachute mines were again a feature. The raid on the Tynemouth and Whitley Bay area was short but sharp and took place in the early hours between 3.00 and 4.00 am.

Shortly before 3.00 am, the raid got underway with a number of explosive bombs which fell in fields around Preston Village (there were no casualties or damage), followed by bombs falling on Whitley Bay. Parachute mines and other bombs dropped in the vicinity of Ocean View and Mason Avenue. The casualties and damage at Ocean View were severe, with fourteen people being killed in the street at five different properties and another woman killed in Mason Avenue. The damage here was very severe because the two parachute mines which fell at Ocean View were very close together, and the rescue parties realized very quickly that there was very little chance of pulling survivors alive from the wreckage. So severe was the damage that, despite the attacks on Tynemouth, rescue parties from there were sent to assist in the recovery of bodies.

Towards the end of the raid, at approximately 3.55 am, several parachute mines were dropped over Tynemouth Borough. One of these fell beside the reservoir at the junction of Rake Lane and Moor

House Road, causing extensive property damage in the New York area and slightly injuring two people (this was the same reservoir that had been used by the fire services during an earlier raid on New York). At approximately the same time, another parachute mine detonated in fields at White House Farm, Preston, but caused little or no damage.

Five minutes later, five more parachute mines fell on the borough, this time with more serious effects. One fell beside the warden post at the Rex Cinema on Billy Mill Lane, causing severe damage and killing air raid warden Hutchinson H. Simpson (47) and firewatcher Charles Edward Grant (58). One of the dead was pulled alive from the ruins but succumbed to his injuries before they could reach hospital. A police constable had just vacated the building, and was undoubtedly lucky to escape the same fate.[11] The damage in the surrounding area was extensive, and included the demolition of Chirton Council School, whilst a number of houses also had to be demolished and others suffered lesser blast damage which rendered them temporarily uninhabitable. Another mine exploded at the corner of Balkwell Avenue and Oswin Terrace, the blast demolishing or badly damaging many houses in this densely inhabited working-class district. Another wardens's post was badly damaged (this time at Collingwood School, which was also an AFS station), though this time without casualties. However, there was one fatality in Balkwell Avenue, where Florence May Carr (56) was killed at number 15. Two Anderson Shelters in Balkwell Avenue were buried by debris and the rescue squad was called. Happily, the seven inhabitants of the shelters were all rescued uninjured from the debris, showing just how sturdy these shelters could be.

At approximately the same time, a mine detonated in the moat of Tynemouth Castle, destroying a stores building, whilst a second fell nearby in King Edward's Bay, causing considerable property damage in Front Street, Percy Gardens and the surrounding area which necessitated more evacuations to temporary shelter. The final mine fell just outside the borough boundary on the main Hartley railway line; it failed to explode, but resulted in delays on the line and the diversion of road traffic until it could be rendered safe.

As a result of this raid, Tynemouth Borough recorded forty-eight properties destroyed or so badly damaged that they had to be demolished, 117 properties which were seriously damaged but where repair was possible and a further 320 where damage was less serious. These figures did not include properties where blasts had simply blown out windows. A total of five rescue squads from Tynemouth were in action during the raid, and the borough also managed to send two squads to Whitley Bay to help at the Ocean View incident. The military were once again called upon to give assistance, and were utilized in directing traffic and preventing looting.

Because of the widespread use of parachute mines, hundreds of people were made homeless due to damage suffered during the raid. Two-hundred and eighteen people were aided by feeding and rest centres in Tynemouth and more in Whitley Bay, and once again information centres were open for several days whilst the clear-up and removal of furniture from damaged properties was enacted. A large number of people again did not depend upon the official organizations, instead relying upon support networks of family and friends.

Due to censorship, the press seldom if ever named towns which had been hit, but the reporting the next day tried to play down the impact of the previous nights' raid. Local newspapers reported that two North-East coastal areas were hit but claimed only five people were killed, although the report admitted that damage to property had been considerable. Seeking to highlight the positives, the report focused on how at one point during the raid four enemy aircraft had been coned in searchlights and 'subjected to an intense barrage'. However, the aircraft were not shot down which the report fails to mention and the report goes on to admit that damage in another 'North East coast town', probably the North Shields incident as it refers to a wrecked hotel, had been considerable. The report added that considering that the attack was focused on an industrial area, 'the amount of damage caused was not heavy. There were few casualties and one workman was killed. Waves of raiders met a terrific barrage from ground defences.'[12] The report concluded that a number of houses in a working-class area had been hit, people had been trapped and that there 'were several casualties'. The press also claimed that two German bombers had been shot down over the North-East, but local reports seem to indicate that only one aircraft crashed in the north of England on this night, and this was most likely a result of mechanical failure.[13]

The next nine nights passed with only minor alerts and no attacks in the area, although the alerts still imposed a strain on the civilian population. On the night of 25/26 April the sirens again wailed out at 9.53 pm, heralding a short raid. In response to the raid, the anti-aircraft batteries on the Tyne were extremely active and the RAF put up approximately 130 night-fighters in an effort to engage the Luftwaffe. However, bombs did significant damage and caused multiple casualties in Tynemouth and Wallsend.[14] The local press later reported that the area had borne the brunt of 'a short but fierce attack by the Luftwaffe … when waves of bombers crossed the coast and dropped incendiary and high explosive bombs indiscriminately over the area'. Confirming what residents had already suspected and probably heard through word of mouth, the account of the raid went on to describe how it was feared that 'casualties were numerous but considering the intensity of the raid the number killed was small'.[15]

The raid opened with bombers dropping rows of flares to light up their targets (this occurred just minutes after the alert had sounded). Bombs and parachute mines almost immediately rained down on the north of Tynemouth Borough, but the majority fell in fields (although one narrowly missed an anti-aircraft battery in a field at the Broadway) and did little damage. Others fell at West Allotment (in fields near the Northumberland Arms public house) and Algernon Colliery (once again in fields nearby). More bombs fell at Percy Main and Cullercoats (once more in fields). Other bombs fell at Shiremoor, where one woman (Flora Charlton (35)) and her child (Eric Charlton (10)) were killed at 20 Louisa Street.

At Wallsend, the situation was more serious as bombs and parachute mines fell in the area of Headlam Street and Ridley Avenue. Sixteen people were killed, including three members of the same family John Simpson Scott (35), his wife Margaret Scott (34) and their young son Robert Scott (6) at number 4 Back Headlam Street.

Very large numbers of incendiaries were also released by the raiders, but no serious fires took hold and damage was slight. The heavy use of parachute mines was somewhat mitigated by the majority falling in unoccupied areas, but many windows were again blown out and required minor repairs. Only one property was so badly damaged to be rendered temporarily uninhabitable, and none were destroyed or required demolition.

The local press acknowledged immediately that damage to property had been considerable, saying that 'Houses were wrecked across a wide area' but praising the efforts of volunteer fire-fighting parties who 'ignored the risk of high explosives being dropped as they concentrated on the job of tackling the flames'.[16] The immediate aftermath of the raid was covered in surprising detail as the report highlighted the damage to a working-class area, the area around Headlam Street in Wallsend, highlighting how two families had been wiped out here and that one of the dead was the wife of a mercantile marine captain who had recently been freed after being held aboard the *Graf Spee*. It also said the damage had rendered scores of people homeless. Reinforcing the necessity of taking to shelters, the account mentioned a Wallsend couple whose shelter was on the edge of the massive crater left by a parachute mine or large bomb. Although the shelter was covered by debris and large baulks of timber, the couple survived and the only injuries were minor facial wounds suffered by the husband.

Further accounts of the raid mentioned how a boy whose house had been wrecked insisted on going back inside so that he could rescue his pet bird, whilst a nearby shop owner whose premises had been badly damaged was salvaging what he could and commented matter-of-factly to a journalist: 'Well, we must carry on, boy.' The devastating results of the attack on some parts of Newcastle were hinted at, but with little detail.

Again, there was a period of relative respite for the area, although on 27 April the fighter catapult ship HMS *Patia* (a converted merchant vessel equipped to rocket-launch a Hurricane fighter) sailed from the Tyne on what was her maiden voyage following conversion to her new role, but was attacked by enemy aircraft whilst sailing up the Northumberland coast bound for Ireland. Following a 'mayday' call, local lifeboats set out from numerous communities and searched for survivors throughout the night. The *Patia* went down, taking the lives of her captain (Commander D.M.B. Baker) and thirty-eight or thirty-nine of her crew, whilst thirty-one crewmen were saved. The *Patia* did manage to shoot down her attacker, the Heinkel *HE111* crashing 35 miles off the Tyne, from where three of the crew were rescued and taken into captivity and for treatment at North Shields. Small numbers of enemy aircraft continued to probe the coast, and on 30 April and 1 May

Junkers *JU88*s sent to bomb Whitley Bay in daylight were intercepted off Northumberland by Spitfires of 72 Squadron and shot down. Again, there were minor alerts which resulted in lost sleep and greater mental strain, but no further casualties or physical damage. Then, just days into May, came a night which has lived on in, and indeed haunted, the memories of many residents of Tynemouth Borough to this day.

On the night of 3/4 May, the Luftwaffe launched a concerted but widespread attack on the North-East of England, with bombs being scattered from north Northumberland as far south as Hull. The raid caused heavy property damage in North Shields and produced the worst incident of the war in the North-East and the worst single bomb incident in provincial Britain when a single German bomber dropped a stick of bombs on North Shields. Since the beginning of the war, many people from the largely working-class eastern part of the town had taken shelter in the deep basement of a local firm, W.A. Wilkinson Ltd. Situated on the corner of King Street and George Street, the shelter had been designated as a public air-raid shelter at the beginning of the war. Believing the shelter to be a safe one, the population were encouraged to utilize it, but the authorities were to be proven tragically wrong. Despite the reassurances of the authorities, many local people did not trust the safety of the shelter. Wilkinson's was a manufacturer of mineral waters and sodas, which necessitated not only a lot of heavy machinery but also the use of large vats of various chemicals, including types of acid. Combined with the fact that the ceiling of the

CAM ship similar to HMS Patia. (Unknown)

basement was not reinforced (it was not until October 1940 that £9 was allocated for defences against blast and shrapnel), many believed that the shelter was in fact a death trap and refused to use it.[17] The shelter itself was divided into three distinct areas, which included an entertainments area and a place for smokers.

On this particular night the alarm sounded just after 11.00 pm, and shortly thereafter there were 192 people inside the shelter, despite the maximum occupancy being 188. The people were marshalled into the shelter by the shelter warden, Mrs Ellen Lee, a popular and well-known figure in North Shields.

Just before midnight, two patrolling Special Constabulary officers heard the unmistakable drone of a lone enemy bomber; a nuisance raider. Special Constabulary Inspector Joseph Stuart could not see the enemy aircraft through the low cloud, but thought it likely to be a Heinkel *HE111* or, more likely, a Junkers *JU88*. Minutes later, Stuart and Special Constable Matthew Layzell heard four explosions. Running to King Street, they were the first people on the scene of a tragedy. Where the factory had once stood was now a ruin of broken masonry and clouds of dust. Screams could be heard coming from the rubble, and Inspector Stuart immediately came to the conclusion that there would be a high death toll. The ARP services were quickly on the scene and, helped by a large crowd of locals, worked for over fifteen hours in extremely dangerous conditions to try to rescue survivors who were from their own community and, for some, included friends and family.

In the aftermath of the disaster, there were mass burials in a part of Preston cemetery which was set aside specifically for victims of the tragedy. Tynemouth Borough Council Emergency Committee met several times in the immediate days following the disaster and interestingly made several recommendations, including the reduction in brightness of signs outside air raid shelters in the borough (although it is unlikely that this played any role in the incident, as there was heavy cloud cover at the time), the removal of 50 per cent of bunk beds from all public shelters and the restriction of numbers in public shelters to just fifty people. At no point in the meetings was Wilkinson's referred to by name.

When the bomb hit Wilkinson's, it penetrated the roof and it is believed went straight through the floor before exploding in the shelter.

The explosion resulted in the roof of the shelter collapsing and the heavy equipment and chemicals falling onto the survivors of the initial blast. The injured were taken to Kettlewell School for initial treatment, whilst the more seriously hurt were transported to Tynemouth Jubilee Hospital and Preston Hospital. A temporary mortuary was opened in nearby Church Street, where shocked survivors and relatives faced the hideous task of identifying the dead. Entire families had been wiped out and many others had lost multiple family members. The survivors included many with injuries, and one young woman, Alice Emmerson Sutherst, was rescued from the rubble after two days when she was found by a dog.

As word spread quickly throughout the borough that a disaster had occurred at Wilkinson's, it became clear that the majority of people who had taken to the shelter that night had been killed. When the final tally was taken, it emerged that of the 192 in the shelter, 107 men, women and children had lost their lives. As the days progressed, macabre stories began circulating in the area as the accounts of ARP workers became more commonly known. Many of the ARP workers who had been present at the shelter were off duty for weeks, shattered by the sights they had witnessed. The day after the raid, *The Journal* reported that a heavy raid in the North-East had resulted in a public shelter being destroyed. It stated that 'About 90 men, women and children were brought out uninjured', although the paper admitted that the death toll 'is feared to be heavy'.[18] In the following days, it would appear that the heavily censored press were ordered to restrict news of the disaster as it quickly disappeared from the headlines and was hushed up to prevent any demoralizing effect.

On the night of 5 May, the air raid warning sirens sounded at 11.25 pm throughout the area, and many could hear that there were a large number of enemy aircraft overhead. Radar stations in the region showed a large raid heading to the coast but, unknown at the time, this force of almost 400 aircraft was on its way to blitz Clydeside in Scotland. Despite this, the all-clear did not sound until shortly after 4.00 am and several bombs were dropped in the region. These included devices which detonated at Heaton Terrace in North Shields, where six people were killed (a Home Guardsman, three women and two children), and Garden Square in Cullercoats.

On the very next night, a much smaller force of less than thirty aircraft launched a raid lasting two hours on Tyneside and parts of Northumberland. Although such raids were unlikely to cause serious damage to vital war industries, they disturbed the sleep of workers and there was always the risk of an enemy bomber scoring a hit on an important target or of bombs or parachute mines causing severe civilian casualties. Several bombs fell in the Tynemouth and Whitley Bay area, with those in the latter causing little damage although several unexploded bombs forced the evacuation of nearby civilians.[19] At North Shields, Heaton Terrace was again hit (between the junctions of Verne Road and Langley Road), along with Cullercoats and in Tynemouth and Howdon, which caused no casualties but damaged more properties in areas which had been hit hard recently. The bombers returned the next night, though the main target was Hull,[20] and more bombs fell in largely open country in the north of the borough, causing further property damage.

This was to be the end of a week-long bombing campaign which affected the area, and although throughout the rest of May there were several alerts, the month passed without any more bombs being dropped in the area and no further casualties were suffered. The respite gave the people and the local authorities time to make good repairs to properties which had been damaged in the recent series of raids, and for people to relax somewhat. Over the next few months, the Luftwaffe were again fairly quiet, although lone raiders and reconnaissance flights were nuisances. These flights were not without danger for the Luftwaffe crews as British defences became stronger; a Hurricane shot down a Junkers *JU88* into the sea off Tynemouth on the night of 2 June. Some bombs dropped by a lone raider on the night of 10/11 July caused minor property damage, but by and large the months of June and July passed fairly peacefully for the area.

The power granted to shipyard workers thanks to the newfound importance of their wartime roles allowed them to take a stronger negotiating stance with their employers, who were unwilling to risk antagonizing them too much and provoking an illegal strike. One such example of this newfound power occurred in July, when workers at Swan Hunter's Wallsend Slipway threatened to strike over the lack of facilities provided for them during breaks. Anxious to avoid strike disruption, the management consulted with the local Factories Inspector, who immediately advised them to build a new canteen for the workers and, furthermore, instructed them that the canteen should be able to house 600 workers and that no less than £15,000 should be spent on it.

The Home Guard continued to develop in the area, and such was the standard of training now being achieved by units in Tynemouth and Wallsend that they were taking on ever more tasks, including relieving regular Army units from guard duties and manning coastal defences. There were, however, ongoing issues with weaponry. Although infantry weapons were now plentiful, there was still a lack of suitable anti-tank weapons. Typically, the Home Guard reacted by falling back on its own initiative, with a number of inventive weapons systems developed and issued. The testing of some of the larger and more experimental weapons could still prove to be somewhat problematic, and even dangerous. During the summer, the testing of a Northover Projector (a simple, and cheap, anti-tank weapon which fired a bottle containing a phosphorous solution) by the very reliable Tynemouth Battalion at Tynemouth Castle resulted in a fire taking hold in some nearby gorse bushes, and the local fire brigade had to be called out. However, as more of the younger members of the force were called up

New recruits training with a Universal Carrier. The training provided by Tynemouth Home Guard had proven useful to those members who went on to join the Army. (*Evening Chronicle*)

1941: THE CONTINUING CRISIS

for regular service, it was reported that the training they had already received during their period of Home Guard service had proven useful.

We have already seen how the men of the rescue squads had attracted the label of being prime rumour mongers in the ARP services. After a scattered raid on the night of 7/8 December had resulted in several deaths up the coast at Newbiggin, members of the rescue squads in Whitley Bay, Tynemouth and Wallsend were cautioned to restrict their conversations when outside of work, as all responses to incidents were to be considered confidential matters. For the men of the Whitley Bay squads, this was followed by a further warning that a relative of one of the victims from a recent raid had discovered that rescue squads had found the deceased's severed head. The relative had overheard this as gossip whilst in a local canteen.

Squadron Leader Denys Gillam had taken over command of 615 Squadron in July after a brief (five-month) spell as a staff officer at 9 Group HQ. In October, he had added to his tally of victories when he destroyed two German seaplanes and was awarded a bar to his DFC. Just a month later, while leading his squadron over Dunkirk, his aircraft was hit and he was wounded in both arms and legs. Nursing his stricken aircraft out to sea, he baled out and managed to struggle into his dinghy. The other aircraft of 615 Squadron stayed over him to provide protection, and Gillam was later picked up by a rescue launch. Whilst he was recuperating, he received an early Christmas present when he was awarded the DSO for his leadership of the squadron.

Notes

1. *Ibid*, p.26.
2. TWAS: DS/SWH/1/7. Minutes from Board meeting, 10 July 1941, p.20.
3. HMS *Calpe* survived the war; HMS *Eridge* was permanently crippled in 1942 and used subsequently as a base ship; HMS *Exmoor*, a replacement for her namesake (built at Vickers Armstrong's Walker Naval Yard) which had been sunk in February 1941, survived the war; HMS *Farndale* survived the war; HMS *Heythrop* was sunk in March 1942; HMS *Hursley* survived the war; and HMS *Lamerton* also survived the war. RFA *Ennerdale* took part in the landings in North Africa, Italy and the Far East, surviving the war despite striking a mine and being damaged in 1945.
4. This incident is covered in more detail in Hudson, Harry C., *Arctic Interlude: Independent to North Russia* (CreateSpace Independent Publishing, 2012), p.87.
5. The target for this night's raid seems to have been HMS *Manchester* and the nearly completed aircraft carrier HMS *Illustrious*, both of which were on

the Tyne. No bombs fell near the ships, although heavy damage was done in South Shields on this night.
6. Mr Thompson had been Junior World Weight-Lifting Champion in his youth.
7. *Shields Evening News*, 15 April 1941, p.2.
8. *Shields Evening News*, 15 April 1941, p.2.
9. *Ibid.*
10. The main target for the Luftwaffe this night was Northern Ireland.
11. The police officer was the father of well-known North-East historian Bill Purdue (who was an examiner when the author submitted his PhD thesis).
12. *Shields Evening News*, 16 April 1941, p.1.
13. The aircraft, a Heinkel *HE111*, crashed at Huby in Yorkshire.
14. This raid had a devastating effect on several communities in Newcastle, notably at Guilford Place where thirty-five people were killed by a parachute mine. The Luftwaffe claimed on German radio that they had made a heavy attack on Sunderland, but not a single bomb fell on that area during this night.
15. *Shields Evening News*, 26 April 1941, p.1.
16. *Shields Evening News*, 26 April 1941, p.2.
17. They included the author's grandfather, who was a fireman in North Shields and whose family lived close by. Shortly before the fateful raid, he forbade my grandmother from using the shelter and thus probably saved her life and that of my mother and uncle, who were children at the time.
18. *The Journal*, 5 May 1941, p.4.
19. The unexploded bombs in Whitley Bay were at Links Avenue, Claremont Road and St Mary's Avenue.
20. This was the first night of a two-night blitz on the city.

CHAPTER FOUR

1942: The End of the Beginning

The fourth year of the war opened quietly in Tynemouth and Wallsend. In Tynemouth, it has been traditional for the New Year to be marked by the firing of a maroon (firework) at midnight, but with the wartime regulations this was impossible; those wishing to welcome in the New Year had to rely on their own clocks or the wireless. Although the celebrations were certainly more muted than in peacetime, there were still several hundred people who went about the borough first-footing. Another tradition, that of crowds gathering in Northumberland Square, North Shields, was also followed. Mr Gilbert Park followed in family tradition by organizing the impromptu celebration, and although there were large crowds the assembly was certainly smaller than in peacetime. Whilst awaiting midnight, the crowd sang popular songs and after the recorded chimes of Big Ben had been heard a bugler sounded the 'Last Post' to commemorate the passing of the old year and then the 'Reveille' to herald the beginning of 1942. After this, people wished each other happy new year and parted to attend various parties. According to reports, there were many house parties heard to be in progress and, for many, the anxieties of the war were completely forgotten amongst the gaiety. However, it was also reported that most people, when expressing their hopes for the New Year, placed victory and peace at the top of their lists.

The New Year had opened fairly quietly, with muted festivities over the Christmas and New Year period. These were disrupted when a large force of enemy bombers made an attack on Newcastle on the night of 29/30 December 1941, but no bombs fell on Tynemouth or Wallsend, although the people there were forced to take to their shelters once more. This was unusual at this time, as the more typical Luftwaffe activity was to continue to send over nuisance bombing raids, often flown by lone Junker *JU88* aircraft. These efforts, however, were by now meeting a far more organized opposition, and were rarely successful. On 16 January, one such attempt was made. The sirens sounded at shortly after 4.45 pm, but just minutes later the raider was shot down by heavy anti-aircraft fire and crashed just off the coast of Tynemouth. The crew were killed, with one body, that of a Leutnant D. Andreson, later being washed ashore at Tynemouth Haven.

In late January, two seamen from North Shields were awarded the Liverpool Shipwreck and Human Society's silver medal for the part they played in rescuing another sailor in December 1941. The two men, George Armstrong of 330 Waterville Road and John Cuthbert Mudd of 86 Stephenson Street, had heard another seaman fall into the water at the rear of their ship, which was berthed at Liverpool. The unfortunate sailor, Seaman Gunner John Galvin, was going ashore but had stumbled over the side of the dock in the extremely dark conditions and, because he was wearing a heavy oilskin coat, had gotten into difficulties. His cries for help were heard by the two Shields men, who without hesitation jumped into the freezing cold water and swam to Galvin. Other crewmen threw in a lifebuoy and the two men managed to get the now unconscious gunner to the dockside, where he was pulled up by other helpers. The two rescuers also climbed out and helped give artificial respiration to Galvin until an ambulance arrived. Galvin was extremely ill by the time he reached hospital and his family were sent for, but he eventually recovered. The award ceremony was well attended, although Mr Mudd could not attend as he was at sea when it took place.

We have already seen how many of the men who had served aboard the North Shields fishing fleet were involved in the extremely dangerous task of minesweeping, and that many of these men paid the ultimate price. In January, the wife of Able Seaman Henry Clay (30) received the news that her husband had been killed in the Mediterranean during an attack on his minesweeping trawler, HMT *Clyne Castle*. Able Seaman Clay was born in North Shields, had worked for a number of years aboard the trawlers of Messrs Richard Irvin & Sons Ltd and left behind his widow and a son.[1]

After recovering from the wounds he had suffered at the end of 1941, Squadron Leader Denys Gillam embarked on a two-month lecture tour of the USA. Squadron Leader Gillam spent this time giving talks to American airmen, many of whom would shortly find themselves fighting against the Luftwaffe in the skies over Europe. After returning to the UK, Gillam was promoted to Wing Commander and posted to Duxford to form the first Typhoon fighter-bomber wing in the RAF. Gillam did a good job, and the wing made its operational debut during the ill-fated Dieppe raid in August that year.

Tynemouth's Mayor had, in 1941, instigated a Russian Red Cross Appeal Fund, and the charitable efforts had proven a great success. It was originally conceived that the fund would finish on the last day of 1941, but the recent announcement of a national competition to salvage waste paper had listed the Aid to Russia Fund as one of its beneficiaries, and it came as little surprise that this led to a change of heart and an extension of the Mayor's fund. On the first day of 1942, a further £42 was donated in the borough, with contributions including £11 from the employees of Messrs Walker (House of Quality) and £7 4s. 3d. from the Spring Gardens Savings Group. This meant that the fund had reached almost £2,500, with at least £200 promised. The Mayor and Mayoress had attended a dance at New York on New Year's Eve to raise money for the fund. The dance was said to have been a big success, although the total raised was not yet counted. Many of the local pubs were in competition with each other to contribute the most. For example, the patrons of the Sir Colin Campbell Hotel raised £6 15s., whilst the Mariners Arms donated £8 0s. 3d. The paper salvage competition and the Mayor's Russia fund were to run until the end of January. It was hoped that the fund might achieve the sum total of £5,000 by its completion date.

The salvage campaigns which ran throughout the war were a source of enthusiasm for many schoolchildren, who eagerly gathered scrap materials such as paper, cloth or metal to be reused. One of the reasons for the enthusiasm many children showed was the offer of prizes for those who collected the most, which were offered by most of the local authorities. The children of Cullercoats seem to have been particularly enthusiastic, as they are mentioned several times as having won prizes.

There was a keen sense of competition between Tyneside communities when it came to find-raising, and at a meeting in mid-January to celebrate the Mayor of Tynemouth's Russia Fund reaching

Schoolchildren in Cullercoats were awarded prizes for their salvage campaigning. (Shields Evening News)

the total of £3,500 the Mayor said that although he applauded the Lord Mayor of Newcastle's appeal for local communities to come together to raise as much as possible, he 'thought Tynemouth has set the pace'.[2] The Mayor declared that the fund had exceeded all of his expectations, and he thanked the people of the borough whilst urging them to even further efforts. The Mayor reserved especial praise for Mr Roy Walker of Messrs Walker (House of Quality) Ltd, who had personally donated £100, and the efforts of the staff canteen of the Shields Ice Company, which had contributed £200. By this point, the area's Licensed Victuallers Association and its members had donated over £264. Other enthusiastic contributors included Mr Tom Welch, whose confectionary company had donated several boxes of sweets and raised approximately £100.

Amongst the early casualties of the year was the death of yet another air gunner in the RAF from the area. Sergeant Reuben Matthew Mander (27), a Wallsend man, was crewing a Bristol Blenheim IV (Z9676) of 82 Squadron along with his pilot and observer at the time of his death on 4 January. The aircraft was at the time on a ferry flight from Egypt to Malta (or possibly vice-versa), and was believed to have been shot down, along with another aircraft from the squadron, over the sea at some point in its journey, killing all three crewmen.[3]

Once the end of January was reached, yet another fund-raising effort began with the Tynemouth Warships Week running from 31 January until 7 February. Past Warships Weeks had been immensely successful (unsurprising in an area so dependent upon shipbuilding), but for 1942 an even more ambitious target was set. The committee intended to attempt to raise the sum of £110,000 to cover the cost of construction of a new destroyer; whilst admitting the total was ambitious, they expressed confidence in achieving it.

We have already seen that the blackout regulations were enforced rigorously and how otherwise law-abiding people could fall foul of the laws surrounding the blackout. In mid-January, one North Shields man, William Goodinson (33) of 25 Verne Road, found himself before magistrates charged with having allowed flames and sparks to come from his chimney during the blackout hours and during an alert. The flames had been seen by a Police Reserve who had cautioned Mr Goodinson. When brought before the bench, Mr Goodinson told the magistrates that the chimney had only been swept three months previously and the magistrates' clerk even admitted that Mr Goodinson was correct when he had said that the incident was one which might have happened to anyone. The bench seems to have taken the view that although this was a breach of the regulations, it was one which was accidental and, although it must be punished, they took a lenient view and fined Mr Goodinson just 10s.

The substantial community of coloured seamen who lived in North Shields had often suffered from a lack of tolerance and understanding from the white community; many struggled to find work, whilst many of their children (a large proportion of whom were of mixed race) had a poor, or in some cases no, formal educational opportunities. One common allegation made against the black community was that they were violent and prone to committing crimes. In January, one such sailor, Alfred Percy Jonathan (29), was charged with having stabbed in the chest and wounded another coloured seaman, James Kennedy, with an intent to maim him. Jonathan was taken into custody, and upon reaching the police station asked the inspector to take down a statement. At a hearing in Tynemouth he was remanded for a fortnight. Jonathan appeared once again at the end of this period, but the police asked for an extension of his remand as Kennedy was still in hospital and would not be released for at least a further fortnight. Despite asking for bail, Jonathan was duly remanded once more.

On 10 February, Jonathan's case was finally heard at Tynemouth magistrates court. It was one of two wounding cases involving three coloured seamen that were heard on that day: the first case in fact shone light on the second. James Kennedy (29) of no fixed abode was the man who had been allegedly wounded by Mr Jonathan in the second case, but in the first he was accused of wounding, on the same day as the incident when he was stabbed, with intent to maim Charles Goldberg Steed by stabbing him in the eye. Due to evidential problems, the police asked the magistrates to reduce the charge to wounding without intent, and Kennedy pleaded not guilty. It would appear that Mr Steed, a ship's greaser, who lived at 13 Union Street, had been at sea for over two months, and upon returning to his home on 12 January had been told by his wife that she had been keeping the company of another man.

Later that night, Mr and Mrs Steed were sitting in their home with Alfred Percy Jonathan and a woman named Linda Dunlop, when two coloured seamen, Kennedy and a man named Goodwin, knocked on the door and asked to see Mr Steed. Upon being refused, they went away but came back shortly afterwards and repeated the request. Mr Steed went to the door, and after a short conversation told Kennedy to go away, at which point Kennedy pulled out a knife and stabbed Mr Steed in the left eye. Mr Steed staggered back into the house and asked the two women to get the police. After examination at Tynemouth Infirmary, Mr Steed had his left eye removed.

Mr Steed said that he had never met Kennedy before, but he had known Goodwin for several years. He denied making any attack on either man, although he admitted that he had a poker with him when he went to the door, but he had put this down before he had answered the door. Mr Steed was then asked if Mr Jonathan had stabbed Kennedy afterwards, but said that he had no idea what had happened in the street after he had been attacked as he had staggered back into his home. Mr Jonathan, giving evidence, said that he had taken the knife from Kennedy and had given chase, and when he caught them they had struggled and when they fell, with Kennedy on top of him, he had stabbed Kennedy in the chest.

When Mr Kennedy was called to give evidence, he said that he had gone to Steed's to see a separate man named Reed, but had known

Steed for a couple of months; he had not gone there with the intent to cause trouble, although he admitted that he was aware that Steed and Goodwin had been arguing about a woman. He alleged that Steed had answered the door holding something and that he had struck him over the head with a poker, and he had reeled back into the street. He denied ever having a knife or stabbing anyone. Goodwin had since gone to sea and could not be called as a witness. The solicitor representing Mr Kennedy said that it would be very unsafe to convict his client on the available evidence, and asked for Kennedy to be given the benefit of the doubt, whilst the police informed the bench that this was the first time Kennedy had been brought before the magistrates.

The magistrates retired to confer and, despite the pleas and the confusing evidence, found Kennedy guilty of the charge of wounding without intent and sentenced him to six months with hard labour.

The second case was then heard, that of Alfred Percy Jonathan (30), also of no fixed abode, accused of wounding with intent to maim Kennedy. Once again the police asked for the charge to be reduced to wounding without intent. Kennedy, who was a ship's fireman, said that he had gone to the house of Mr Steed at 9.30 pm on 12 January in the company of another seaman named Goodwin, with whom Mr Steed had been arguing over a woman. A quarrel had developed in the passage of the house between Steed and Goodwin, but he stated that he had played no part in it. He said that he had left the house and gone into the street, where he was followed by Jonathan. He alleged that Jonathan had got hold of him from behind, and he saw that he had a knife in his hand. He said that during the initial scuffle he had received a cut on the palm of his hand. The two continued to struggle before they fell to the ground, with Jonathan on top. Kennedy then alleged that Jonathan had stabbed him in the chest and left him there. Kennedy said he lay there for five or ten minutes before he managed to get up and walk away, propping himself up against the wall of the Alnwick Castle public house. He was found there by two men and taken to the police station, where a police sergeant who saw him took him to hospital.

Under cross-examination, Kennedy admitted that it had been he who had been staying with Mrs Steed whilst her husband was away at sea, but once again denied quarrelling with Mr Steed or possessing a knife.

He denied that the cut on his palm had occurred when Mr Jonathan had taken the knife off him.

Mr Steed repeated his version of events before his wife, Mary Elizabeth Steed, gave evidence. She agreed that there had been a quarrel in the passage and that her husband had staggered back into the house having been injured, telling her to fetch the police. Mrs Steed said that whilst she was going for the police, Mr Jonathan left almost immediately and she saw him pursuing Kennedy with a flashlight in his hand. Upon being asked if Mr Jonathan had a knife in his hand, she said, 'I didn't see anybody with a knife.'

Called to give evidence, Dr Fleming of Tynemouth Infirmary said that when he saw Kennedy he was very ill with shock, and that his clothing was soaked with blood. He determined that Kennedy had lost at least a pint of blood and was suffering from a wound an inch-and-a-half long on the left side of his chest, with a deep cut on the palm of his left hand. Further examination had shown that the wound to Kennedy's chest had not hit any vital organs. Under cross-examination, the doctor testified that the wound to the hand was entirely consistent with Jonathan's account of having taken the knife from Kennedy.

PC Wilson testified that when he reached 13 Union Street, having been summoned by Mrs Steed, he saw Jonathan standing there with a knife in his hand. He asked him to hand it over and he immediately did so, saying that he had not been the cause of the trouble. PC Wilson said that the handle of the knife was sticky with blood when he took it from Jonathan.

Superintendent Logan said that when he arrested Jonathan the next day, the accused had immediately volunteered to give a statement which he wished to be written down. Logan said that Jonathan had been 'very anxious to make a statement and was very straightforward about it'. In his statement, Jonathan said that he was a native of Cardiff and lived there, but was visiting Steed. He witnessed Kennedy stab Steed in the eye before making off, and when Steed asked his wife to fetch the police he also asked him to follow Kennedy. Having borrowed a torch, he left the house to do so. He acknowledged that he produced a pocket knife, but said that the knife produced in evidence was much larger and was not his but the one used by Kennedy to stab Steed. Jonathan said that when he realised he was being followed,

Kennedy had rushed at him with the knife in his right hand. Jonathan had ducked, causing Kennedy and himself to fall. Whilst struggling on the ground, Kennedy tried to stab him in the throat and Jonathan grabbed his wrist. At this point he alleged Kennedy changed the knife to his left hand, but Jonathan said he snatched it from him. He acknowledged stabbing Kennedy, but said, 'What I did I did in self-defence ... because he was trying to do it to me.' Jonathan said that after being stabbed, Kennedy had run away and he had walked back to Steed's house, where PC Wilson found him. Under examination from Chief Inspector Radcliffe, Jonathan said that he had stabbed Kennedy in the same movement with which he had snatched the knife from him. After conferring over the case, the magistrates declared that Jonathan had acted in self-defence and dismissed the charge against him.[4]

On 14 March, yet another vessel came to grief at the mouth of the Tyne. This time the victim was the Belgian steamer SS *Brabo*, which collided with the SS *Poznan* and sank roughly halfway along the north pier. Working from previous experience, efforts were made to construct a dam to protect the vessel from the waves, but poor weather intervened and high waves smashed into the vessel, causing it to break up.[5]

The shipbuilding communities of Wallsend followed the exploits of 'their' ships throughout the war, with many of the officers and men on board sending souvenirs that reflected their adventures at sea. In December 1938, Swan Hunter's had completed the Tribal Class destroyer HMS *Somali* and the men who had worked on her construction followed the career of the ship keenly, reacting with pride when she became the first British ship to capture a German merchant vessel on 3 September 1939. HMS *Somali* saw widespread service, taking part in the Norwegian campaign before spending the winter of 1940/1941 as leader of the 6th Destroyer Flotilla, kept busy patrolling home waters during this dangerous time. In the spring of 1941, she had boarded a German weather ship and captured valuable Enigma machine instructions and code books. Her active service life continued in 1942 when, in August, she took part in Operation Pedestal in the Mediterranean and rescued the whole 105-man crew of a torpedoed American cargo ship. Just one month later, HMS *Somali* found herself escorting convoy QP14 to Russia in company with several of her sister ships (including the Swan Hunter-built HMS *Eskimo*). She had a new captain on this journey, Lieutenant Commander Colin Maud, as her old commanding officer, Jack Eaton, had been taken ill. On 20 September, HMS *Somali* was hit in the engine room by a torpedo from a German U-boat (during the same action, HMS *Eskimo* was described as having 'torpedoes all around her seemingly in dozens. With all her guns blazing she turned and twisted in "avoiding action"').[6] Without power and in very heavy seas, sister ship HMS *Ashanti* managed to secure a tow; for several days and in appalling weather conditions, which prevented the crew being taken off the stricken destroyer, the two vessels struggled to reach home. On 25 September, the damage and severe seas took their toll as HMS *Somali* broke her back and sank. Of her 102-man crew, only thirty-five were rescued from the freezing waters. These included the commanding officer, who was saved by the courageous actions of Leading Seaman Goad of HMS *Ashanti*, who dived into the freezing and churning waters to rescue him. Included amongst the lost from HMS *Somali* was Willington Quay man Petty Officer Ralph William Gilpin (24). The news of the loss of Petty Officer Gilpin was

HMS Somali. *The men who built her followed her career keenly until she was sunk in 1942.* (Public Domain)

received by his parents at their home at 60 St Peter's Road, Willington Quay. The loss of the ship was met with great sorrow amongst the workforce of Swan Hunter's.

During the year, the Wallsend yard of Swan Hunter completed ten naval vessels, including the massive 43,000 ton King George V Class battleship HMS *Anson*, two 11,000 ton Colony Class light cruisers HMS *Newfoundland* and *Gambia* the Hunt Class destroyers *HMS Bolebroke, Border, Grove, Melbrake* and *Modbury*, the Q Class destroyers HMS *Quality* and *Queensborough*, as well as the V Class destroyer HMS *Vigilant*.[7]

HMS *Anson* was launched in February 1940, but there had been delays in commissioning the battleship caused by the fitting of fire-control radar and additional anti-aircraft guns. In the month of her launching, the battleship had its name changed, as prior to this she was to have been called HMS *Jellicoe*.

Six of the warships completed during the year subsequently served with Allied navies. HMS *Gambia* was transferred to the Royal New Zealand Navy in 1943, whilst three of the Hunt Class ships (the

HMS Anson. (Public Domain)

HMS Newfoundland. (Public Domain)

HMS Quality. (Public Domain)

exceptions being HMS *Grove* and *Melbrake*) were transferred to the Hellenic Navy in 1942 and renamed (*Bolebroke* became *Pindos*, *Border* became *Adrias* and *Modbury* became *Miaoulis*). The former HMS *Border* achieved some level of fame as *Adrias* when, in 1943, she hit a mine and had her bow blown off, whilst sister ship HMS *Hurworth* was sunk. After taking on the survivors of her sister ship, the *Adrias* managed to beach in Turkey before setting sail for Alexandria (600 miles away), although she could only move at night due to the threat from enemy bombers. Several days later, she steamed slowly into Alexandria, where this remarkable feat of seamanship was met by ringing cheers from all of the naval crews present. Her captain, Commander Toumbos, received the highest award for bravery that the Greek navy could grant, whilst a message of tribute was dispatched to Swan Hunter's thanking the workforce for the construction of such a durable ship. Both of the Q Class destroyers finished in this year also saw foreign service, although this was not until after the cessation of hostilities; both were transferred to the Royal Australian Navy in 1945.

Adrias *(formerly HMS* Border*) on the Tyne in 1942 after transfer to the Hellenic Navy.* (Public Domain)

We have already seen how Wallsend engineering firm Charles Crofton & Co. Ltd had taken on large numbers of female workers and introduced other innovative measures. The firm continued to offer opportunities for work, but demanded good educational backgrounds. In August, for example, the firm was advertising for a youth to work in its order office, insisting that the applicants have a technical school education.

Minor problems with drunkenness, especially amongst industrial workers and servicemen, continued throughout the year. A typical example occurred in February, when three servicemen were accused of criminal damage and drunken and disorderly behaviour at North Shields ferry landing. The three men, naval ratings Ronald Miller (22) and Norman Dinsdale (22), and soldier Ernest Herbert (29), had been drinking heavily in North Shields, and when they got to the ferry landing they smashed a window at the terminal. A bridgeman employed by the Tyne Commission overheard the commotion, saw the three men moving away from the scene and reported the matter to the police. The collector at the ferry terminal said that the men were indeed drunk when they passed through the turnstile and that one of them threatened him with a torch, at which point he snatched up a spanner to defend himself but was disarmed by another of the men. Responding to the incident, PC MacDonald testified that the three men were acting in a drunken and disorderly fashion on the ferry landing and refused to quieten down after he cautioned them, so he took them to the police station. In doing so, he noticed the spanner taken from the collector lying beside one of the automated ticket booths, which also had a window smashed. All three men denied the offences, Dinsdale claiming that he could not remember anything and the other two merely admitting that they had been drunk as a result of too much beer. Miller went on to admit to the magistrate that he consumed a large amount of beer and did not know what he was doing on the night; he remembered seeing Dinsdale with the spanner but had no recollection of how he had come by it. Dinsdale then admitted being guilty of the drunk and disorderly charge but denied any knowledge of the criminal damage, whilst Herbert simply repeated that he had been drunk. Despite the testimony from an officer from the ship commenting on the two ratings' previous good character, the magistrates were obviously unimpressed by the behaviour of the servicemen and fined each of them 10s. for drunkenness and £1 5s 2d. for the damage caused.

With the battle to maintain Britain's seaborne supply routes at its peak, the magistrates and authorities were apt to be extremely disapproving of those who failed to make their ships at the appointed time of sailing, handing down some severe penalties in an effort to impress upon them the necessity of maintaining shipping schedules during this time of national crisis. Two North Shields men suffered the full wrath of the magistrates when they appeared before them for just such an offence in February. John Longton Gonsales (22) of 13 Upper Norfolk Street and Osten Persson (20) of 55 West Percy Street had been engaged to sail as able seamen, but had absented themselves from their ship without permission and gone home, replacements having to be found at the last moment so that the ship could sail. When asked by the magistrates why they had left their vessel without permission, they answered that they were on leave, but under questioning admitted that they did not have permission. The magistrates' clerk told them that they could not just leave the ship when they felt like it. Despite the fact that both men had, in the time between being charged and appearing in court, been back to sea and had handed themselves in at the police station when they heard about the charges facing them, the magistrates (headed by Mr Arthur Bilton; the Bilton family were prominent in North Shields, owning trawlers and running T.B. Bilton & Sons Ltd coppersmiths works at Bell Street in the town) took an extremely hard line with them. Partly as a lesson to others, they fined them each £10 (over £432 today), with one month to pay or face imprisonment.

Even in 1942, local authorities in the area were planning for infrastructure redevelopment in peacetime. In February, the joint committee for the construction of a new road tunnel under the River Tyne from Howdon to Jarrow were getting ready to submit their proposals for the scheme to the government (along with a proposal for a new bridge at Scotswood).

We have already seen how bombing raids could quickly overwhelm individual local authorities, and coordination and cooperation were essential. The three main local authorities in the area (Wallsend Municipal Borough, Tynemouth County Borough, and Whitley and Monkseaton Unitary District) seem to have developed a strong system of mutual cooperation. This even ran to the voluntary organizations, and the WVS formed several Mobile (Mutual Assistance) teams consisting of members skilled in cooking, first aid, gathering and disseminating information, and organizing and providing clothing. These teams, of which there were forty-one in 1942, were provided with transport and could locate from area to area as required.

For the people of Tynemouth, yet another disturbed night occurred on 26 March when the alarm sounded at 8.50 pm as a force of enemy aircraft approached the coast. The raiders seem to have been tasked with bombing areas around Newcastle, but little bombing actually developed (many of the planes were possibly forced to abandon their attack as a result of the defences) and no bombs dropped on Tynemouth or Wallsend. The alert was lifted shortly after 10.30 pm. The Luftwaffe once again paid a price, as the anti-aircraft defences of Tynemouth claimed another victim; this time a Dornier *DO217* which crashed into the sea off Tynemouth.

Although the number of raids had fallen away, it was obvious that Tynemouth and Wallsend were still vulnerable to attack by enemy aircraft. The authorities continually urged residents of the area to remain vigilant and not to let their guard down through negligence. The failure to completely observe the blackout regulations continued to be a source of many prosecutions in the area throughout the year. Given the heavy bombing which had affected the area in April 1941, it is no surprise that the authorities were keen to make examples of those who flouted the blackout and caused risk to themselves and their neighbours. Repeat offenders, especially, could expect stern measures to be taken against them. In April, Tynemouth magistrates fined two women from the same house 10s. apiece for separate blackout offences. In the first prosecution, Mrs Thomasina Macciochi (27) of 67 Blackthorne Crescent was fined for having no blackout up in her scullery. An ARP warden had seen a light shining through the window and had notified the police. Mrs Macchiochi pleaded that the blackout had been torn and she was going to get a new one, but was found guilty. In the second case, Mrs Lily Bennett (27), a lodger at the same house, was fined for having no blackout up at her bedroom window while having an electric light on. Her excuse that she had forgot to put up the blackout curtain was not accepted, as the warden had gone around some time after first warning her, only to find the light still shining.

The Empire Youth Rally which was held in North Shields on 25 April was hailed in the press as a great success, showing the number and variety of youth organizations present and active in the area. The rally and church service were preceded by a procession of over 550 boys and girls from the following organizations: Army Cadet Corps (North Shields); Air Training Corps (Tynemouth); Women's Junior Air Corps (which was the largest contingent); ARP Messengers; and the Boys' Brigade. They were joined at the church by groups from: North Shields Boys and Girls Club; North Shields Youth Centre; Christ Church Youth Club; the Young People's Guild; Tynemouth Municipal High School; Ralph Gardner Senior Girls; and Percy Main Parish Children.

Fund-raising had continued unabated throughout the year, with Red Cross campaigns and official government campaigns to provide funds for war materials including ships, aircraft, tanks and guns proving very popular in the area. In October, for example, Tynemouth raised over £30 during the borough's Tynemouth Tanks for Attack Campaign. The gift was accepted and a message of thanks from the Chancellor of the Exchequer relayed to the local authorities.

The contribution of Tynemouth Borough residents to the National War Savings Scheme was particularly impressive. It was announced that from the scheme beginning in November 1939 until 18 April 1942, the borough had contributed almost £3 million, equating to an average of £52 0s. 1d. per person.

Some individuals made charitable gifts which would serve the hard-working men and women of the ARP and civil defence services, whilst others donated medical equipment and even entirely equipped ambulances to the borough. A typical example of this sort of charitable donation came when it was announced that Councillor Mrs G.I. Frater of North Shields had gifted a mobile canteen unit to the borough at the end of April.

We have already seen the contribution made to the war effort by many North Shields trawlermen who were serving in the Royal Navy, but for those who continued with their civilian careers, the war greatly increased the threat in what was already an extremely dangerous job. Trawlers were very vulnerable to mines and attack by enemy aircraft, most having only minimum armament with which to defend themselves against attack. On 27 April, two members of this industry were honoured in a ceremony at the Fish Quay after the morning sales had taken place. Skipper David Pawse McRuvie of Kitchener Terrace and deck hand William Charles Jarman of Upper Queen Street had been aboard the Messrs R. Irvine & Sons trawler *Ben Screel* when it was attacked by a pair of German aircraft. The first bomb tore off the trawler's rudder, whilst the head-on attack of the second aircraft caused further damage. This second bomber, however, paid for its attack when it was hit and probably destroyed by return fire from the Lewis gun manned by Jarman. This was despite the deck hand, who was sheltered from fire only by a wooden shield, being blown from his gun before resuming his post. McRuvie used the starboard trawl-board as a makeshift rudder and managed to steer his trawler head-on into the swell whilst holes were patched and damage made as good as possible. The skipper was then able to make his way some 20 miles to an examination vessel, from where the trawler was towed back to port. For their actions on this day, the two men were awarded the Lloyd's War Medal for bravery at sea by the Mayor. It was also announced that McRuvie was to be awarded the MBE and Jarman the BEM.

With bombing attempts now far more limited than in 1941 and the spring weather a deterrent, the Luftwaffe restricted its main efforts to minelaying in the North Sea, with numerous attempts made to block the key Tyne approaches and counter-efforts by the minesweepers, which went out on a daily and nightly basis. Some of the aircraft engaged in minelaying also carried a few bombs and flew over the coast to drop these on targets of opportunity, seemingly at random. Just such a raid took place on the night of 15/16 April,

Skipper D.P McRuvie and Deck Hand W.C. Jarman, who were rewarded for their heroics during an attack on their trawler. (Shields Daily News)

G.U. (Charlie) Minto (right) at Colonial Rest House, North Shields. (IWM D10714)

and although no bombs fell in Tynemouth or Wallsend, yet again the presence of enemy aircraft resulted in a lengthy and anxious night in the shelter for the residents of this area as the alarm lasted all night from shortly after 9.30 pm to around 6.30 am.

On 30 April/1 May, what was described as a small force of bombers was spotted flying north from Ostend. Upon being joined by others from the direction of the Dutch coast, the raiders concentrated on the North-East, with aircraft plotted between Tyneside and Teesside. Although this was obviously an attempt at a concentrated raid, it never developed and the bombing, as had become typical, was widely scattered and largely inaccurate. There were, however, casualties in many communities in the area, including Wallsend. Bombs which may well have been aimed at the shipyards proved to be inaccurate and instead fell on the residential streets of Holly Avenue and Willow Grove, killing eleven people, including a Home Guardsman. Tynemouth Borough was more fortunate, only four bombs recorded on this night. They fell on the wagonway beside Allotment Farm, West Allotment, but caused little damage.

Death Toll in Wallsend, 1 May 1942

Name	Age	Address	Notes
Annie Elizabeth Anderson	64	43 Willow Grove	
Elsie Anderson	19	43 Willow Grove	
James Anderson	65	43 Willow Grove	
Elizabeth Ann Anderson	36	159 Holly Avenue	
Stanley Anderson	36	159 Holly Avenue	Home Guard
Stanley Anderson	11	159 Holly Avenue	
Arthur Dempsey	29	156 Holly Avenue	
Margaret Gallantry Duffy	32	156 Holly Avenue	
Margaret Elliott	22	157 Holly Avenue	
Nicholas Lee	1	157 Holly Avenue	
William Alexander Lee	1	157 Holly Avenue	

We have already seen how the war had a polarizing effect on attitudes towards foreign nationals. Distrust of enemy aliens continued throughout the war, although some, who were obviously working for the Allied cause, were accepted in the area. The monitoring of non-enemy aliens was also a matter of great concern for the local police forces: they were forced to register and many also faced curfews and other restrictions on their free movement. The attitude towards non-enemy aliens was often determined largely by race. There were significant populations of non-enemy aliens in the area. North Shields, in particular, had a large number of Scandinavian and a smaller but still significant number of African seamen, whilst across the river, South Shields had a very large Yemeni population. Whilst the Scandinavians had largely become an accepted part of the community in North Shields, this was not the case for the Africans: a report by the Colonial Office into attitudes in the town claimed that 'colour prejudice in this town was quite unbearable. Coloured men on land remained in a perpetual state of un-employment, as the white man considered them only fit to perform the most menial task in a segregated atmosphere of a cargo ship at sea.'[8] Efforts were made by members of the black community to integrate themselves within the town. In May, the International Coloured Mutual Aid Association was set up in the town by Mr C.U. Minto (known widely as Charlie Minto) of Calabar, Nigeria.

Minto, a former welterweight boxing champion who had lived in North Shields for some time, witnessing the 'very poor living conditions' amongst the black population, approached several local figures to secure their support and suitable premises for his organization. One of his key supporters was a former Mayor of the town, Mr Stanley Holmes, who became a patron and, together with Mr Minto, set about gathering support for the scheme. By charging a small fee of 2d. per week from each member, the group was able to initially rent some rooms and put on a series of workshops, meetings and lectures. The association quickly grew and began to raise more funds, with members from as far afield as Nigeria, Barbados and Sierra Leone.

A key to the success of the association was the appointment of a steering committee which included Mr Minto as President, Mr Benjamin (from Sierra Leone) as Vice-President, Mr Provensal (from the Gold Coast) as Secretary and Mr Thomas (from Liberia) as Treasurer. One of the first decisions the committee made was that a prime goal of the association should be to encourage greater 'understanding between the white and coloured people' of the town.[9] Other aims of the committee included the supply of funds to those black seamen and their families who were experiencing hardships, fostering good relations within all communities and the raising of funds for the education of black children in the town.

The association became a huge success in a remarkably short time, the Colonial Office being particularly impressed with the leadership, determination and vision demonstrated by Mr Minto. Before the establishment of the association, a large proportion of the children of black residents many of whom were from mixed marriages between, according to *The African Standard*, black seamen and white women 'from the lowest walks of life' (i.e. prostitutes and former prostitutes) did not attend school. This began to change as funds were supplied and attitudes changed. There were also, of course, black women and women of mixed race present in the town in some numbers, and until the formation of the association these people too had an extremely difficult time securing work to support themselves and their families. An early success for the association came over just such an issue. Upon learning that two black women had been turned down for positions at a local fish factory purely on the grounds of their race, Mr Minto secured a meeting with the manager and convinced him to give the young women a chance. After a period of a few months, the manager reported to Mr Minto that he found the women's attitudes to be very good and that he was extremely pleased with them. This news spread throughout the town and resulted in increasing numbers of managers being willing to engage black women in their workforces.

A follow-up report by the Colonial Office into black affairs in North Shields found that almost solely through the work of Mr Minto and his association, attitudes towards the black community in the town were markedly improved. As a sign of this, the members of the black and coloured community were 'daily receiving increased support' from the white community, with the lives of blacks in the town being 'considerably improved', leaving 'little anxiety for the future'.[10]

By 1942, the Tynemouth Home Guard contained a large percentage of men of military service age who had been deferred from conscription as they were engaged in important war work, with most being in reserved occupations in industry. However, by October the leaders of the Home Guard were growing increasingly anxious due to the rumour which suggested that the government was considering cancelling the reserved status of many of these men and replacing them in war work with over-40s who were currently engaged in non-essential work (despite many impracticalities therein), as they felt that it would prove

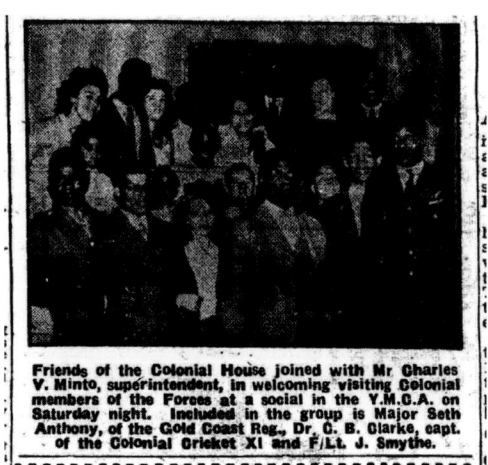

Charlie Minto and friends of Colonial House shortly after the end of the war. (*Shields Daily News*)

impossible to replace these younger men within the ranks of the Home Guard. The leadership of the Home Guard felt that their organization was making a worthwhile contribution to the war effort, but the need for men in the services was reaching a critical point and they would find it difficult to argue with the government on this point.

The Tynemouth Battalion of the Home Guard had established a reputation for itself as an efficient and well-trained unit, and this was recognized in May 1942 when men of the battalion were manning a 'Z' battery of anti-aircraft rocket projectors stationed beside the Park Hotel. This weapon had been developed amidst great secrecy, with training facilities located in Tynemouth Borough. The use of men from the Tynemouth Home Guard in training on and helping to develop such a top-secret weapon demonstrated the official recognition of the skills of the guardsmen and officers of the battalion. The Home Guard gunners succeeded in bringing down at least one enemy aircraft with the new weapon during this period.[11] As well as the 'Z' batteries of anti-aircraft rockets, the men of the battalion also manned more traditional anti-aircraft guns.

We have already seen how large numbers of women wished to play a more active role in the defence of Britain by joining the ranks of the Home Guard, but were forbidden to do so by officialdom. By mid-1942, the unofficial Women's Home Defence organization had formed groups in London; in October, the first detachment of this organization outside London was formed at Whitley Bay. Led by Mrs F.M. Pelton of 2 King's Drive, Whitley Bay, and Miss M. Taylor, thirty volunteers aged 25–40 had been formed into two groups of fifteen and were receiving instructional lectures from members of the Home Guard. The leaders of the group were defiant in their belief that women should be able to play a larger and more active role in the defence of the country, and told a local reporter that regardless of whether the organization was legalized or not, they would continue with their sessions. Basic training included instruction in areas such as: cooking for troops in the field, first-aid, unarmed combat, signalling, fieldcraft, anti-gas techniques, camouflage, map reading and firearms drill.

Mrs Pelton said that the women wished to play a larger role and to assist the Home Guard in the event of attack, 'even to the extent of picking up a rifle and shooting the enemy'. Mrs Pelton also said that although the decision had been made that the organization would not wear a uniform, they did have a badge which consisted of crossed rifles and a pistol with the initials WHD. Each member, upon joining, paid the sum of half-a-crown, which paid for her badge and left some money for administrative costs.

Mrs Pelton praised the local Home Guard for the assistance and instruction which they had so far given to what was formally the Whitley Bay and Monkseaton Women's Home Defence. This demonstrated that many in the Home Guard also felt that women should be allowed to make a more active contribution to the war effort. It was claimed that there had been many enquiries regarding membership, but that the numbers could not be increased until suitable accommodation for a larger group could be arranged. Mrs Pelton also expressed the hope that the group would soon be able to use the rifle ranges for marksmanship practice and musketry drill. Emphasizing that these were women who were already leading busy lives, the leaders of the group were keen to let people know of the difficulties of women meeting up during the day. They also expressed their pride in the fact that many members were already fire watchers or members of the ARP services. A large proportion of the women were the wives of servicemen or Home Guardsmen and, according to the reporter, they showed especial enthusiasm for their role. The reporter was impressed by the keen grasp of military ideas shown by the members of the group and, in a rather sexist comment, revealed his surprise at the women's 'willingness to submit themselves to orders'.[12]

With petrol rationing in force and people being urged not to travel unless it was absolutely necessary, it is no wonder that boredom became a factor in everyday life. One initiative to challenge this, especially during the traditional summer holiday weeks, was the Holidays at Home campaign which became a feature of British wartime life for many. Organized by local authorities and volunteers, the programme enjoyed great success in providing entertainment to relieve the otherwise drabness of wartime life in Britain. In Wallsend and Tynemouth, the schemes proved a great success and demonstrated a strong community spirit.

Activities during the Holidays at Home periods were very varied, with sports, music and patriotic competitions at the forefront. It was announced in June that the Wallsend summer programme would run for five weeks, from 13 June until 8 July. Music was a strong feature of the events, with a performance from the Royal Netherland Band at Wallsend Park being a highlight. Other musical performances were given around the borough by the Rising Sun Colliery and Wallsend Shipyard bands. Dancing would be a feature of all of these performances. The North-Eastern Electric Supply Company Ltd had agreed to supply their welfare ground for a number of sporting competitions, including ladies' and men's bowling, tennis and putting.

Although the threat from enemy bombing had lessened, there were still occasional hit-and-run raids attempted by lone bombers which came in at low level to avoid radar detection. On 8 August, a raider dropped several bombs on Cullercoats and Tynemouth. One of these hit St John's Methodist Church in Cullercoats, demolishing the building and killing 13-year-old Denis Thomson Armstrong, who was practising the organ at the time. Other bombs fell at various locations on Marden Avenue, Mast Lane (where the naval sick quarters was hit), and near Beaconsfield House at Tynemouth and Kennersdene Farm (both of which were near the main railway line).

Whilst the war changed the lives and available opportunities for many women in the area, in some things traditional attitudes still prevailed. The NAAFI provided a welcome and valuable service to the men and women of the services and ARP and civil defence units. In October, an appeal was made for more women from the area to come forward for such duties. It asked them to consider being trained as a NAAFI cook, claiming that although the women of the area were renowned for their 'high standard of home cooking' and those that had come forward were particularly valued, more were still needed. The appeal promised a six-week paid course, with travel and billeting allowances available.[13]

Throughout the year, the shipyards of the Tyne were working at full capacity and turning out both warships and merchant vessels at a prodigious rate. Amongst the warships completed in 1942 was HMS *Petard*. The P-Class destroyer had been launched in 1941 before completion work was finished in July 1942 and it formally became a Royal Navy ship. Its largely inexperienced crew was initially under the command of Lieutenant Commander Stephen Beattie, although he was quickly replaced by Lieutenant Commander Mark Thornton, DSC.[14] HMS *Petard* began her wartime career as an escort to a Middle East-bound convoy, but seems to have initially suffered from ill-luck as the convoy escorts shot down two British Sunderland flying boats and one of the destroyers collided with a merchant vessel in foggy conditions. After serving the convoy, HMS *Petard* joined the 12th Flotilla, operating in the Mediterranean from a base at Port Said. On 30 October, the *Petard*, along with four other destroyers, was hunting for a reported U-boat off the Nile Delta. Dropping depth charges, they forced the submarine to surface, where *Petard* and HMS *Hurworth* engaged the vessel with gunfire. With the U-boat sinking and the crew having abandoned her, three men from *Petard* went across to the submarine and carried out a search. They were First Lieutenant Anthony Fasson, Able Seaman Colin Grazier and NAAFI canteen assistant Tommy Brown. The latter was a 16-year-old from North Shields and had followed the other two across voluntarily. They discovered important documents and, crucially, the code books for the new four-rotor Enigma machine. Tommy Brown had left the submarine when it sank quickly, the other two men being lost with the enemy vessel. For his courage, Brown was awarded the George Medal, whilst Fasson and Grazier were both awarded the George Cross posthumously.[15]

HMS *Petard* continued operations in the Mediterranean, her exploits closely followed back on Tyneside by the yard workers who had constructed her (Thornton occasionally sent back souvenirs of her service). In November, the destroyer took part in the operation to resupply Malta, which was under siege from Axis forces. During Operation Stoneage, *Petard* rescued five RAF men from a dinghy before taking the cruiser HMS *Arethusa* under tow after it had been hit by a torpedo which had crippled it and killed over 150 crewmen. The towing process was an arduous one because the damage to the cruiser was severe, and the bridge crew on *Petard* got no rest for three days and nights as they monitored and adjusted the tow and fought off repeated aerial attacks. By noon on 19 November, two tugs from Alexandria took over the tow. The commanding officer of *Petard* learned that Operation Stoneage had been a success, with the first resupply convoy in two years successfully reaching Malta.

The *Petard* continued her escort duties, rescuing further RAF men and shooting down a German bomber before sinking an Italian submarine on 15 December whilst on her way to Malta from Benghazi. The action took place in darkness, with the submarine (*P-35*) firing two torpedoes at *Petard*. The destroyer successfully evaded the torpedoes before launching two depth charge attacks (along with one from her partner, the Greek destroyer *Queen Olga*) and forcing the submarine to surface. This was followed by shelling the enemy vessel and subsequently ramming and sinking her. News of the engagement spread rapidly, and the two destroyers received a rapturous welcome when they reached their destination. The damage to the bows of HMS *Petard* resulted in her spending some time in dry dock in Alexandria.

A tale of the great courage and coolness under extreme circumstances shown by an 18-year-old North Shields merchant seaman was related to the people of the area in September. Second Mate Ralph William Armstrong was at the time an apprentice mate aboard a merchant vessel sailing from Singapore to Australia when the ship was attacked and hit by Japanese dive-bombers, causing severe damage and many casualties. Amongst the casualties were the master and mate (who were both seriously injured), and all other officers were either killed or seriously injured. Ralph had already distinguished himself during the action by pulling two wounded men from the wreckage, and on being informed that there were no officers left in a fit condition he immediately took the initiative and began to organize and rally the crew. After successfully extinguishing the onboard fires, they turned the ship around and made for Singapore, but hours later were attacked and hit yet again. This time it was clear that the battered ship was sinking. Ralph once again took charge, organizing the crewing and launching three lifeboats which he then kept together, making for Singapore. The journey took ten days, with Ralph also caring for the injured master and mate in his own boat. All three boats successfully reached Singapore, where the injured were treated. When the Japanese invaded Singapore and it became clear that the island was going to fall, Ralph and three men of the crew made their way by lifeboat to safety. At the end of September, it was announced that Ralph was to be awarded the British Empire Medal for his courage and cool leadership. The investiture took place the next year, when Ralph was presented with his medal by King George VI at Buckingham Palace.

In many ways, 1942 was the year when traditional conflicts between employers and employees were renewed. Whilst 1939 and 1940 had been relatively peaceful, with only minor stoppages in 1941, there were signs that workers were increasingly ready to take illegal strike action to further their own ends or defend themselves against what they perceived as injustices. The shipyards and engineering works of North Shields and Wallsend were particular sources of industrial unrest, with a long history of strike action. For many workers, the increased negotiating power which they held due to the importance of their work during wartime, combined with prior examples of the government being unable or unwilling to take harsh measures against striking workers who were vital to the war effort, encouraged them to bolder actions. On Tyneside, however, not all strikes were made against employers, with several stoppages in the engineering and shipyards of Wallsend being because of disputes between local trade union members and national trade union leaderships.

Ralph William Armstrong, Merchant Navy, was awarded the BEM for his incredible coolness in saving his ship's crew after Japanese attack when aged only 18. (Shields Evening News)

In September, the growing signs of industrial unrest once again showed through the patriotic gloss of a nation united at war. The drillers employed at the Wallsend firm of Parsons Steam Turbine Company Ltd came out in a dispute over their rates of pay, and were quickly supported by men from other local engineering firms. By mid-September, the strike had spread to some men from Swan Hunter's Neptune Works and negotiations were proving very difficult, despite the intervention of the conciliation officer from the Ministry of Labour and National Service. The dispute was eventually resolved, with some concessions being made to the drillers.

Other strikes which occurred in the area during the year involved not only engineers but trades represented by unions such as the National Union of Heating and Domestic and General Metal Workers, the

Amalgamated Society of Woodworkers (Tyne District), the National Society of Painters, the Plumbers, Glaziers and Domestic Engineering Union and the Amalgamated Slaters and Tilers Provident Society. Many of these stoppages were about pay rates or working conditions and were typically short-lived, but they remained a worrying sign of growing industrial unrest.

October brought further industrial action to the area with a strike which has been called a watershed moment in wartime strike action. For some time the shipyard owners had been experiencing severe shortages in available and suitably trained clerical staff alongside an increased workload. They had approached the main engineering unions, the AEU and CSEU, during the summer and asked if they would consider an alteration in how their members were paid. They suggested that instead of paying on a Friday to Friday basis, as was the case, it would be easier for clerical staff to pay on a Saturday to Saturday schedule. The unions realized that this would mean their members losing out on two days' pay in the initial week of any such arrangement, and suggested Sunday to Sunday. This was agreeable to the employers, and both national unions agreed to the alteration. On 5 September, the Tyne District Secretary of the AEU, Jack Bowman, wrote to members informing them that the union had accepted this suggestion. Although the workers would lose out on one day's pay, the employers had agreed to pay this in advance, with it being reclaimed over the next five weeks' pay packets.

On the face of it this was a small matter and, given the demands placed on the clerical staff, a sensible one, but for the Tyne engineers it was the final straw in a year of simmering issues, and the reaction amongst local branch members was furious. Local branches complained immediately to their regional representatives, the main bone of contention being that the national unions had simply accepted this change without even bothering to consult with their membership. Accusations that the national executives had overstepped their mandates were made, and feelings ran increasingly high. On 10 September, some attempt at reconciliation was made when a local deputation met with national CSEU leaders and, in an attempt to dampen down the situation, the employers immediately agreed to extend the period during which the extra day's wages would be claimed back to twelve weeks. This seemingly reasonable suggestion failed to mollify the workers, and the situation and mood amongst Tyne workers became increasingly volatile.

On 5 October, workers at several yards refused to begin work and the strike action quickly spread up and down the river, affecting all of the major and minor shipbuilding and repair yards. The strikers received remarkably little support, with both the Communist Party and the *Catholic Herald* being particularly vehement in their opposition. The leader of the Communist Party, Harry Pollitt (himself a former boilermaker), even journeyed to Tyneside in order to encourage shop stewards with communist sympathies to do their utmost to bring the strike to an end. The press was also vehemently against the actions of the strikers, with the *Shields Daily News*, for example, describing the action as being viewed by the people of Tyneside as 'crazy'. Ernest Bevin, the Minister of Labour, dubbed the strike 'unwarrantable and unjustifiable', but amongst the communities where those who took action lived there does appear to have been support for their argument.

A typical example of local press hostility towards the striking men can be found in an editorial of the *Sunderland Echo* which stated that the 'strike to the everlasting shame of all concerned, still continues'. After commenting that men were going to the gates every morning (some from as far as Wearside) to grumble and then disperse, the editorial went on to opine that 'it is inconceivable that British workmen knowing the vital industry in which they are engaged can absent themselves over so nebulous a grievance as these men possess. It is difficult to find words to convey its sense.'[16]

Curiously, attitudes towards the employers remained largely non-hostile amongst those taking action. The strike, after all, was not primarily aimed at the employers, but instead at the seemingly high-handed actions of their national union leaders and district representatives in accepting a deal without consultation. Several of the local councillors and Mayors of Tyneside communities were increasingly worried and exasperated by the lack of progress, and made attempts to mediate. On 8 October, workers at several premises in North Shields met at Swan Hunter's with the Mayor of Tynemouth, Councillor Joseph Mayo, to discuss possible compromises, and agreed that they would return to work if an independent inquiry looked into the matter and the workers at other yards agreed. The other workers rejected this suggestion and the strike continued.

Attitudes hardened, and when several men reported for work on 6 October they were met by a crowd of women at lunchtime when they filed out for their break, being called blacklegs and other abusive terms by the women. The men refused to return to work the next day. The majority of the significant numbers of women employed in the yards refused to back the strike officially, although those who did so seemed to be the most determined strikers of all. The majority of apprentices were not affected, although there were limited walk-outs in support.

On each day of the action, workers filed down to the yard gates to hear from their stewards if there had been any change in the positions of employers or unions, only to walk away again upon being told that there had not. With a lack of support from their own national and district organizations, alongside complete hostility from all sections of the press, it was clear that the strike could not be maintained for long. It continued in a haphazard but determined manner for almost a fortnight before a meeting was arranged (with the help of several of the Mayors of local communities) at Wallsend for all shop stewards on 12 October.

At this meeting, the shop stewards of the Central Strike Committee voted to advise their members to return to work by a majority of 75 to 22, and this was accepted by the large numbers of workmen who had gathered outside. The Central Strike Committee, through the Mayor of Wallsend, Alderman T. Black, thanked the other Mayors for their help in reaching a conclusion to the strike. By 14 October, all of the yards were back at work.

Although a relatively short strike, the 'Total Time' or 'Lying-on' strike, as it came to be known, was nationally important as it was the first real area-wide strike and as such raised considerable alarm both locally and nationally, with the authorities becoming increasingly concerned over the morale of industrial workers and their attitudes towards the war. The strike also highlighted once more an interesting facet of industrial action on the Tyne. The workers in the area had a capacity for long terms of relative harmony followed by sudden and extremely determined prolonged periods of industrial action, during which a strong feature was the ability of Tyne workers to organize themselves in unofficial local bodies which showed a marked contempt for 'blacklegs' and other attempts at strike-breaking. This was to remain a feature of wartime industrial action in the area.

Although the strike was over, resentment continued to fester and the Central Strike Committee remained in existence. With acrimonious accusations directed between members of local branches and the district committees, it was clear that anti-official feeling still ran extremely strongly amongst Tyne workers. As a response to this, the strike committee asked all of its own members to resign from their positions as shop stewards and called upon those who had remained anti-strike to do the same, thus forcing a mass re-election of shop stewards in the yards. The results were startling, all of the strike committee being re-elected whilst the vast majority of anti-strike shop stewards lost their positions. However, there were repercussions when some of the pro-strike stewards were thrown out of the union and also lost their reserved occupation status upon resignation, to the approbation of the left-wing press.

The aftermath of the strike also highlighted the ambivalent position in which the Communist Party found itself on Tyneside. Refusing to back the workers and, indeed, vehemently opposing and taking active steps to break the strike, the party lost a great deal of respect amongst many of its erstwhile sympathizers and supporters. The Trotskyists made the most of this, with the Workers International League (WIL) claiming that many members left the party en-masse because of this issue and that the influence of the party amongst the shipyard workers on the Tyne was 'almost wholly shattered'.[17]

We have already seen how the mix of nationalities in the area was increased by the war and how, sometimes, this could lead to tensions and even criminal acts. Late in November, three members of the Greek Navy were involved in a murder case when one of their number was stabbed to death on Wallsend High Street West. It had begun when one of the Greek sailors, Costas Frezaulis, arranged to meet up with a young ATS girl, Private Isobel Gilchrist, with whom he had been in regular contact by letter. The two met at the Robin Hood Hotel in Wallsend, where they went into the music room with several other Greek sailors and girls. Private Gilchrist described how they had been sitting together when a small Greek sailor whom she did not recognize pulled a face at her jokingly, and she answered back in similar fashion. Her partner noticed this and spoke to the other sailor in Greek, whereupon an angry exchange took place before the two men went out into the passage with some other Greeks. When her partner returned he was smiling, but she believed there had been some sort of fight. The two continued with their night and left by the back door at around 9.50 pm. Once outside, Private Gilchrist found herself pushed aside roughly and realized that the other sailor, Spiros Karpathios (25), was again there and was fighting with her partner. Describing a ferocious fight, Private Gilchrist testified that she had run back inside the pub, told another Greek sailor, Nikolous Valoyiannis, that the two men were fighting again and asked him to stop them. She stayed inside for some time.

Outside, Valoyiannis attempted to get between the men, and in doing so was forced to strike them both. Karpathios at this point pulled out a knife and stabbed Valoyiannis in the stomach. Valoyiannis exclaimed that he had been stabbed and fell to the ground, dying almost immediately. Karpathios turned and fled, despite being hit on the head with a piece of concrete by Frezaulis. When Private Gilchrist re-emerged from the hotel, she found Valoyiannis lying dead on the ground and noticed that Karpathios had dropped both his greatcoat and paybook, which gave his name. The police quickly arrested Karpathios and established that there had been an ongoing grudge between Karpathios and Frezaulis. However, the knife was not found. Committed to Northumberland assizes in February 1943, the charge was later reduced to manslaughter and Karpathios was found guilty and sentenced to six months' imprisonment.

Notes
1. Able Seaman Clay was killed on 18 January 1942 and is buried at Gibraltar (North Front) Cemetery.
2. *Shields Daily News*, 13 January 1942, p.3.
3. Sergeant Mander's body was never found and he is commemorated on the Alamein Memorial. Also, see 1944.
4. *Shields Daily News*, 11 February 1942, p.3.
5. The wreck buoy for this vessel was not removed until 1979.
6. *The Journal*, 30 September 1942, p.4.

7. HMS *Grove* was sunk by a U-boat in June 1942, but the other ships all survived the war, although HMS *Melbrake* suffered heavy damage in 1944 when a bomb destroyed her bridge and wheelhouse.
8. NA: CO 876/41. 'Social Welfare among the Coloured People on the Tyne Side', a report by R. Dunbar to Sir D. Cameron, 1942.
9. *The African Standard*, 29 May 1942, pp.45.
10. NA: CO 876/41. 'Social Welfare among the Coloured People on the Tyne Side'. So encouraged were the Colonial Office by the results achieved by Mr Minto and his association that they used much of his work as a basis for the opening of a hostel for African seamen in Newcastle.
11. *The Shields Evening News*, 10 January 1945, p.3.
12. *Shields Daily News*, 16 October 1942, p. 6.
13. *Evening Chronicle*, 8 October 1942, p.8.
14. Beattie would later win the VC for his actions during the raid on St Nazaire. His replacement had a rather odd reputation for his eccentric behaviour. Because of the poor radar equipment with which *Petard* was outfitted, he emphasized the importance of keeping a good look-out, to encourage which he would often tie himself to the mast. He would also throw small items at officers whom he felt were not maintaining a good enough look-out, and some took to wearing steel helmets at all times! Other examples of eccentric behaviour included covering the deck with soap to make it slippery and giving the ship an artificial list to represent possible battle conditions.
15. Tragically, Tommy Brown did not live to collect his medal as he was killed trying to rescue his sister from a house fire in North Shields in 1945.
16. *Sunderland Echo*, 10 October 1942, p.2.
17. *Socialist Appeal*, October 1942. Quoted in Croucher, R., *Engineers at War 1939–1945* (Merlin, 1982), p.186.

CHAPTER FIVE

1943: A Year of Victories and Attrition

The New Year (the fourth of the war) was welcomed in a traditionally boisterous manner, with first-footers and house parties to the fore. There were a very large number of first-footers out and about, but there was disappointment in Northumberland Square when the special wartime ceremony hosted by Mr Gilbert Park had to be cancelled, even though a large crowd had assembled. There was a catalogue of catastrophes at the ceremony, as first the bugler had to cancel due to illness and could not be replaced, followed by the breakdown of the loudspeaker assembly which was to relay the sound of Big Ben to the crowd. Despite the disappointment, the crowd was the largest since the beginning of the war and made the most of the night by singing and dancing and wishing each a happy new year before dispersing to first-foot and take part in privately arranged entertainment. 'Happy parties tramped the streets lustily singing and making calls for several hours,' it was reported.[1]

The Mayor of Tynemouth, Councillor G.C. Murray, wished all residents of 'canny Shields' a happy new year and expressed his hopes for the year, saying that the beginning of the year brought positive war news and he hoped for victory and peace soon.

Although the majority of people in Tynemouth and Wallsend had enough on their minds thinking of their own situation, there was a keen awareness of the suffering of those allies who found themselves occupied by the enemy, and fundraising campaigns to aid refugees were popular throughout the war. The previous year had seen a focus on Greece, as it became clear just how dreadful the Axis occupation was proving for the Greeks. A combination of looting by the occupiers, the confiscation of transport, mass unemployment and hyperinflation had led to a catastrophic famine in Greece, with hundreds of thousands dying from malnutrition. In 1942, this had led the British to lift their naval blockade of the country in order to allow the Red Cross to bring in grain supplies. The situation in Greece had quickly become public knowledge, and many communities across Britain held charity events and campaigns to raise funds to supply food to the embattled Greek population. In late February, it was announced that Tynemouth Borough would host a special Aid to Greece campaign which would run until 6 March. An exhibition was set up in an empty North Shields shop on the corner of West Percy Street and Bedford Street, which was opened in a ceremony where the guest of honour was the Greek consul, Mr S. Antonaropulos. The exhibition displays had been created by members of the Greek community who were living locally, and featured photographs and information relating to the campaign in Greece (including the powerful resistance movement).

Councillor G.C. Murray, Mayor of Tynemouth, wished 'canny Shields' a happy New Year. (Shields Evening News)

A meeting was also held by the United Nations Committee and the Ministry of Information at the Municipal High School, where the keynote speaker was the secretary to the Greek Legation, Mr S.L. Hourmouzios. Mr Hourmouzios was born in Cyprus but had lived for many years in Athens before moving to Britain to study at London University, and had been secretary to the Greek Legation in London for over eight years. At the outbreak of war, however, he had immediately resigned his post and elected to join the British Army, in which he served as a gunner in a heavy anti-aircraft battery.

The Greek community in exile was appreciative of the efforts of the residents of Tynemouth. The president of the Greek Red Cross Executive Committee, Mr A.P. Cawadias, wrote to the Mayor expressing his 'deep gratitude', adding, 'It is with great emotion that I have just heard that you are launching an appeal in your town on behalf of the Famine Relief Committee in aid of the people of Greece.' He concluded by thanking the British people and pledging that the 'gallant help from the British Government and the British people ... shall never be forgotten'.[2]

The voluntary service of many of the men and women on the home front is apt to be forgotten, but for some of those the rigours of heavy work combined with overwork could be dangerous: there are numerous examples of volunteers being injured or even dying whilst on duty. One such sad case occurred at the Wallsend NFS (National Fire Service) station in February, when one of the maintenance staff, William Henry Simmonds Dixon (33) of Ravensworth Street, Willington Quay, collapsed and died whilst inspecting one of the service's vehicles.

The men and women of the ARP services and Home Guard already cooperated in many ways, such as the Home Guard lookout post in Tynemouth Borough. However, with the falling number of paid ARP workers it became more vital than ever that the two groups worked together more closely. The Regional Commissioner, Sir Arthur Lambert, ordered all services to come up with plans to set up mobile columns consisting of both ARP services and Home Guard which could be moved quickly to areas which had suffered bombing. To enable this system to work, Lambert proposed that every member of the ARP and Home Guard should spend at least sixteen hours a month practising skills used by the other service. Thus the Home Guard, especially, were turning their hands to even more duties beyond their original remit. The scheme was envisaged as going even further, with the NFS and police all becoming involved in the cross-training and mobile columns.

Throughout the first weeks of the year there had been a spate of damage being caused to air raid shelters, but finding the culprits had proven to be a difficult task. When asked about this, Sir Arthur Lambert said that 'he did not know what to call the people who deliberately damaged the shelters', adding that magistrates in the area had been told to 'inflict severe penalties on anyone found guilty of such an offence'.[3]

Incidents of bombing became fewer throughout the year, but vigilance could not be relaxed as the Luftwaffe was still capable of mounting attacks. On the night of 12/13 March, a small raid was launched against various targets along the Tyne. Although there were deaths and significant property damage in other communities, Tynemouth and Wallsend escaped relatively unscathed. However, incendiary bombs were again dropped on North Shields gasworks, with further incendiaries falling on Preston Cemetery and in open ground on the northern boundary of the borough. There were no casualties and only very slight damage, with the majority of incendiaries extinguished very quickly.

Ten nights later, another minor raid developed which again caused significant damage in other communities, but left Tynemouth and Wallsend largely undamaged. On this night, explosive and incendiary bombs fell in the north of the borough at Rake House, whilst two explosive bombs fell at Cullercoats, one on the beach and the other on rocks beside the south pier, again causing no damage. Just two nights later, the attempt was repeated and this time bombs fell on Alexandra Road at the junction with Hawkey's Lane; whilst there were no serious casualties, there was a considerable amount of damage caused to housing, necessitating widespread use of rest centres.

Despite the recent attacks, it was clear that bombing was becoming less of a threat on the home front, especially during daylight, and some traditional gatherings which had been abandoned during the early years of the war began to be reinstated. In March, with Easter approaching, it was agreed that the traditional Good Friday procession could once again be held (it had been in abeyance since the start of the war). The police and District Sunday School Union had agreed on a route to and from Northumberland Square, North Shields, where a large open-air service would take place. The procession had been a cherished tradition in the borough and had always been looked forward to and well-attended. The open-air meeting had always been especially keenly anticipated, with large attendances, and displays of banners and accompaniment by a brass band bringing entertainment to the proceedings. The cancellation of the procession and meeting had been a source of contention to many in the borough, who could not understand why that meeting should be postponed when the Mayor's Sunday procession and parades on national days of prayer and for savings campaigns had been allowed to take place.

The war, with its risks and excitement, encouraged many young couples to marry, and amongst the rash of wartime marriages were many involving those who were serving in uniform. In mid-March, the *Shields Evening News* carried information on three such marriages which had all taken place at Holy Saviour's Church in Tynemouth. One was of a young Spitfire pilot from North Shields and his Tynemouth ATS sweetheart (of which more later). The second marriage was that of another RAF man, Harold Hardy of Sheffield, and a Scarborough woman serving in the WRNS, Miss Viola Kenward. As was common, the bride wore her service uniform, and after a reception at Link House in Tynemouth the couple set off for their honeymoon in the bride's hometown. Miss Kenward was presumably serving in Tynemouth, which is why the marriage took place there. The third marriage was that of Third Officer Norah B. Williamson, WRNS, and Lieutenant D.W. Barnes, RNVR.

As had happened during the First World War, incidents of venereal disease had increased sharply in wartime Britain. The authorities were growing increasingly alarmed about such cases removing men and women from active service, as well as the loss of working days by employees in vital war work. The government proposed to make cases of VD compulsorily notifiable in an effort to shame people into taking adequate precautions, but the *Shields Evening News* of 26 February reported that the controversial Archbishop of Canterbury, Dr William

3rd Officer N.B. Williamson, WRNS, and Lieutenant D.W. Barnes, RNVR: a typical wartime marriage. (Shields Evening News)

Temple, had addressed a conference of the Central Council for Health Education cautioning against this, claiming that the primary problem was a moral one and not a medical one. Dr Temple suggested that there should be more emphasis placed on the sacredness of sex, the duty of abstinence and on providing more wholesome employment for both sexes in civilian or military life to eliminate boredom, which he considered a prime factor in the loosening of moral principles. Dr Temple was particularly concerned with what he viewed as the misuse of alcohol in the forces. He went on to say that 'Inducements to indulge in alcoholic drinks should be removed as far as possible. He had heard of dances and other entertainments for men and women of the Forces where none but alcoholic drinks had been in evidence. That seemed little short of criminal.' Dr Temple also encouraged a healthy family life, more suitable housing and living arrangements, and the 'wise upbringing of their children'. He advised that the authorities should handle cases of VD by expressing 'the conviction that misconduct roused the condemnation of all decent citizens and the "dreadful admonishment of God"'.[4]

As we have seen, Tynemouth Borough attracted a justified reputation for generous contributions to the various charitable campaigns which were launched both nationally and locally. In 1943, it was the turn of the borough to host the Wings for Victory Week to raise funds for the RAF. This was a very popular theme, as the people of the area still keenly remembered the sacrifices made during the Battle of Britain and were eagerly following the progress of the campaign by Bomber Command to strike back at Germany's towns and cities. The council was therefore relatively confident of being able to raise a substantial sum, and so set its target figure high. It was announced that the borough's intention was to raise enough money to build ten Lancaster Bombers and 20 Seafire fighter aircraft (a naval version of the Spitfire which was capable of taking off from an aircraft carrier, a popular option given the threat from raids on convoys and the offensive against Japan). The first of 11,000 programmes listing the numerous events and ways to invest was ceremonially purchased by the Mayor, Councillor Murray, on 19 April. The campaign would begin on Saturday, 1 May.

The campaign began with a large parade involving all of the services, the Home Guard and many other organizations. It was said

1943: A YEAR OF VICTORIES AND ATTRITION

to be the grandest such occasion that had taken place in the borough since the beginning of the war, and attracted substantial crowds. The parade assembled at St Edward School before marching through much of the town. The order of the parade was: band of the Royal Northumberland Fusiliers; a Naval Detachment including members of the WRNS; Merchant Navy; detachment from the Army including Home Guard, ATS and Army Cadet Corps; Newcastle City Police Band; an aeroplane fuselage along with members of the RAF, WAAF, ATC, Women's Junior Air Corps (WJAC) and GTC; Tynemouth Police; National Fire Service; a collection of Civil Defence squads; Tynemouth & Cullercoats lifeboat crews; Royal National Lifeboat Institution; Tynemouth Volunteer Life Brigade; NFS pipe band; Ambulance Brigade; Red Cross; British Legion; WVS; Sea Scouts; Boy Scouts; Boys' Brigade; and Girl Guides. When the parade reached Northumberland Square, it passed a small stand and the salute was taken by Group Captain P.H. Cummings, DFC, accompanied by the Mayor and Mayoress and a number of other dignitaries. After this, the parade proceeded to the playing field of the Municipal High School, where the official opening of the campaign was to take place.

Hundreds had lined the route, many of whom joined the large crowd of spectators who had gone straight to the school. The Mayor and Mayoress presided and there were many dignitaries (including the Mayor of Wallsend, Councillor J.H. Malia) on the dais along with

WJAC members marching in Northumberland Square, North Shields, during the launch of the Wings for Victory Campaign, 1943. (Shields Evening News)

The Pipe Band of the National Fire Service at the Tynemouth Wings for Victory event. (Shields Evening News)

invited officers from the RAF. The RAF ensign was draped over the dais, followed by the playing of the national anthem and a flourish of trumpets before 300 pigeons were released from under the dais. Telegrams from the Air Minister and the Chancellor of the Exchequer were read out by the Mayor before he announced that he had received a letter from someone simply signing themselves as 'an old soldier's widow', wishing the campaign every success and enclosing a postal order for 5s. towards the campaign. The Mayor said that it moved him to realize that this widow had sent what could represent a large part of her weekly income, which should act as a spur to the rest of the borough in its aim to raise £500,000.

Group Captain Cummings was then asked to formally open the campaign. In his speech, he made a number of rather bland and contestable claims regarding the Battle of Britain. At the beginning of his speech he made the probable error of stating that two-and-a-half years ago the battle had taken place over south-east England. Whilst the majority of fighting had of course taken place over this part of the country, there had been fighting over other areas, including the North-East. This might have served to alienate some of his audience, but did not seem to have had this effect. He went on to claim that this was Hitler's first defeat (a contentious claim amongst historians) and that it had given Britain the chance to build up its strength (which was true). He added that Britain owed its survival to that 'small but gallant command' and claimed that many thousands owed their lives to the men of Fighter Command of 1940. This may have been popular at the time, but it fails to mention the immense sacrifice that was being made by the men of Bomber Command, who were targeting the Channel invasion ports on a nightly basis and suffering severe casualties as a result.

The latter part of Group Captain Cummings' speech was rather more inspired, as he compared the task facing the people of Tynemouth to that which faced the aircrews of Bomber Command. He said that the aircrew were fully briefed before each raid and instructed on the importance of the target and how to get there, and that the people of Tynemouth had also been fully briefed on the importance of their target and how they could reach it. Closing his speech, he said that he was confident that the people of Tynemouth would reach their target 'and, if necessary, exceed it'. He concluded by wishing the people of the borough, as he would a pilot setting off on a mission, 'Good luck, good trip and happy landings'.[5]

The MP for Tynemouth, Sir Alex Russell, thanked Group Captain Cummings before comparing the situation that year to the previous one, when he was present at the opening of Tynemouth Warships Week. He claimed that in the previous year the mood had been bleak, as Russia was being pushed back and 'Tynemouth itself was in a sad heart for it had lost in recent raids many of her own townspeople'. Comparing that mood with the present one, he said he was glad to see the people in a buoyant mood after the good war news of 1942 and the fact that 'Germany was upon the defensive and her people shivering in their beds wondering where and how the next attack will be made – whether from the air or by sea in the form of an invasion'.[6] Concluding by saying that the war had melded the people of Tynemouth, and indeed the country as a whole, into one solid team determined to secure victory against Nazism, his speech was met with hearty applause. Following the speeches, there was musical entertainment from the various bands present, including the Royal Scots' fife band, and the opening ceremony concluded.

The following day being a Sunday, a church parade had been organized, with a route and make-up following similar lines, although on a far smaller scale, to that which had preceded the opening ceremony. When the dignitaries, again including Group Captain Cummings, took the salute in Northumberland Square, a formation of RAF aircraft circled overhead at low altitude, thrilling the crowds that had lined the route. At the culmination of the route, the congregation packed out Tynemouth Parish Church, where the Rev Noel M. Kennaby, vicar of Tynemouth, conducted the service, assisted by RAF chaplain the Rev R.L. McCulloch.

A number of posters and flyers were also designed to encourage the people of Tynemouth to contribute to the campaign. Some of these were somewhat jingoistic and even bloodthirsty. One insisted that people remembered the sinking of the *City of Benares*, 'that shipload of kiddies you "liquidated"', along with the *Arandora Star* and countless other 'little ships you sent to the bottom without warning ... the tankers and tramp steamers, grain ships and cargo vessels. We remember the lifeboats you gunned and the crews you set adrift.' After listing these terrors, the poster grimly stated that 'this is for them, Jerry. This is yours! This is the end of your career of murder and piracy!', before sarcastically adding, 'How the world will miss you!' The small print reminded readers that the RAF was hitting back at the U-boats, Fighter and Bomber Command at their docks, shipyards and facilities which produced raw materials, whilst Coastal Command was sinking them and chasing them back to their bases. The poster urged everyone in Tynemouth to contribute everything they could to this cause. The poster itself featured a bomb heading for a U-boat, alongside a message accusing the U-boat crews of being 'glamour boys' (ironically, considering that the men of RAF Fighter Command were often accused of this) for whom nothing but the best was good enough. It added, 'So here it comes Jerry ... a nice big "cookie" to share with your friends.'[7]

Because of the complexities of the multitude of savings schemes which were launched during the war, the authorities were keen to explain to members of the public exactly how their contributions aided the war effort. There was thus a meeting of the North Shields Townswomen's Guild on 4 May, at which the Assistant Regional Commissioner for National Savings, Mr J. Scott, addressed members on how the various schemes functioned. The meeting, at the Wesleyan Memorial Church Hall, heard a general survey of all the schemes before Mr Scott addressed two key issues. The first was whether all of the

1943: A YEAR OF VICTORIES AND ATTRITION

Tynemouth Wings for Victory poster. (*Shields Evening News*)

Wings for Victory poster. (*Shields Evening News*)

schemes were truly necessary. Mr Scott told the assembly that he was unhesitating when he told them that the special weeks of fundraising were vital as they not only, for example, secured funds for the RAF, but were also a demonstration of the organization and determination of the British people, and were thus useful for propaganda purposes both at home and abroad. To reinforce his second point (how useful was the scheme?), Mr Scott praised Tynemouth Borough for having raised over £4 million already in war savings and told the meeting that this amounted to over 8s. per person, per week, and almost £73 per person since the scheme started in 1939. Before the meeting, the guild held a bring and buy sale in aid of the Wings for Victory campaign. This seems to have been a small affair, as only three stallholders were mentioned by name. In a sign of the times, the majority of items on sale were fruit and vegetables.

On 4 May, it was announced that £76,345 had been donated, bringing the total by the morning of the 5th to £248,935. This meant that the fund had almost reached the half-way point. Commenting on this, the Mayor said it demonstrated that the borough was 'keeping pace ... but in this matter it would be better to be ahead of time'.[8] To encourage the people of the borough further, he reminded them to think back to the time when the drone of aircraft engines sent them hurrying their children to the air raid shelters, but now it was RAF bombers going out to hit Germany. If they wished to support this effort, then they had to donate to the scheme.

Given that it was the Wings for Victory Week, it should come as no surprise that the local press threw their full weight behind the campaign, throughout the week highlighting the bombing campaign which was continuing against Germany and its allies. On 5 May, for example, the *Shields Evening News* carried on its front page several accounts of bombing raids. One of the main headlines was 'Bomber Command's Very Heavy Raid on Dortmund'. The report related how visibility was good, aside from ground haze, and that early reports indicated that concentrated bombing had led to heavy damage in the city. The report admitted that thirty of the British bombers had failed to return and were missing. It then highlighted the industrial importance of Dortmund, telling readers that the city of 500,000 people contained several vital synthetic oil plants.

The raid had consisted of 596 aircraft in what was the 'largest "non-1,000" raid of the war so far and the first major attack on Dortmund'.[9] In fact, some of the backing-up marking by the pathfinders went astray and a large decoy fire site also fooled several bombers into attacking it. Having said that, over 50 per cent of the force did bomb within 3 miles of the specified aiming point and severe damage was inflicted, with more than 1,200 buildings destroyed and twice that number heavily damaged, including several important factories and industrial concerns. At least 693 people were killed in the city (including 200 PoWs). The reporting in the newspaper was fairly accurate, although thirty-one bombers had actually been lost in the attack, with a further seven crashing in England due to poor weather.

It was reported that this was the first major attack in several days, but that there had been ten heavy night attacks mounted on 'arms centres and ports' in April, the chief targets being Berlin, Duisburg, Essen, Kiel, Mannheim, Rostock, Stettin and Stuttgart.

The front page also featured a couple of photographs of bombing raids. As RAF Bomber Command attacked almost overwhelmingly at night, photographs were very difficult to obtain, so the newspaper instead showed the efforts of US B17 bombers attacking Tunis. Other stories on the front page included a brief mention of British heavy bombers attacking Taranto in Italy and an account of RAF fighters mounting attacks on Japanese transport and troop concentrations in Burma.

At the conclusion of the Wings for Victory Week, the Mayor announced that the target figure had been exceeded by a considerable amount, with the total so far being £571,499. He was at pains to point out that this was not the final tally, as late payments had still to counted and he was confident that the figure would rise considerably. Once again, the reports praised the efforts of the people of the borough and said that many had been motivated by the debt owed to the RAF for its service during the Battle of Britain. The Mayor commented that he thought that it was a 'marvellous figure and a remarkable achievement'. He added that this was evidence that it 'does not bespeak the fact that the people in this town have large purses, but rather does it reflect the

USAAF B-17 bombers on a raid. (Shields Evening News)

fact that they have very big hearts'. He praised the enthusiasm reached during the week-long campaign as a big factor in achieving such a goal.[10]

By the time the final counting had been performed, the Mayor was proven correct in his estimates, as the total sum amounted to £608,956 (£25,480,388 today), which was £108,956 (£4,559,000) above the already ambitious original target and more than paid for the construction of ten Lancaster bombers and twenty Seafire fighters.

In his final report on the Wings for Victory Week, the Town Clerk, Mr F.G. Egner, was able to state that Tynemouth led the way in small savings, having beaten every other participating community in Northumberland and Durham. The average contribution per head was over £11, whilst the average small saving was almost £6 per person.

Mr Egner was quick to praise the people of the borough, saying, 'Never before in my experience have I known such enthusiasm during any campaign in the town. Never can the citizens of Tynemouth be more proud than today.'[11]

Even whilst the people of Tynemouth were making herculean efforts to raise funds for the war effort, there were those in the borough who were falling foul of the legal system. At times the actions of the authorities could seem rather pernickety and harsh. In May, a case dating back to the previous month was heard at Tynemouth Borough juvenile court. The case was that of a 14-year-old boy who had been accused of taking cabbage leaves and crust scraps from waste bins on Linskill Street, North Shields. The accuser was a council employee who had the responsibility of emptying the bins, who claimed that on the previous day they had been full but when he went to empty them the next day he noticed that one was not as full as it had

Mr. F. G. Egner, Tynemouth's Town Clerk, who reported on the success achieved in the borough's Wings for Victory Week and paid tribute to the hard work put in to achieve the target.

Mr F.G. Egner, Tynemouth Town Clerk, was fulsome in his praise for the results of Wings for Victory. (Shields Daily News)

been. As there was a warning notice on all the bins and nobody had the authority to empty them apart from the council, he informed the police. The police then questioned the boy (unfortunately there is no mention of how the police came to suspect this particular youth) and he confessed to taking the items, which he claimed were to feed his rabbits. The magistrates told the boy that he knew he should not have taken the scraps and warned him not to do it again before dismissing the case, with 4s. costs, under the Probation of Offenders Act. Whilst the boy had committed an act which under wartime regulations was illegal, with pressure on families to produce their own food it is no surprise that some felt that scraps could legitimately be taken for their own uses.

The next case to be heard by the court was more serious, involving the theft of a schoolgirl's bicycle by a 16-year-old Wallsend youth. The girl, Miss Atkinson from The Quadrant, Balkwell, North Shields, had left her bike in the shed at Ralph Gardner School, but when she returned at lunchtime it had been stolen. The next day, Wallsend Police contacted North Shields to say that they had confiscated the bike (along with several others) and arrested three youths (the other two were dealt with for crimes at Wallsend, with one being sent to an approved school as a result). One was the young man who was in possession of Miss Atkinson's bike. Upon being questioned, the youth immediately admitted the offence, saying merely that he had taken the bike to go for a ride. The magistrates asked Miss Atkinson why the bike had not been locked, and she replied that she did not have a lock, despite her school teacher telling her to get one. After advising Miss Atikinson to invest in a lock, the bench heard evidence about the accused.

He had been before the courts five times and was at the time of his appearance on probation. The magistrates heard how, in December 1941, he had been bound over after being found guilty of larceny of milk and housebreaking at Wallsend, and then bound over yet again at Wallsend a year later for housebreaking and theft. Calling for evidence from the boy's probation officer, the court was informed that there had been a group of four boys from the same Wallsend street who had proven troublesome. Of these, one had just been sent to an approved school, one other evacuated and the other was in the process of moving out of the area. The probation officer therefore thought the group had been split up and that there would be a reduction in trouble from the remaining member of the four (the accused). The magistrates were keen to set the boy an example and told him that as he was becoming a regular offender, they were going to try to stop his behaviour by giving him a fortnight to pay the fine of £1 plus 5s. costs (£52 today in total) due to damage to the bike (the chain guard had been removed), telling him that if he appeared before the court again he would be sent to an approved school.

A further case involved two 15-year-old boys who were caught chopping wood in a condemned house in Silver Street, North Shields. After being chased by the police, one boy was caught and told them the identity of his accomplice, although he said that the other boy had not chopped any wood or taken any, only being there to hold the sack for him whilst he chopped up the doorframes and fittings. The boy who had been caught admitted what he was doing and confirmed that both axes which were recovered belonged to him.

The alleged accomplice was represented by a solicitor and denied the charges of theft, saying that he did not chop any wood; he was merely asked by the other boy to hold the sack for him and was not going to take any profit from the sale of the wood for firewood.

The other boy had been before the courts on four occasions, the first for the unlawful wounding of an old man with an iron bar in December 1942, and was on probation. His accomplice was previously of good character and had never been in trouble before. The accomplice was placed on probation and his case dismissed on the payment of a 7/6d. fine. The main offender, however, was described as having 'a bad record' and the magistrates sent him to the approved school and ordered his parents to pay maintenance to the school at a rate of 7/6d. per week (a considerable sum for a working-class family).

Part of the success of the Wings for Victory campaign lay in the fact that the RAF was seen as the most glamorous of the services, carried a certain mystique and had bolstered this with its performance in the fateful summer of 1940. Service with the RAF possessed a certain glamour for many young men and women, especially after the Battle of Britain had made heroes of the pilots of Fighter Command. Many preferred to serve in the RAF rather than what they viewed as the miserable and, at times, boring life in the Army. However, the majority of men who passed the stringent medical required for duties as aircrew found themselves not as pilots and certainly not as fighter pilots, but were instead trained for other aircrew roles such as gunners or navigators, posted to Bomber Command (or Coastal Command) which was, from 1942, engaged upon its great offensive designed to crush Germany.

Amongst those who had joined the RAF were two brothers from North Shields. The Goulden family was well-known in local sporting circles, with Mr Thomas C. Goulden being the groundskeeper for Tynemouth Cricket Club and his eldest son, Thomas, the opening batsman for the club as well as playing for Northumberland; he was also a good rugby player who played at stand-off half for Percy Park and represented the county in the sport. Before the war, Thomas had been a marine engineer, having served an apprenticeship at the North-Eastern Marine Engineering Company at Wallsend, but had decided to join the RAF. After training in the USA, he was posted back to Britain as a single-engined aircraft pilot at the beginning of 1942. By 1943, Thomas was flying Spitfire photo-reconnaissance aircraft with 541 Squadron from RAF Benson. During a period of leave, he found the time to marry his Tynemouth-born sweetheart, Lance Corporal Thelma Robson of the Auxiliary Territorial Service (ATS), at Holy Saviour's Church in Tynemouth on 17 March. However, like many wartime marriages, this one ended in tragedy when Mr and Mrs Goulden received notification at their home at Cricket Field Cottage, Preston Avenue, that their eldest son had been posted missing. On 28 May, Thomas, then a Flight Sergeant, had been flying a photo-reconnaissance mission to Lubeck in a Spitfire PRXI (EN411), but failed to return and there was no news of him.

As tragic as this news was for the family, it must have created further worry as Thomas' brother, Donald, was also serving in the RAF as an air gunner with Bomber Command. Whilst most of Bomber Command's campaign consisted of the bombing of city targets, it also undertook precision attacks, and one such attack was ordered for the night of 17/18 August. It had been established that the Baltic island of Peenemunde was the site of the development of Nazi rocket weapons and posed a risk to the British Isles and the war effort. Given the distance to Peenemunde, the only realistic option was a night-time precision attack by the heavy bombers of RAF Bomber Command. The force sent that night consisted of 596 aircraft (324 Lancasters, 218 Halifaxes and fifty-four Stirlings, with a force of Mosquitoes launching a diversionary bombing attack on Berlin). Amongst the Halifax force despatched was the 10 Squadron Halifax II (JD200, ZA-S) of Flight Sergeant A.J.E. Long, one of eighteen aircraft sent by the squadron that night; the mid-upper gunner was Sergeant Donald Goulden. Taking off from RAF Melbourne just after 9.00 pm, nothing further was heard from the aircraft or its crew and it failed to return to base. It seems probable that the aircraft was the thirty-ninth to be shot down whilst over Peenemunde, and its eight-man crew (an inexperienced second-pilot was being given his first operational experience) were all killed. The crew had an average age of just 23 and had already flown eight operations.[12]

Once again the Goulden family received a telegram informing them that another son had been posted missing whilst involved in aerial operations; the second in just over three months. The family would receive little comfort, as neither son's body was ever found. They are both commemorated on the Runnymede Memorial to the missing, in Surrey.

We have already seen some of the brave acts carried out by local men who had before the war served in the fishing fleet at North Shields. Amongst these was Skipper Robert Armstrong who, before the war, had been one of the youngest skippers in the North Shields fleet. A member of the RNR, he had been called up shortly before the war and made the skipper of the 339 ton HMT *Derby County*, a minesweeping anti-submarine warfare (ASW) trawler. Serving aboard this vessel from the start of the war to late 1940, Armstrong was then transferred to the command of another ASW trawler before taking over command of the 433 ton HMT *Kingston Crystal* (another ASW trawler) in early 1942. Aboard this ship, Armstrong served both at home and in the Mediterranean, and in the summer of 1943 whilst in the port of Taranto (which the Allies had just captured) was responsible for depth-charging and sinking an Italian miniature submarine which was attempting to penetrate the port defences. For this action Armstrong was mentioned in dispatches, as this was amongst the first such craft to be successfully engaged. After this incident, Armstrong was promoted to Acting Skipper Lieutenant and again transferred, this time to the large (593 ton) minesweeping trawler HMT *Lilac* in summer 1944.[13]

With the alarming losses of shipping in the Atlantic, the local authorities, keen to ensure redevelopment on the Tyne, attempted to persuade the government to reopen some of the defunct Tyne shipyards (Palmers at Jarrow being one). When the Town Clerk of Tynemouth, M.F.G. Egner, heard that a delegation from Jarrow had been granted an audience with the Admiralty to discuss reopening Palmers, he wrote to the Admiralty stating that if there was a move to reopen Tyne yards, then the Northumberland Yard at Howdon should be considered. His letter was supported by politicians from Tynemouth and Wallsend.[14] The problem with reopening yards in the North-East was primarily the shortage of available manpower. Indeed, at the time, the Admiralty estimated that 'On the Tyne we could use at least a thousand more men.'[15] The Admiralty's claim was reinforced by a report that had been published in 1941, which concluded that Wallsend Slipway was suffering from a lack of available labour and

HMT Derby County, *seen here as a pre-war trawler. The author's grandfather skippered her during the war.* (Public Domain)

HMT Lilac, *a minesweeper commanded by the author's grandfather.* (Public Domain)

that this had led to delays in production.[16] When Jarrow politicians claimed that there was an abundance of labour in the town, their counterparts in Tynemouth and Wallsend immediately demanded that, rather than use this labour to reopen the defunct Palmers Yard, the men should instead be transferred to a recently reopened shipyard on the north bank of the Tyne which was still 50 per cent below strength.[17] The Ministry of Labour weighed into the growing debate, backing the Admiralty and declaring that whilst there was no shortage of unskilled labour, the shortages of skilled shipyard labour would prevent the reopening of the Palmers Yard and other yards on the Tyne. However, they concluded that a small yard producing prefabricated modules or landing craft would probably be viable in Jarrow.[18]

The boom in the shipyards also gave more scope to those who wished to gather money from illegal sources. Minor fraud and petty thefts from the shipyards were increasingly commonplace, although there were concerted efforts to crack down on them and punish offenders more harshly. One typical case came before magistrates at Tynemouth in the first days of the year when a labourer, Henry James (44) of 20 Beaumont Street, North Shields, pleaded guilty to stealing a small amount of scrap metal at Smith's Dock valued at 10s. James was arrested by a detective from the River Tyne Police who had seen him carrying a heavy sack to a marine store at Dock Road, North Shields. Once arrested, James confessed that the sack contained scrap from Smith's and conceded his guilt, saying 'Well, I can't say anything.'[19] It would appear that James had acted impulsively and out of character (it was his first offence), and James admitted to magistrates that he had no excuse but said that he had 'got the wind up and was going to take it back to the yard where I got it from'. Hearing that James would lose his £4 a week job as a result of the offence and that he had two children at home, both of whom were employed, the magistrates decided to act with leniency and fined him the sum of £1 with a fortnight to pay.

Once again the Holidays at Home period saw a wide variety of entertainments taking place in Tynemouth Borough. With the Holidays at Home scheme taking place from 19 June to 18 July, there was plenty on offer. In May, a number of events were announced to the public, including several days of open-air dancing in Tynemouth Park and cabarets one night per week at the same venue. The Grand Hotel had announced that it was planning a large dance, whilst Tynemouth Golf Club was to have a number of competitions which members of the public who were not members of the club could also enter. The Tynemouth Boy Scouts' Association announced its intention to mount a Scouts Week in the final week of the period. The Joint Services Committee, which was responsible for the representation of all service personnel based in the area, had said that it was organizing a large intra-services sports meeting for 19 June, and was also planning a services football match at Appleby Park, the home of North Shields FC.

Sports played a substantial role in the Holidays at Home schedule, with a table tennis tournament being held at the youth centre on 23 June, followed a week later by a services swimming gala. The semi-finals of the Tyne area service basketball Summer Trophy championship were scheduled for 7 July, and a week later there was a swimming gala pitting the forces against teams from the police, civil defence and NFS, whilst that day would also see the final of the basketball competition. Local schools got very involved in the sporting programme, with elementary school sports days taking place at Murton School, New York, on 23 June, Linskill on 8 July, Collingwood on 13 July and Smiths Park on 15 July. Two days after the Holidays at Home programme, the Municipal High School was to host its own athletics sports day. A sports meeting at Smith's Park on 26 June was also organized by the Women's Junior Air Corps (WJAC).

Other events announced at this time included a parents day at Lovaine House open air school, whilst entertainment of a more genteel kind consisted of two plays at Linskill Senior Girls' School and a series of short plays at the Municipal High School.

Over the weekend of 4/5 July there was a dance at Tynemouth Park at which the RAF Broadcast Band would play, followed by the music of W. Moutney and his Hawaiian Swingtet. Other events included a drama evening at the youth centre, an amusement fair at Collingwood View field, a cycle ride from Christ Church, North Shields, to Todburn (Northumberland), with lunch and tea at Longhorsley, a Christian meeting at the Albion Cinema on the theme of the 'Sword of the Spirit', pony rides at Smith's Park, a driving competition at Tynemouth Golf Course, a concert by the NFS band at Tynemouth Park (on the Sunday) or in the public air raid shelter if the weather was poor. The fun extended into the Monday when Reco Bros Empire Circus was at Collingwood View field, the pony rides were at Linskill Terrace field and there were dances at both Murton School, New York, and at Tynemouth Park.

The Home Guard also got involved in the festivities of the Holidays at Home programme when they organized an extensive demonstration of their history and capabilities on Tynemouth Promenade and in front of St George's Church, Cullercoats. Part of the event was a pageant which recalled the history of the Home Guard from its earliest days as the LDV, 'with emphasis on the lack of uniforms and equipment leading up to the high state of efficiency now attained with an abundance of first-class weapons'. This was followed by a realistic demonstration of the Home Guard in action, with the men of the battalion using many of the weapons available to them, including machine guns, spigot mortars and Northover Projectors (improvised anti-tank guns). This was followed by a demonstration of firepower, with targets being engaged by weapons such as rifles, machine guns, Northovers, spigot mortars and Browning automatic rifles. There were also demonstrations of camouflage techniques, unarmed combat, fieldcraft and signals, along with a display of the weapons of the Home Guard in the sunken gardens.

The Home Guard were also now being used to man anti-aircraft defences in the area, as well as coastal defences and their regular patrol and guard duties.

Unbeknownst to the residents and the authorities, the final bomb to be dropped on Tynemouth Borough fell on 25 March. This was the last bomb of over 300 high explosive bombs, 18,000 incendiaries and at least nineteen recorded incidents involving parachute mines from when the first bomb dropped on 22 June 1940. During this period, the borough had suffered an estimated 225 fatalities and 500 people injured, at least 150 of them seriously.

The shipyards of the Tyne continued to work at full capacity throughout the year, the men and women who laboured in the yards faced with an exhausting schedule of extended hours of intensive work. Although undoubtedly tired, the majority of workers were sure in the knowledge that they were making a very important contribution to the war effort. As we have seen, strikes had affected production at times, but these were often of short duration and over local issues. The increased pay levels and spirit of contributing to the war effort was enough for most of the workers. Some, however, did show what can be termed recalcitrant and negligent behaviour. There had been persistent allegations of the slow pace of many workers and the inefficient use of labour in some of the yards, but these had never been proven. There were also bad apples and malingerers who disliked the work which they were expected to perform. In April, one such man, George Sidney Stephenson (23) of South Shields, appeared before Tynemouth magistrates charged with absenting himself from work without reasonable excuse on two occasions and being persistently late for work without a reasonable excuse on many occasions. Mr Stephenson had been assigned work at Smith's Dock in North Shields and was obviously deeply unhappy with his lot. The Ministry of Labour and National Service alleged that Stephenson had been late on thirty-six days between November 1942 and February 1943, and that he had been absent on seventeen days. Mr Stephenson had been warned and interviewed by the Yard Committee at the end of November, and had said that he didn't like working in the yard. The head timekeeper at the yard said that the warnings had no effect on the defendant, with his behaviour not improving at all. When interviewed by the National

Service Officer in March, he had refused to give any statement and, in the opinion of the Ministry, there was 'no excuse whatever for his conduct'. When questioned by the magistrates, Stephenson, who admitted his guilt on all charges, simply said 'I didn't like working in the yard' before adding that he had been trying to go away to sea and was awaiting word. The bench took a hard line on the offences and were unimpressed with Mr Stephenson's attitude, fining him a total of £9.[20]

One of the more unusual vessels to be completed at Swan Hunter's during the year was the 13,000 ton Nairana Class escort carrier HMS *Vindex*. Originally being constructed as a merchant vessel, the Admiralty took her over and the company was ordered to begin conversion work to turn her into an escort carrier. Commissioned in December, she performed useful work, with her Fairey Swordfish aircraft sinking four U-boats.[21] Other naval vessels finished during the year included the U Class destroyers HMS *Grenville* and *Ulster*, the

HMS Vindex*, one of the more unusual wartime vessels to be completed at Swan Hunter's. (Public Domain)*

HMS Grenville *on the River Tyne, May 1943.* (Public Domain)

HMS Tyrian, *1943.* (Public Domain)

S Class destroyer HMS *Tyrian*, the T Class destroyer HMS *Tuscan*, the V Class destroyer HMS *Virago* and the Castle Class corvette HMS *Portchester Castle*.[22]

With the tide of the war beginning to change, the centralized control of industry and the increasing importance of the coal industry to the war effort, the Wallsend engineering firm of Charles Crofton & Co. Ltd was allowed to switch much of its focus back to its original lines of specialized equipment for the mining industry. This allowed the firm to become one of the leading suppliers nationally, and it also began to forge tentative foreign links looking to the post-war market.

As has been mentioned, the local youth organizations provided a worthwhile pastime for many younger people in Tynemouth and Wallsend, and both the Boy Scouts and the Girl Guides were very popular during the war years. For boys, the Scouts offered some sort of quasi-military pastime in which fieldcraft was heavily practised, whilst there was also the thrill of danger as many Scouts assisted the ARP services as messengers during raids and others worked with the first-aid services. For the Girl Guides, there was the knowledge that they too were being trained in skills to assist both the war effort and their local community, and many helped out at local hospitals and first-aid posts. In June, the Tynemouth Guides and Brownies held a mass rally at the Municipal High School to demonstrate their skills and celebrate their accomplishments. The guest of honour on this occasion was no less than Lady Baden-Powell.

Lady Baden-Powell, guest of honour at Tynemouth Guides' mass rally. (Shields Evening News)

Lady Baden-Powell inspecting some of the Brownies who paraded at the Scouts and Guides Rally held at Tynemouth Municipal High School, on Saturday.

Throughout the war, local hospitals were forced to adapt to wartime conditions and an increase in their workload as they nursed both civilians and members of the forces, as well as being focal points for the civil defence first-aid services in their area. For Tynemouth Infirmary and Preston Hospital, both in North Shields, the workload was substantially increased by the fact that the town was a common landing point for mariners who had suffered the loss of their vessels, had been taken ill or had been wounded in the many attacks by the Germans on East Coast shipping. Airmen who had come down in the sea and subsequently been rescued were also landed at the port and taken to one of the hospitals for assessment and treatment. All of this meant that the staff at the hospitals were overworked, being expected to make sacrifices of their own time to provide care for patients. Both hospitals developed a very good team ethic amongst their staffs, who also dedicated some of their time to supporting local charities and fundraising efforts. In July, the efforts of some of the nursing staff from both hospitals was rewarded when several nurses were given a variety of awards for their wartime services.

The Mayor and Mayoress of Tynemouth (Coun. and Mrs G. C. Murray) with nurses from Tynemouth Infirmary and Preston Hospital who won awards during the past year.

The Mayor of Tynemouth and local nurses. The nurses in local hospitals made a huge contribution to the war effort. (*Shields Evening News*)

The men from Tynemouth and Wallsend who were in the armed forces were fighting across a large number of fronts which spanned the globe. Although there were many in the Army who were in Britain training for the long-awaited invasion of Europe, there were also a large number who were fighting against the Japanese in Asia and, equally, a significant number fighting against the Afrika Korps in the deserts of North Africa. Throughout 1943, the fighting in North Africa continued unabated, featuring many men from the area in the various services. On 27 August, yet another young Tynemouth man lost his life in this theatre of action. Lieutenant Keith Angus of the Royal Scots Fusiliers died of wounds sustained whilst attached to the 1st Battalion, Gordon Highlanders. Keith was the 21-year-old youngest son of John Laws Angus and Mabel Isabella Angus of 11 Latimer Street.

Although many of the RAF casualties were suffered in action, any service in the wartime RAF could prove extremely hazardous, with training accidents commonplace and claiming many lives. On 24 March, such an accident claimed the life of Tynemouth man Pilot Officer George Brian Gibson. Gibson was a 23-year-old air gunner based at 16 Operational Training Unit (OTU) at Upper Heyford, Oxfordshire. The OTUs were responsible for the final training of aircrew destined for service squadrons, 16 OTU being a bomber crew training unit equipped with Vickers Wellingtons. For many embryonic airmen, the culmination of their training at an OTU was a short operation over enemy territory or a mission to lay mines in enemy waters. Many of the raids were to drop not bombs but propaganda leaflets over occupied countries (such missions were codenamed 'Nickels'), and it was on one of these operations (to the Orléans region of France) that Pilot Officer Gibson and the five other airmen of his crew lost their lives. Little is known of the cause of the loss of Wellington

Lieutenant Keith Angus, Royal Scots Fusiliers, died of wounds in the Middle East. (Shields Evening News)

1943: A YEAR OF VICTORIES AND ATTRITION 137

III (X3991), but it is known that the aircraft crashed at Pontgouin in France, where all six are now buried.[23]

Buoyed by the year's successes during the bombing of Hamburg and the Battle of the Ruhr, RAF Bomber Command's next target was the German capital. The Battle of Berlin was to be a sustained campaign which aimed to destroy the capital, erode morale in Germany and force a collapse of the Third Reich. The first raid was launched on the night of 18/19 November and consisted of a force of 440 Lancasters and four Mosquitoes, whilst a diversionary raid by 248 Halifaxes, 114 Stirlings and thirty-three Lancasters was made on Mannheim/Ludwigshafen. Weather over the target was poor, and although a large number of bombs fell on Berlin the raid was scattered over the vast city and there was no concentration of bombing. Amongst the nine Lancasters to be lost on the operation was the 9 Squadron Lancaster III (DV284, WS-G) piloted by Pilot Officer G.A. Graham, RCAF (Royal Canadian Air Force). The wireless operator/air gunner in this crew was 20-year-old Sergeant Arthur Fenwick Williamson from Northumberland Terrace, Tynemouth. The Lancaster was shot down by anti-aircraft fire and crashed shortly before 10.00 pm at Burgwerben, killing all eight crewmen, who were subsequently buried at the Berlin 1939–1945 War Cemetery.[24]

It was not only the airmen of Bomber Command who were suffering losses: the crews of night-fighters were also killed due to enemy action and the inherent difficulties of flying at night, sometimes in poor weather, with limited technical aids. A Tynemouth man had made something of a reputation for himself in night-fighting circles. Squadron Leader Dudley Ormston Hobbis, DFC, had joined the RAF in 1939 before being posted to 219 Squadron at Catterick in 1940. When the unit converted to night-fighters (initially with Bristol Beaufighters, which were quickly replaced by de Haviland Mosquitoes), Hobbis, then a flying officer, remained with the squadron. His first success came when he shot down an unidentified enemy aircraft off Portsmouth on 27 April 1941. His second 'kill' came on 1 June of the same year when he shot down a *JU88* over Brighton before a third success against a Heinkel *HEIII* off Winchelsea a fortnight later. For these he was awarded the DFC, whilst his radar operator sergeant was awarded the DFM.

During the spring and summer of 1942, Squadron Leader Hobbis commanded 530 Squadron, flying the experimental (and ultimately unsuccessful) Turbinlite converted Douglas Havoc. Rested for a period, he was then posted as 'A' Flight commander of 488 (New Zealand) Squadron, flying the Mosquito, in April 1943. On the night of 25 November, Hobbis and his radar operator, Pilot Officer O.L.R. Hills, took off and were over Bradwell Bay when Hobbis radioed that one of his engines was on fire and he had ordered his radar operator to bail out. It was assumed, but never confirmed, that Hobbis followed him out of the aircraft, but a subsequent search failed to find either airman. Hills' body washed ashore several months later, but that of Squadron Leader Hobbis was never found and he is commemorated on the Runnymede Memorial.

Squadron Leader Hobbis was 33 when he lost his life and had been married for just over three months. Originally from nearby Benton, Hobbis married Jean Lillington Henderson on 11 August and the couple settled in Tynemouth, his wife's home town. Hobbis had been educated at Rutherford Technical College in Newcastle and had a reputation as a keen amateur tennis player; he and his wife had met when they both represented Northumberland in the sport.

For the many men from the area who had been captured by the Japanese, horrors awaited as they were used as forced labour and subjected to terrible brutality and inhuman treatment by their captors. Even without this, there were the everyday tragedies of war. On 29 November, the Japanese ship SS *Suez Maru* was transporting several hundred sick and wounded Japanese soldiers, along with 548 British and Dutch prisoners, when it was torpedoed and sunk by the American submarine the USS *Blowfish*. Although 200 of the prisoners managed to escape, the first vessel to find them

Squadron Leader Hobbis, DFC. The pioneering night-fighter pilot was killed due to a mechanical failure. (Unknown)

was a Japanese minesweeper and the captain refused to pick up any of the European prisoners, instead ordering his crew to shoot them with rifles and machine guns whilst in the water, before ramming those who were aboard boats or clinging to wreckage; the massacre took over two hours to complete. Amongst the prisoners was a Whitley Bay man, Corporal C.P. Dron, a member of the Royal Air Force Volunteer Reserve (RAFVR). Despite an inquiry into the incident after the war, there was no action taken against the captain of the minesweeper or the lieutenant in charge of the prisoners who was ordered to supervise the massacre.

As 1943 ended, the local mood was grimly determined. The people of Tynemouth and Wallsend had been buoyed by much of the war news through the year and there was a strong belief that victory was now very likely, but also awareness that there was still a long and bitter struggle ahead. Many more sacrifices would be likely from amongst the people of the area. Happily, the threat from enemy bombing had receded and people took this as another sign of the tide turning.

Notes

1. *Shields Evening News*, 1 January 1943, p.3.
2. *Shields Evening News*, 26 February 1943, p.3.
3. *Shields Daily News*, 26 January 1943, p.3.
4. *Shields Evening News*, 26 February 1943, p.3.
5. *Shields Evening News*, 2 May 1943, p.3.
6. *Ibid*.
7. *Ibid*. Poster from Tynemouth Savings Committee. A 'cookie' was a 4,000lb high capacity bomb commonly used by RAF Bomber Command in its attacks on German towns and cities.
8. *Shields Evening News*, 5 May 1943, p.1.
9. Middlebrook, M., and Everitt, C., *The Bomber Command War Diaries. An operational reference book 19391945* (Midland, 1996), pp.38485.
10. *Shields Evening News*, 10 May 1943, p. 1.
11. *Shields Evening News*, 21 May 1943, p.3.
12. The eight-man RAF crew consisted of: F/S A.J.E. Long (pilot); F/O C.L. Barbezat (second-pilot); Sgt D.A. Galloway (flight engineer); Sgt J.J.V. Heal (navigator); Sgt J. Cooper (bomb aimer); Sgt L.H. Sefton (wireless operator); Sgt D. Goulden (mid-upper gunner); and Sgt F. Willetts (rear gunner). Although the average age of the crew was just 23, the second pilot whom they took along with them that night was aged 34. All are commemorated on the Runnymede Memorial.

13. Acting Skipper Lieutenant Robert Armstrong was in fact the author's grandfather. The plaque which he was given signifying his mention in dispatches was mislaid after his death.
14. Letter from Town Clerk of Tynemouth CBC, 26 May 1943, *ibid.*
15. National Archives: ADM1/152260. Minutes of a Meeting between the Financial Secretary and a Deputation from Jarrow, 18 May 1943.
16. TWAS: DS/SWH/1/7. Swan Hunters minute book, Board meeting, 2 September 1941, p.27.
17. Letter from Tynemouth CBC, 12 June 1943, *ibid.*
18. Letter from Ministry of Labour and National Service to the Admiralty, 22 June 1943, *ibid.*
19. *Shields Evening News*, 4 January 1943, p.5.
20. *Shields Daily News*, 9 April 1943, p.7.
21. HMS *Vindex* had a long life. After being sold for commercial use to the Port Line in 1947, she was renamed *Port Vindex* and was not scrapped until 1971.
22. Both HMS *Grenville* and HMS *Ulster* had exceptionally long service careers: *Grenville* was not paid off from RN service until 1974 and scrapped in 1983, whilst *Ulster* was withdrawn from RN service in 1977 and scrapped three years later. HMS *Portchester Castle* was featured in the iconic 1952 movie *The Cruel Sea*.
23. The other crewmen were: Pilot Officer V.N. Ballard, RAAF (Royal Australian Air Force) (pilot); Pilot Officer P.W. Masters, RAF (second pilot); Pilot Officer A.R. Dicker, RAF (navigator); Sergeant J.E. Jones, RAF (bomb aimer); and Sergeant H.R. Kinder, RAF (wireless operator).
24. The other crewmen were: Pilot Officer G.A. Graham, RCAF (pilot); Flight Sergeant J.G. McComb, RAF (second pilot); Sergeant W.G. Statham, RAF (flight engineer); Flying Officer D. MacDonald, RAF (navigator); Sergeant R.M. Inness, RAF (bomb aimer); Flight Sergeant H.F. Altus, RAAF (mid upper gunner); and Sergeant K. Mellor, RAF (rear gunner). It is likely that Graham's crew were well advanced in their tour of operations, as they were trusted to have an inexperienced second pilot with them.

CHAPTER SIX

1944: The Beginning of the End?

The New Year once again opened with the traditional celebrations and festivities, but it was clear that people were now growing increasingly weary. For some, the signs that the Allies were winning the war caused their thoughts to turn to a possible peace. An article in the *Shields Daily News* expressed these thoughts, saying that a great many people in the area were concerned that peace would bring a return to the economic and industrial slumps that had characterized the inter-war years and had proven so painful for the area. The paper expressed the belief that people were not reassured by repeated but bland messages that this would not be allowed to happen again, and wanted action that would safeguard a peacetime future for the area. Although the article expressed disbelief that widespread unemployment would be a problem after the war, it acknowledged that concrete plans must be put in place to 'bring to this area the new industries which are the best guarantee of steady prosperity after the war'.

Once again the people of Tynemouth and Wallsend made the best of the situation and tried to maintain the traditions of first-footing and welcoming in the New Year. Parties were again held, with many of the forces personnel who were based in the area being invited to the homes of friends they had made locally or celebrating in their off-duty hours at the many forces canteens and other establishments in the area.

Amongst the locals who were mentioned in the New Year's honours list was a Cullercoats-born Royal Navy Commander who had served for twenty-six years since joining the Dartmouth Naval School aged just 13. Commander Charles Arthur de Winton Kitcat was the son of the former superintendent of the Tyne-based training ship and correctional school HMS *Wellesley*. Since 1935, he had been commanding officer of a number of destroyers. This was the second time in three years that Commander Kitcat had been mentioned in dispatches. The first occasion was after his actions in the evacuation of Namsos in 1940. Since then he had taken part in the relief convoy to Malta and several Russian convoys. In September 1943, his ship was attacked and sunk by German aircraft and he received a severe head injury. At the time of the announcement of his second mention in dispatches, he was still at home at 21 Beverley Gardens, Cullercoats, recuperating from this injury.

For the families of many of those men who had been unfortunate enough to be taken prisoner by the Japanese, the waiting to hear news of loved ones was interminable. In some cases it could take years for the authorities to confirm the fate of such men. On 1 January, the family of Sergeant William Langton Wilson of 106 Wallsend Road, North Shields, received confirmation that he was being held prisoner in Thailand. Sergeant Wilson had been posted missing in February 1942 and, although his family must have been relieved to hear positive news, their anxieties must have remained as rumours and reports of Japanese poor treatment of Allied prisoners had already reached Britain. Thankfully, it would seem that he survived the ordeal of his capture and returned to Britain after the war.

Having already seen how committed the people of the area were to raising funds for the war effort through contributions to the various schemes that made up the national war savings effort, it should come as no surprise that at the start of the year Tynemouth was proud to be able to boast that its residents had raised a total of £5,352,479 (a massive £217,814,410 today). This amounted to an average contribution of over £103 for every person resident in the borough (or £4,191 today).

Even at this point in the war, people were still expected to have fully maintained gas masks and to carry them at all times. It was still felt that, in desperation, the Nazis might employ gas-filled bombs on civilian targets, or that new terror weapons might be under development to deliver poison gas. Inspections of gas masks were common in the workplace and at schools. Of course, the masks did deteriorate over time and required replacement or repair. In mid-January, the pupils of Tynemouth Municipal High School had one such inspection and those whose masks required replacement parts were sent to the local ARP stores to have them fitted as necessary. This was yet another

Tynemouth High School pupils at a gas mask fitting and repair check. (Shields Evening News)

way in which the men and women of the ARP served and provided a comforting and reassuring presence.

As the Home Guard continued with its duties throughout the long winter, a welcome night of relaxation came on 14 January when the 7th (Tynemouth) Battalion, Northumberland Home Guard, held its second annual dance at the Grand Hotel in Tynemouth. The dance attracted a large crowd, with members from all of the services present as well as those who had played a part in the formation and running of the battalion. Included amongst these was Lieutenant Colonel Shrive, MBE, MC, Royal Artillery, and Lieutenant Colonel and Mrs Stanley Holmes (he was responsible for the initial organization of the unit as area commander). The dance was a great success, with music provided by Jack Moor and his band along with competitions in aid of the Red Cross. The social side of serving in the Home Guard was lively and vitally important to the maintenance of morale in a service which faced no relaxation in what was an increasingly heavy workload alongside its members' regular work.

The Home Guard continued in its duties throughout the year, and by this point of the war such units in this area were a very skilled and professional body of men. The equipment shortages of their early months were far behind them, and they now possessed equipment which would, in many cases, have been the envy of a regular battalion in 1940. We have already seen, for example, how in 1940 a Tynemouth Home Guard patrol was reprimanded for firing five rounds of ammunition. This contrasts strongly with the fact that by the time the battalion was stood down it had almost one million rounds of ammunition and access to artillery pieces that had been in use by the Regular Army until 1943.[1]

One of the increasing roles of the Home Guard in the area was that of anti-aircraft defence. In Tynemouth, some members of the Home Guard were given the task of manning the Z Rocket Battery that was emplaced near the coast next to the Park Hotel. The Z Battery consisted of multiple launchers designed to bring down low-flying raiders, and the unit had at least one success confirmed. The weapon had been tested extensively on Tyneside earlier in the war, amidst great secrecy,

A Mobile 'Z' Rocket Battery was later placed in the area. (Public Domain)

SA tatic 'Z' Rocket Launcher similar to those located beside the Park Hotel (this one is on Merseyside). (Public Domain)

and was a favourite of Winston Churchill, who had forced through its development.

Minor crimes committed by servicemen when under the influence of alcohol continued to be problematic. A special meeting of Tynemouth Police Court heard that on 14 January, the same night as the dance mentioned above was taking place, two naval ratings, Albert Frank Dean (21) of Liverpool and William Usher (20) of Gateshead, had been apprehended carrying two stools along Wellington Street, North Shields, by Detective Wilkinson. They had confessed that they stole them from a public house, but could not remember which one as they were both drunk. Detective Wilkinson arrested the men for theft and made enquiries which revealed that the licensee of the Clock Vaults, Mr Robert William Lawson, had found two stools to be missing and subsequently identified the stools carried by the two men as his (they were valued at 10s. 6d. each). The defendants expressed their regrets and apologies, and insisted that they would never have stolen the stools if they had been sober. The magistrates appear to have accepted the excuses and taken a lenient view of the offence, for they dismissed the charges under the Probation of Offenders' Act and ordered them to pay 7s. 6d. each in costs.

Drunkenness was again used as an excuse by two men from Walker appearing at Tynemouth charged with having stolen a police officer's bicycle at North Shields. Robert Mark Thompson (22) and soldier Robert Lucas (22), who seem to have been habitual troublemakers, claimed that they had been drunk and had stolen the bike simply out of a sense of mischief. However, the court heard that Thompson had been before the bench on five previous occasions. In 1936, he had served a period of probation after being convicted of theft and, as a former merchant seaman, had been fined several times for being absent from his ship or having failed to join his ship in time for sailing. At the time of this latest act he was employed as a labourer in a local shipyard. Lucas also had a criminal past, having been sent to prison for two months for breaking into a shop, and was currently absent without leave from his unit. The two men had met recently and had been sleeping rough in various air-raid shelters in Newcastle and North Shields. Each man was fined 40s., with Thompson given fourteen days to pay and Lucas two months. As he was absent from his unit, Lucas was also handed over to a military escort for return to it and punishment.

Although conditions on war-torn Tyneside could be grim, many people had their morale boosted by news of Allied victories and it was clear that the tide of war had changed. The end of January brought news of the landing of over 40,000 Allied troops at Anzio in Italy. Amongst the forces to land on the first day was the 1st Battalion, Duke of Wellington's (West Riding Regiment), which went ashore at Peter Beach, 6 miles north of Anzio. A week or so after the initial, largely unopposed landing, the Allies launched an offensive against the now reinforced and dug-in German troops. The British 1st Division launched its attack towards Campoleone. The attack made ground, but attempts to take the town failed and at the end of the battle the 1st Division was occupying an exposed and dangerous salient. The fighting during this short-lived offensive was fierce, with a large number of casualties suffered by the 1st Division. Amongst them was Private Patrick McMullen, 1st Battalion, Duke of Wellington's, who was killed on 31 January aged 21. Private McMullen was a Wallsend man, one of a number of men from the town to be killed in the fiercely fought Italian campaign.

One of the most keenly supported wartime campaigns was that of RAF Bomber Command against the cities and towns of Germany. For years, the men of Bomber Command had been the only real way of taking the offensive against the Germans and, given the suffering of British people under Luftwaffe bombs, the bombing of Germany found great favour amongst most members of the Tyneside public. As 1943 had been particularly successful for Bomber Command, the expectation now was that Berlin would be the next major target. Indeed, a sustained assault on the German capital began in the autumn of 1943 and continued into the first months of 1944. With the Bomber Command campaign against Berlin reaching its terrible conclusion, its men were suffering dreadful casualties on an almost nightly basis. For the families of these men, there was little comfort or certainty as they generally received only a telegram telling them that their loved one had failed to return from operations and had been posted missing, with a vague promise of further information if it was forthcoming. This resulted in an anxious wait as relatives nourished hopes that their loved one had managed to survive and was either evading the Germans with the help of the various resistance movements or had been taken prisoner. This wait could last months or years before some scrap of information, or simply the lack of any further news, led the authorities to inform the family that their loved one must now be presumed to have been killed.

Mr Leslie Forster and his wife, Isobel, received the dreaded telegram informing them that their son, Sergeant Douglas George Forster, had failed to return from operations on 22 January, and the anxious wait then began. It was not until nine months later that they received a telegram advising them that it was now presumed that Douglas had been killed. Sergeant Forster was aged 20 and was well-known in the area, having been educated at Tynemouth Municipal High School before working at the North Shields branch of the Prudential Assurance Company. He was also an active and enthusiastic member of the YMCA. Sergeant Forster was the wireless operator/air gunner in a Halifax II (LM274 DY-R) which had taken off from Pocklington near York shortly before 8.00 pm as part of a force of 648 aircraft tasked with bombing the German city of Magdeburg. This was the first major raid on Magdeburg, but the new tactics employed by the German night-fighter force once again proved very effective: German fighters got into the bomber stream before the RAF crews had even crossed the German coast. Losses were very heavy, with fifty-seven aircraft failing to return (8.8 per cent of the total) and the lower-flying and obsolescent early model Halifaxes suffering very badly indeed, thirty-five being lost (15.6 per cent). Sergeant Forster's DY-R came down off Flamborough Head, killing all seven men on board, although it is not known if this was on the outbound or inbound flight. It would appear that the bodies of both air gunners washed up at a later date, which allowed the authorities to confirm the probable death of Sergeant Forster.[2]

Although the Battle of Berlin was not quite over, Bomber Command, after its recent heavy losses over the German capital, switched its attentions to other cities. On 24 February, for example, the command launched its first major raid on Schweinfurt, the base of Germany's ball-bearing manufacturing industry. The raid consisted of a force of 734 aircraft, including 554 Lancaster bombers. The Pathfinders of 156 Squadron based at Warboys in Huntingdonshire (now Cambridgeshire) dispatched a number of aircraft, amongst which was Lancaster III (JB721, GT-F) piloted by Flight Lieutenant J.A. Day, DFC. Its wireless operator was Dunston-born Flight Sergeant Jack William Goulbourn (23). Flight Sergeant Goulbourn's aircraft took off shortly before 7.00 pm but failed to return. The aircraft had exploded in mid-air whilst over

Sergeant D.G. Forster, RAF Bomber Command, was missing following a raid on Magdeburg. (*Shields Daily News*)

Mosquito FB IV of 613 Squadron. (Ringway Observer)

Briey in north-eastern France, killing five of the seven-man crew. The pilot and flight engineer were flung out of the aircraft by the explosion and were taken prisoner, whilst three crewmen are buried at Briey Communal Cemetery, one at Abbeville and one at Choloy.[3]

It was not only the campaigns of Bomber Command which was costing the lives of locally born RAF men during this period. On 13 March, Flying Officer Charles Harrison Pigg (26) was killed along with his navigator whilst engaged in an operation over France. Charles was the pilot of a Mosquito of 613 Squadron, a day and night tactical strike unit which was used in both night intruder operations and precision strikes in daylight as part of 2 Group's (TAF) efforts to pave the way for the D-Day invasion. Flying Officer Pigg had been a keen golfer and was a well-known member of Tynemouth Golf Club (where he is commemorated), and left behind his parents and a younger brother at their home at 8 Algernon Terrace.[4]

The awful grinding campaign of Bomber Command continued throughout the first three months of the year before the force was switched to less challenging (though still very dangerous) targets to prepare the way for the invasion of France. On the night of 22 March, Bomber Command dispatched 816 aircraft in what was the second major attack on the city of Frankfurt in five days. Amongst the 184 Halifaxes which were sent was the 78 Squadron Halifax III (LW512,

EY-Q) piloted by Sergeant S. Hampson. The aircraft was intercepted by a *JU88* night-fighter over the German town of Trier at 18,000ft. Shot down by the German fighter, the Halifax crashed to earth with only the rear gunner having time to bail out of the stricken bomber. The bomb aimer in the Halifax was Sergeant Richard Alan Renwick, a Tynemouth man who was 23 at the time of his death; he is buried alongside his crew in Rheinberg War Cemetery in Germany.[5]

The commander-in-chief of Bomber Command, Air Chief Marshall Arthur 'Bomber' Harris, was keenly aware that his command would be ordered to mount raids in preparation and support of the Normandy landings. However, still convinced that the war could be won by bombing, he was keen to make one last grand raid before this happened, especially now that he had admitted defeat in the campaign to destroy Berlin. On the night of 30/31 March, the men of Bomber Command were briefed for a raid on the distant target of Nuremburg in southern Germany. On the bomber bases there was consternation at this announcement, as the moon would be quite full (they usually avoided distant operations during the full moon period) and the route was a fairly straight one, with little to confuse the German defences. Several commanders also raised concerns that the route took the bombers dangerously near to a fighter assembly beacon. However, the raid went ahead as planned and 795 aircraft took to the skies, aiming for Nuremburg. For this raid, 640 Squadron, based at Leconfield, dispatched sixteen aircraft. Included amongst the force was Halifax III (LW555, C8-L) piloted by Flying Officer C.E. O'Brien, RCAF. On its way to the target, the Halifax came under attack by the Messerschmidt *ME110* of Oberleutnant Martin Becker and was shot down, crashing near Westerburg and killing all seven men aboard. The rear gunner in the crew was Sergeant Terrence Christopher McFadden (21) of Wallsend, who along with his crewmates is buried in the Rheinberg War Cemetery. McFadden and the rest of the inexperienced crew (they were on only their fourth operation) had been particularly unlucky in having run into Becker, an established and very experienced night-fighter ace who scored seven kills on this one night alone.[6]

Given that the people of Tynemouth and Wallsend had a noted reputation for the success of fund raising projects during the previous years of the war, it is no surprise that the authorities expected this to continue throughout 1944. Indeed, the year had begun with a well-received appeal for the collection of scrap materials and continued attempts to raise funds for organizations such as the Red Cross.

Tynemouth set an ambitious target for its Salute the Soldier Week, which was to run from 6 May. It had been decided that Tynemouth Borough would attempt to raise sufficient money to fully clothe and equip an entire brigade of the 50th (Northumbrian) Division, with the bar set at a target total of £500,000 (£20 million today). This was the same target that had been set, and exceeded, in 1943 for the borough's Wings for Victory Week. It would require an immense contribution from both small and large investors, and would be a test of the public's morale during the sixth year of the war, during a period in which there had been considerable industrial unrest in the area.

Key to the week-long campaign was the small investor, who had, in the previous year, donated a very significant sum; the local authority was keen to ensure the involvement and enthusiasm of ordinary people in following and taking part in the campaign. The area had already been divided into distinct areas of street groups, each with its own captain who was responsible for much of the organization and administration. In such voluntary ways did people continue to make a substantial contribution to the war effort. The target for the street groups alone (there were numerous other groups involved) was extremely ambitious. Even the partial list published in the *Shields Evening Post* on 28 April represented a target of almost £5,000 (over £203,000 today), with contributions targets varying according to the wealth of the area and past performance, ranging from £1 (£40) in Lawson Street West and the well-named Thrift Avenue to £500 (£20,347) in Sheringham Avenue and Lynn Road. In total, some eighteen street groups planned to raise £100 or more (over £4,000), and from these, eleven had agreed to raise at least £200 (over £8,137).

Salute the Soldier Campaign 1944: street group targets for Tynemouth Borough (partial list)

Street Group	Target (£)	Street Group	Target (£)
Addington Crescent	10	Heaton Terrace	70
Holywell Road & Juliet Avenue	200	Mowbray Road	15
Orlando Road	23	Sheringham Avenue & Lynn Road	500
Surrey Road	18	Verne Road (1)	30
Verne Road (2)	25	Willoughby Road	60
Glanton Road	50	Balkwell Green (1)	20
Balkwell Green (2)	8	Marden Terrace, Marden Avenue, St. Oswin's Avenue & Hudlestone Street	100
Eleanor Street, Percy Avenue, Dove Street & Station Road	40	John St, Eskdale Terrace, Elizabeth St, Simpson St & Belle Vue St	70
Beverley Terrace & Beverley Gardens	200	The Laundry	25
Sibthorpe Street	20	Borough Road & Gardner Street	50
Little Bedford St & Lower Rudyerd St	50	Waldo Street	25
Yeoman Street	20	Tennyson Street	15
Cardonnel Street	20	Lawson Street	20
Seymour Street	100	Collingwood Terr & Trinity Terr	5
R. Spendiff's Group	60	Wilson Street	19
Vicarage St, Henry St & Waterville Rd	15	Upper Elsdon St, Elsdon St, Howdon Rd & Penman St	200
Trinity Street	10	Thrift Street	1
Victoria Street	5	Lawson Street West	1
Collingwood View & Victoria Crescent	100	Hopper Street & Hopper Street West	50
Brannen Street & Lovaine Place	8	Sidney Street, West Percy Street & Nelson Street	100

1944: THE BEGINNING OF THE END? 153

Street Group	Target (£)	Street Group	Target (£)
Beaumont Street	10	Hylton Street, Hylton Terrace & Belle Vue Terrace	10
William St & William St West	5	Algernon Terrace & Livingstone View	85
Edith Street	80	Albury Park Road	200
Denwick Terrace	25	Brislee Avenue & Hulne Avenue	50
Horsley Terrace & Shipley Road	30	Beanley Crescent	30
River View	400	Mariners' Lane	50
Birtley Avenue	50	Broadway (South)	25
Seacrest Avenue	300	Sunlea Avenue, Sandhurst Avenue & Medhurst Avenue	200
Wansbeck Avenue	300	Links Avenue & Links Road	40
Seacombe Avenue	130	Shoreston Avenue	50
Broadway (North)	50	Newton Avenue	25
Burnside Road	20	Hatharton Avenue	100
Hoghton Avenue	200	Foxton Avenue	200
St. George's Road, Mast Lane & Longston Avenue	150	Addison Street	10
Appleby Street	3	Coronation Street	10
Dene Street	5	Dene Terrace	10
Laet Street	10		
		TOTAL (£)	4,921

A very varied programme of events was incorporated into the Salute the Soldier Week campaign, which opened with a parade held at the Municipal High Scool at North Shields. The parade included representatives from the Royal Navy, Army, Royal Air Force, Home Guard, Civil Defence and other services, as well as a variety of local organizations, and was accompanied by music from no less than six bands. Before reaching the school playing field, the parade and bands had marched through the town, where large crowds lined the route. After initially assembling at King Edward School, Preston Avenue, the parade route took in much of the town and included Northumberland Square, where Major-General Clement A. Milward, accompanied by the Mayor and Mayoress, took the salute.

When the salute had been taken and the various groups taking part in the parade were drawn up in front of the dais, which held a large number of dignitaries, the Mayor, with the aid of loudspeakers, read out letters of encouragement and appreciation from both the Chancellor of the Exchequer and the Minister of War. In front of what was described as a huge crowd, the Mayor then invited Major-General Milward to open the campaign. In doing so, the general spoke of how proud he was to be invited to open the Tynemouth Salute the Soldier Week, adding that it was a vitally important cause and urging all residents to give whatever they could to the government so that the Army could be properly equipped to finish the war in victory.

The Mayor's speech alluded to the recent industrial unrest on Tyneside when he said that 'in these days when we had our occasional

General Milward opens the Tynemouth Salute the Soldier Week, 1944. (Shields Evening News)

ups and downs in industry, it was very pleasing indeed to be there to salute the soldier, for he was the man who could not strike, and would not, if he had the chance – except of course, at the enemy'.[7] In mentioning this, the Mayor perhaps risked alienating some of those who had supported or taken part in recent industrial action, and it was probably not the occasion to make this point when trying to encourage everyone to get behind the campaign.

After the speeches, a display of unarmed combat was given by four junior NCOs of the 7th (Tynemouth) Battalion, Home Guard, followed by a display of pipes and dancing by men of the 9th Battalion, Home Guard.

Another event to open the week of campaigning was the launch of an exhibition of the latest military equipment in the Memorial Methodist Hall, North Shields. Opening the exhibition, Colonel L. Sawyer, DSO, said that the idea behind it was to show the general public exactly what their contributions were being used to purchase and to reassure the people of Tynemouth that the equipment of the British soldier was at the cutting edge and was the best available. Amongst the displays which attracted greatest interest were the 'Walbike', which was a miniaturized folding motorcycle dropped for the use of airborne troops, a new 4.2in mortar and a portable one-man receiver/transmitter wireless set. Interspersed with the displays of military equipment were a series of eleven impressive paintings of events in both the current war and the First World War. The exhibition remained open all week and attracted a considerable number of people.

Amongst the many groups to vigorously support the Salute the Soldier campaign was, unsurprisingly, the 7th (Tynemouth) Battalion, Home Guard. On the first night of the campaign, the battalion, accompanied by the local Army Cadet company, held a parade, under the command of Major F.H. Baume, through the central and eastern parts of the borough. Starting from the junction of Military Road and Albion Road, and led by five motorcycle dispatch riders, they were seen off by a large cheering crowd. Indeed, crowds lined the entire route of the march. The march progressed via Military Road, Brandling Terrace, Linskill Terrace, King Edward Road, Percy Park and Queensway to Tynemouth Front Street. When they paused at Front Street to hear a selection of military marching tunes from the

Tynemouth Home Guard parade during Salute the Soldier Week, 1944. (Shields Evening News)

Tyne North Sector Home Guard Military Band, the crowd was several hundred in number. From overheard comments, it would seem that the public were very impressed with the military bearing and smartness of the Home Guardsmen. After the musical interlude, the parade set off back to the Drill Hall, pausing to pay their respects at the cenotaph at Tynemouth, via Manor Road, King Edward Road, Linskill Terrace and Drummond Terrace.

Their grandest event to raise funds for the year's campaign was the holding of a military dance at Roselyn Hall in Stephenson Street, North Shields, on Friday, 12 May. Music was to be supplied by the band of the Royal Northumberland Fusiliers and admission was by ticket only. Tickets could be purchased, for 2/6d., from the Drill Hall on Military Road or the office of the *Shields Evening News*; refreshments at the dance were not covered in the ticket price and all proceeds went to the Salute the Soldier campaign.

Such was the enthusiasm displayed by the public that by the end of just the second day of the campaign, a total of £174,815 had already been donated. This was almost £3,000 more than had been raised by the corresponding point in the earlier Wings for Victory Week. The

1944: THE BEGINNING OF THE END? 157

Officers and guests at a military dance at Roselyn Hall in aid of Salute the Soldier Week, 1944. (Shields Evening News)

Mayor of Tynemouth, Councillor J.W. Hogg, was appreciative of the efforts already made, but reminded people that there was still some considerable way to go before the target amount was met and urged 'townspeople to remember that it is the small saver on whom this drive counts and that on him the success of the campaign entirely depended last year'.[8]

The enthusiasm continued, and on the third day of the campaign a total of £53,605 was donated; hopes were beginning to be expressed that the target total of £500,000 might even be exceeded. Amongst the events on the third day of the campaign was a whist drive hosted by the Mayoress at Holy Saviour's Parish Hall. The guest of honour at the drive and subsequent dance was the Lady Mayoress of Newcastle, and a large number of guests attended. The dance which followed attracted over 140 guests, including the Mayor and Mayoress and the Deputy Mayor and Mayoress, and there were several prizes given out, including one of some fresh eggs. A considerable sum was raised for the campaign as a result of the two events.

The campaign was supported by an extensive series of advertisements in the local press, as well as by a poster campaign mounted jointly by

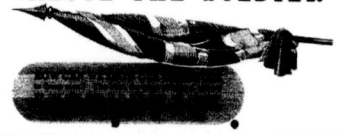

Salute the Soldier campaign poster, 1944. (TWAS T15 1516)

Salute the Soldier campaign poster by Tynemouth Savings Committee, 1944. (TWAS)

the local and national authorities. One feature of the campaign was the setting up of selling centres by the lady members of the street groups. These centres sold bonds and managed to raise £29,852 for the cause. These centres were the brainchild of Mrs Bainbridge, who received official thanks for her efforts from the organizers of the campaign.

    The local schools also played a role in the campaign, and had set themselves a combined target of raising £10,000 by the end of the week. A part of the programme within the schools was a series of talks given by an Army Education Officer, Major H.D. Badger, who on the fourth day of the campaign gave talks at several schools, including

1944: THE BEGINNING OF THE END? 159

Major Badger, Army Education Officer, talking to Percy Main schoolchildren as part of Salute the Soldier Week, 1944. (Shields Daily News)

A pet competition at Percy Main cricket field during Salute the Soldier Week, 1944. (Shields Evening News)

Percy Main Council School, Percy St John's School and Ralph Gardner Senior School. After these talks, the pupils were treated to music from the (seemingly everywhere during the week) band of the Royal Northumberland Fusiliers. These talks and music events continued throughout the week: the next morning it was the turn of St Cuthbert's and St Joseph's Catholic Schools.

Other events held on this day included a pets competition at Percy Main cricket field, a combined whist drive and dance at Laws School of Dancing and a dance at Roselyn Hall, organised by Welch & Sons Ltd (music was, again, by the RNF band). By this point, some organizations had realized that the initial targets which they had set themselves had been inadequate and had already been exceeded. Tynemouth Conservative Club, for example, had set itself a target of £200, but had already passed this and had revised the target to a more challenging £750. Also on this day, £10,000 was donated to the campaign by the North Shields branch of the Liverpool Victoria Insurance Company.

With the campaign due to close on Saturday night, it was announced on the Saturday morning that the target of £500,000 had been easily reached and exceeded; it was hoped that the total might exceed the £608,456

Councillor J.W. Hogg accepting a cheque from Tynemouth and Cullercoats YMCA during Salute the Soldier Week. (*Shields Evening News*)

that was raised during the Wings for Victory Week. By Friday night, the tally stood at £524,624, and there had been substantial donations from several local organizations and companies on the preceding day. These included £50,000 from Tynemouth Corporation, £5,000 from Tynemouth Victoria Jubilee Permanent Building Society, £5,000 from the National Association of Local Government Officers, £2,000 from North Tyneside Co-Operative Bakeries, £1,000 from the Wesleyan General Insurance Company, £1,000 from F.W. Woolworth & Co. and £1,000 from James Hogg & Sons. Amongst the smaller donations given on that day was £8 from the patrons and staff of the Albion Grill and an anonymous donation of £10 handed in at Cullercoats. The campaign closed with yet another dance at Roselyn Hall, this time the Hello Girls dance. By Saturday evening the total stood at a hugely impressive £618,635 following late donations from such groups as the Newcastle & Gateshead Gas Co., which contributed a further £5,000.

As promised, the council had counted the amounts raised following the week-long campaign and had arrived at the total of £673,335 (over £27,400,000 today), exceeding their target by over £175,000. This was an improvement on the 1943 Wings for Victory Week, which had raised £608,956. Jointly, these two week-long campaigns in the borough had raised an impressive £1,282,291 (over £52,181,000 today).

By June, the figures had been further tallied and, at a meeting in the Town Hall, it was announced that the street groups had managed to raise a total of £100,000 (over £4,069,000 today), which was approximately the same as the previous year. Mrs Bainbridge, who was in charge of the supervision of the street groups, announced that two groups had managed to contribute over £10,000 (over £469,000). In all, some £221,320 had been raised during the Salute the Soldier Week by small savings alone, without the donations made by organizations and companies. Although the authorities were pleased with this and had high praise for those who had organized and run the campaign, they did feel forced to comment that small donations were down for the year and compared the total in small savings raised to the £293,767 that had been raised in the Wings for Victory Week. Under the auspices of the national services campaign, the borough had raised £673,335 in 1944, which worked out at an average of over £12 per head (which was an increase on 1943).

Due to the fact that Tynemouth had reached its target, a trophy in the form of a plaque had been awarded to the local Savings Committee. All the groups who reached their target would also receive a special certificate to reward them for their efforts. In all, the week had been a great success and the honorary secretary said that the 'citizens of Tynemouth can be justly proud of their splendid achievement. Every voluntary organisation, every school, every industry, every officer, the churches, the Police, National Fire Service, Civil Defence and allied services, the Licensed Victuallers and organisations in the town took an active part [in the campaign].'9

Tragedy struck on 28 May when another Wallsend-connected airman lost his life. Flight Sergeant Thomas Dowens Purves was born at Tweedsmouth but had married a Wallsend woman and settled in the town. He had initially served with the Northumberland Fusiliers before being transferred to an engineering unit, given his experience of working as a railwayman. Later discharged from the Army, Thomas had once again volunteered, this time for the RAF. Trained as a flight engineer, Thomas had flown many missions over Germany. In May 1944 he was a flight engineer flying Short Stirlings with the secretive 299 Squadron based at RAF Keevil in Wiltshire. Since April, the special duties squadron had been responsible for dropping Special Operations Executive (SOE) agents and supplies over occupied countries in Europe. On 28 May, his wife received the dreadful news that her husband had been killed in a cycling accident. Flight Sergeant Purves (32) left behind his wife, Mary, and a young son, and was buried in Wallsend.

Wing Commander Denys Edgar Gillam, DFC (and bar), DSO, returned from another tour to the USA and in April was given command of 146 Wing of the 2nd Tactical Air Force (TAF). The wing flew Typhoon fighter-bombers and would play a crucial role in the build-up to the invasion and during the subsequent fighting in Normandy. Wing Commander Gillam proved a popular commander and the wing enjoyed a string of successes under his leadership. As a result, he was awarded the bar to his DSO in August.

Having first seen the opportunity in 1943, there had been considerable pressure from the local authorities on Tyneside to have several defunct shipyards reopened to help replace the severe losses that had afflicted the merchant fleet. Despite this pressure failing to influence the government, it was decided that a committee should be formed to make further representations. Tynemouth and Wallsend councils were particularly keen to make the attempt. The committee met in January and decided to make the case for the reopening of the Northumberland Shipyard at Howdon and the Palmer's Yard across the river at Jarrow. Both yards had been victims of the Depression and had closed in the 1930s. Much of the equipment, however, remained on site and it would have been possible to reopen the yards, although it would no doubt have been costly. The committee was led by the Town Clerk of Tynemouth (Mr F.G. Egner) and included such luminaries as Sir Alexander Russell MP (Tynemouth), Councillor J.W. Hogg (Mayor of Tynemouth), Alderman Richard Irvin (Tynemouth), Alderman C.H. Smith (South Shields) and Mr H. Ayrey (Town Clerk of South Shields).

Sir Alexander West Russell had been Conservative MP for Tynemouth for thirteen years but lost his seat in the 1945 General Election. (Public Domain)

As we have seen, workers in the area, especially in the shipbuilding and engineering trades, had been increasingly willing since 1942 to launch illegal strike action if they felt they were being exploited or were in conflict with the agreements and policies of the national leadership of their respective unions. The high watermark of strike action was 1944, which saw one of the most dramatic and important strikes; one which resulted in politically motivated prosecutions and marked the 'high point of industrial militancy during the war'.[10]

Ironically, the strike was not motivated by grievances against either employers or unions, but against government policy. By 1944 there was a severe shortage of labour in the coal mines of Britain (which had also been badly affected by strikes) and, with the armed forces swelling daily, the government decided that 10 per cent of all young men called up would, instead of joining the forces, be directed to work in the mines. They became known as Bevin Boys. The policy was never popular with those who were directed down the mines because mining, outside of mining communities, was apparently seen as both dirty and dangerous whilst lacking the glamour or glory of armed service. However, it was even less popular with those young men who were serving apprenticeships in the shipyards. For these men, the thought of swapping what had seemed to be the first rung on a promising career ladder for a short period of enforced work in a dirty and dangerous industry in which they had no interest, and which had no future for themselves, was abhorrent. The fact that the majority of apprentices would not be eligible for the scheme did not matter, nor were they convinced by the promise that their current employers could apply for a deferment on their behalf.

Before this, the apprentices had not been a traditionally militant group: many were not even members of a trade union. This changed with the threat of being sent down the mines. There was a local tradition of forming strong local labour groups to fight for local issues when necessary. The apprentices quickly formed their own organization, the Tyneside Apprentices Guild (TAG), under the leadership of a young apprentice named James William Davy. The TAG was quickly seen as a group which consisted solely of apprentices and fought solely for apprentices. However, the TAG was from its inception an organization with strong political links and, although the vast majority of apprentices did not have serious political leanings, Davy himself was thought by the authorities to have had strong pro-communist ideals. There were also proven links between the TAG and some leading members of the local Independent Labour Party (ILP), including such notables as T. Dan Smith. It was also discovered that the formation of the TAG had been influenced by members of the Workers International League.

The TAG expressed its viewpoint on the possibility of apprentices becoming Bevin Boys well in advance of any threat of industrial action. However, the concerns of the guild and its members appear to have met with stony silence from all quarters, probably because both the employers and authorities refused to recognize the TAG as a legitimate organization, seeing the group as a bunch of rabble-rousers and malcontents.

The TAG sent a delegation of five to London in an effort to engage in negotiation with Ernest Bevin and the trade union leaderships. Both Mr Bevin and the trade unions refused to meet with the delegation (although some talks were held with what were described as minor functionaries). Despite this disappointment, the delegates addressed a large open-air meeting upon their return, from which the press were excluded. The meeting was held at Swan Hunter's recreation ground at Wallsend. With no negotiations forthcoming, the leadership of the TAG held a vote and, with the backing of both their workmates and their families, announced that it would take immediate strike action.

Even before the strike had begun, there were allegations that political subversion was at work. Two former members of the TAG, J. Stubbings and R. Johnson, claimed, according to the *Evening Chronicle*, that they had played 'a leading part in the formation of the Guild' and had resigned some time previously as they had become aware that the TAG was being influenced by 'two political organisations'. They said that it was not being run as they had originally intended, they could not make their points at meetings as they were opposed by members of the TAG who were representatives of the two political organizations and were trained political speakers, and that they were excluded from some meetings. However, it seems, by their own admission, that Stubbings and Johnson's 'leading part' had consisted of sending out a circular to all apprentices in the Tyne area. This was hardly a leading part in the formation of the Guild.

The *Evening Chronicle* took up the evidence of Stubbings and Johnson, and claimed that its own unnamed 'representative' had investigated and quite clearly uncovered links with 'two organisations, popularly termed "extremist"'. The newspaper, however, failed to give any of the clear evidence which it claimed to have obtained, and admitted that 'It may be that the Guild is no longer connected with a political organisation.'[11]

The strike had polarized opinion in the area, as the letters pages to local newspapers reflected. The majority of people who lived in the largely shipbuilding dominated communities of Wallsend and, to a lesser extent, parts of North Shields were sympathetic to the apprentices, whist the views of those from outside these communities seem to have ranged from mildly sympathetic to virulently anti-apprentice. Oddly, and disappointingly, there are no letters from residents in the mining communities of the area such as Shiremoor. The letters page of the *Shields Daily News* was taken up throughout the course of the strike by an at times intemperate argument over the strike.

On just one particular day, for example, there were five separate letters; three against the apprentices and two for them. The letters against were particularly ill-tempered and accused the apprentices of sedition, amongst other allegations. Mr Alfred E. Hill, of D. Hill and Carter Ltd, North Shields, wrote that previous letters from apprentices had shown patriotism and a sense of duty, but he wished to ask the apprentices if they would be satisfied in the future to 'recall that in the hour of their country's need they came out on strike? Have they never heard of Nelson's famous signal?' Writing as 'Be British', another contributor did not agree with a previous letter which said the apprentices were striking with the object of having a good time, but then argued that in his belief the apprentices were 'being thoroughly misled by agitators', at the risk of their future careers. In a rather patronizing tone, he then exhorted the apprentices to return to work, saying, 'Come along boys, get back to your machines and other work', before showing a remarkable degree of paranoia when stating that 'We are surrounded by traitors'.

This was all rather muddled thinking and unlikely to have much effect on a group of young men who thought that they were being railroaded against their will, with the effect that a career for which they had worked long and hard was being snatched away from them.

The next two letters berating the apprentices (from 'Private' and 'Soldier's Wife No. 2' respectively) focused on the sacrifices of the members of the armed forces, as opposed to a rather narrow and resentfully unfocussed view of the lives of the apprentices. 'Private' wrote a two-sentence letter replying to one from an apprentice that simply said that 'a couple of months in the Army would teach him a lesson', and advised him to 'Take a tip and stick to your cushy job.' 'Soldier's Wife No. 2' agreed with some previous letters before asking how many of the strikers 'sitting by the fire side, discussing these trivial things, think of the millions who are being killed or maimed'?

Clearly this was an emotive subject, especially for those who had loved ones in the forces or who had suffered a loss in the conflict, but for people to describe the issue as trivial or to assume that the life of an engineering apprentice was 'cushy' is utterly foolish. The apprentices themselves were keen to get their own views across, and there was an almost equal balance in the letters, although many of those from the apprentices seem to have been far more reasoned and well-thought-out.

'Three Apprentice Shipwrights' wrote in reply to a letter from 'Disgusted Sailor', laying out some facts to counter his arguments. They made the point that approximately 75 per cent of the apprentices on Tyneside had, at some point, applied to join the forces but had been rejected as they were engaged on work of national importance, but the government would 'put us down pits we know nothing about and don't want to be in'. They added that, 'Nobody likes striking but it was the only action we could take because our negotiations with Mr Bevin were to no avail.'

The second pro-apprentice letter was in response to a previous letter from 'Soldier's Wife' which alleged that the apprentices were striking over a petty grievance. The letter, written by someone signing himself as 'Apprentice', argued that the parents of apprentices had made their own sacrifices to buy books and equipment for their sons, whilst the apprentices themselves had made their own sacrifices such as attending evening classes (and working long hours) in order to secure a brighter future for themselves and their family.

The third letter in favour of the apprentices' cause was yet another reply, this time to a letter by someone who rather pompously signed himself as 'Patriot'. This letter once again took offence at the allegation that the matters over which the apprentices were striking were trivial. The letter argued that being directed into the mines and losing one's apprenticeship after four years served was anything but trivial, and added that if 'Patriot' 'thinks I am a traitor after volunteering for the RAF, doing Home Guard duties, and working excessive hours, the same as the majority of Tyneside apprentices, then I sign myself – Traitor'.[12]

The unions, unsurprisingly given their recent wartime track record, refused to support the strike, and throughout the industrial action refused to acknowledge the TAG as a legitimate representative organization. This was probably for two reasons: firstly, the unions, as discussed, had remained largely on the government's side throughout the war; and secondly, the unions probably saw the rise of a highly organized apprentices' guild as a threat to their dominance of the industry's workforce. In the first days of the strike, a huge open-air meeting at Wallsend attended by an estimated 5,000 apprentices reached an impasse when the unions refused to countenance any form of negotiation with the TAG members.

Neither surprised nor discouraged by this, the apprentices gained even more determination to see the struggle through and were described as being in an 'aggressive mood'.[13] Links were forged with apprentices' movements on Clydeside and at Huddersfield, and, encouraged by the TAG, apprentices at these locations also walked out. However, the Clydeside and Huddersfield apprentices quickly returned to work and, despite support in their own communities, the leadership of the TAG found itself isolated. The strike formally lasted only a fortnight, and by 11 April, some 70 per cent of the Tyneside apprentices were back at work. However, the TAG had made its point and very few Tyneside apprentices were subsequently sent down the mines against their will.

The strike also caused some polarization within the ranks of the TAG itself. Some apprentices (most notably at No. 22 Shed at Vickers Armstrong in Newcastle, and at Parson's in Wallsend) refused to take strike action, whilst others became less enamoured of the reasons for the strike when they realized that the TAG was asking for deferment for all apprentices, and not just those employed in shipbuilding and engineering. By 5 April, there was a slight drift back to work of those who disagreed with this policy. The local press made the most of this perceived weakness, with the *Evening Chronicle* using the example of one Wilf Robson (20), an apprentice from North Shields, who was said to have been involved in the creation of the TAG but who disagreed with the all-apprentice deferment cause and said that he had thought it applied only to engineering apprentices. The newspaper argued that Robson had influenced a large number of apprentices at North Shields to return to work.[14] This response by the newspapers blew it out of all proportion, as, by and large, the strike remained strong.

The government and local authorities had been severely rattled by the strike. Most sinister of all, in official eyes, were the links between the TAG and what were viewed as subversive political elements. It quickly became the official line that the membership of the TAG had been conned into taking illegal industrial action by these political subversives. This was patently false as, although there were links between the TAG and these groups, the apprentices were striking only on a matter of principle and anger at government policy. The refusal by the authorities to acknowledge this served them in a twofold manner: they could ignore the fact that the Bevin Scheme was so unpopular, and it allowed them to take investigative and, possibly, legal action against what they viewed as dangerous political subversives.

The belief that there may have been Trotskyist motivation in the strike became paranoia in official circles, and a complex but not entirely objective or thorough police investigation was launched. The threat of Trotskyist manipulation of young apprentices was one which was taken very seriously by the local and national authorities, especially given their suspicions over the strike at Swan Hunter's in 1941.

The main suspects in this case were the Revolutionary Communist Party (RCP), and local police intelligence reports concentrated on the activities of members of this group, along with the suspected links to ILP members such as T. Dan Smith and members of the TAG leadership, especially Mr Davy. Workplace and outside meetings were closely monitored, whilst there were also attempts to infiltrate the local shop stewards movement in order to gather intelligence.

By the summer arrests were made, with four locally prominent members of the RCP charged with conspiring to incite the apprentices to strike and having acted to further an illegal strike. In their effort to gather evidence for the charges, Newcastle City Police (who were in charge of the investigation) brought Mr Davy in for questioning. In their zeal, they ignored their legal obligations and overstepped their authority. Mr Davy was not advised of his rights, nor was he formally cautioned, whilst the officers questioning him, over a period of twenty-four hours, had made thinly veiled threats to Mr Davy, hinting that he would be arrested and imprisoned and that in future his name would be blacklisted, preventing him from finding work. It seems clear that Mr Davy had been 'threatened and cajoled' into giving a statement incriminating the RCP for its involvement in the strike.[15]

The four members of the RCP to be tried were Lambert Heaton Lee (organizer of the RCP), Rawling Tearse (Secretary of the Militant

Workers' Federation, or MWF), James Ritchie Haston (national Secretary and organizer of the RCP) and Angel Rosalie Keen. The trial at Newcastle Assizes was held in June. The judge presiding made it very clear that the apprentices had been striking purely on a matter of principle on behalf of all apprentices, and that they had been aware from the start that the majority of them would not be affected by the Bevin Ballot. The judge even went so far as to say that the strike was basically motivated by the apprentices' view that they had a right to continue in their chosen profession, whilst the government had no powers to ride roughshod over this right. Despite this commentary from the judge and a lack of positive evidence, all four of the accused were found guilty of furtherance of a strike but not guilty of incitement. Mr Lee, who was a South African national, and Mr Tearse were both sentenced to a year in prison, whilst Mr Haston was sentenced to six months and Mrs Keen was released immediately after serving a nominal sentence.

The trial, however, backfired on the authorities, as many people on Tyneside saw the allegations as ludicrous and contrived, whilst the national publicity simply served to bolster the self-importance of the RCP and brought attention to the group. The public's suspicions over the findings of the trial were proven when, only three months later, all the convictions were quashed at appeal.

With the engineering firm of Charles Crofton & Co. Ltd having made a significant contribution to the war effort, at the expense of its normal business, and with one of its original founders serving with the Ministry of Supply, it should come as no surprise that there were changes within the company. In April 1944, Mr Crofton decided to officially retire from the business, which was handed over to his partner, Mr Mann, and several senior employees. As a result, it was decided that the company should be renamed, and the obvious choice was Victor Products (Wallsend) Ltd (it was also felt that this name would help in the post-war market).

With the relentless demands of work, along with continued rationing and shortages, the general public were becoming increasingly warweary in the sixth year of the conflict. Holidays at Home gave the public of Tynemouth and Wallsend the chance to relax somewhat and enjoy themselves. The schemes were organized and run by the local authorities, and were very varied. The summer programme in Tynemouth for 1944 included (amongst others) a six-a-side football tournament, school swimming gala, what was described as village sports at the youth centre and a Home Guard demonstration which included patriotic scenes and re-enactments of events from British history.

Holidays at Home was not the only scheme put in place to allow people some relaxing leisure time during the war. At the same time as the Holiday at Home programme was in full swing, Whitley Bay also held its Victory Garden Week in aid of the Red Cross. There were a variety of events planned for the week, including bowls tournaments, bring and buy sales and a children's day. The week culminated in several shows in the morning and flower, fruit and vegetable shows in the afternoon and evening, at which the Duchess of Northumberland was the guest of honour. The week raised over £2,000 for the Red Cross. The residents of Whitley Bay had a strong history with this event, having finished thirteenth in the country in 1943 for raising funds through its garden week.

Although the Holidays at Home schemes run by various local authorities in the area continued to be very popular with most people, the various events could sometimes be costly for the authorities to put on. When the accounts for the 1944 Tynemouth scheme were tallied, it was found that there was a deficiency of £371. This was well below what the council had estimated (£1,000) and was a significant improvement on previous years, as that in 1943 had been £695 and in 1942 it was £1,201. Many of the costs could be defrayed with grants.

As the Allied forces pushed their way inland from the Normandy coast after D-Day, the British faced an increasingly hard fight against a determined and stubborn foe. Casualties in the fighting were heavy, and at home in Tynemouth and Wallsend the initial euphoria over the success of the landings began to turn to the grim realization that the fighting would continue to take a heavy toll of local men. The 8th Battalion, Royal Northumberland Fusiliers, had already experienced a particularly rough war, suffering very heavy losses in 1940 before being evacuated from the beaches of Dunkirk. In November 1940, the battalion had changed role and been assigned as a motorcycle battalion in the 3rd Infantry Division. Just six months later, it was transferred to the Reconnaissance Corps and renamed the 3rd Battalion, Reconnaissance Corps, then just over a year later renamed again as the 3rd Regiment, Reconnaissance Corps, before finally transferring to the Royal Armoured Corps on 1st January 1944 as the 3rd (Royal Northumberland Fusiliers) Reconnaissance Regiment. Throughout this time, it remained a part of 3rd Division. The regiment landed on Sword Beach on D-Day and fought throughout the Normandy campaign before pushing up through Holland and later taking part in the invasion of Germany, ending the war in Bremen.

By August 1944, the British Second Army was in positions to the west of Caen. The Germans had moved the 2nd Panzer Division and were preparing to move the 21st Panzer in order to attack the American forces, which had just launched Operation Cobra to break out of the Normandy bridgehead. The British Second Army, taking over a sector where it was faced by lightly armed German infantry, took the opportunity to launch another attack, codenamed Operation Bluecoat, in order to tie down the German armoured units and capture the important road junction in the town of Vire and the nearby heights of Mont Pincon. The offensive went on for over a week after its launch on 30 July. The fighting was bitter, but on 6 August Vire and Mont Pincon were captured by the Allies. The operation had been a success, pinning the German armoured units in place and continuing the process of wearing down the German defenders in Normandy. This meant that the planned German counter-offensive against the Allies failed due to lack of resources, and the Germans were left with no option but to retreat. The cost was high: VII Corps of the Second Army, for example, lost over 5,000 casualties during the fighting. On the day that Vire and Mont Pincon fell, one of the casualties was a North Shields man. Trooper James Norman Nicholson (20) was serving with the 3rd (Royal Northumberland Fusiliers) Reconnaissance Regiment when he was killed. Trooper Nicholson was buried at St Charles de Percy War Cemetery in Normandy.

With the continuing advance of Allied forces, the defeat of the Luftwaffe and the threat of the flying bombs eliminated from all areas apart from southern England, the government felt that the blackout which had been in force over Britain for over five years could now be relaxed (although London and the South-East continued to be blacked out for some time longer). Officially, the blackout was partially lifted from the night of 17 September. The new policy was quickly termed the 'dim-out'. In practice, this meant that some street lights would be lit at reduced power and people could now take down the heavy blackout curtains. However, houses were expected to obscure their lights so that no shafts of light escaped and objects could not be seen from outside. This advice was a little unspecific, and Wardens were urged to pass on to residents any instructions or admonitions resulting from the new regulations in a friendly manner, at least initially. Residents were also to be told that if a Warden gave the order or if the sirens sounded, they would have to immediately replace their blackout or turn off all lights.

Some local authorities had already been briefed on the new regulations, and it would seem that some in the North-East jumped the gun. Tynemouth had reportedly brought in its new lighting scheme on the night of 15/16 September, with some lights along main streets and bus routes being lit at 15-watt power or its gas equivalent. This meant that only a few streets were lit in such a manner, but on the following nights the scheme was expanded.

It was decided that the white lines which had been painted on many roads in the area as an aid during the blackout would be retained as a safety measure when the dim-out was over. In Tynemouth Borough, the council began a process of renewing these markings, starting with those on Albion Road in North Shields. The white markings on pavement edges which had been put in place as a guide to pedestrians, however, were not to be retained, as they were felt to be unnecessary.

As the campaign in Europe loomed and the battle against Japanese forces continued, the shipyards of Wallsend continued to be extremely busy throughout the year. During the course of 1944, Swan Hunter's completed a variety of naval vessels. These included the tank landing ship LST *3019*, the Battle Class destroyer HMS *Barfleur* (which saw action against the Japanese), the Loch Class frigates HMS *Loch Shin* and *Loch Morlich*, and the corvettes HMS *Rushen Castle* and *Shrewsbury Castle*.[16] Three other, more unusual, vessels were completed during the year. HMS *Bullfrog* and HMS *St Margarets* were built as cable laying ships, with *Bullfrog* seeing use as a harbour defence vessel and her sister ship taking part in the D-Day invasion. The final vessel was surrounded by a great deal of secrecy.

HMS Bullfrog, *a cable-laying ship built by Swan Hunter.* (Public Domain)

HMS Loch Morlich. (Public Domain)

Landing Ship Tank 3019. (Unknown)

1944: THE BEGINNING OF THE END? 175

HMS Rushen Castle. (Public Domain)

HMS *Cyrus* was a trimaran vessel built using steel lattice trusses and was to be used as a mine destructor vessel, being towed through minefields to detonate pressure mines with the belief (largely proven correct) that because of her construction she would detonate the mines but not be badly damaged by the blast. The work to build the unusual vessel was surrounded by great secrecy, with workmen forbidden to talk about her and the official line being that the ship was designated as an Algerine Class minesweeper. HMS *Cyrus* and her sister ship,

Cybele, proved themselves during Operation Overlord, but *Cyrus* was wrecked in the Seine Estuary in December 1944.

The long-awaited invasion of France on 6 June was greeted with great enthusiasm once it had become clear that the initial landings had been successful. The invasion, however, came at a cost, with men from Tynemouth and Wallsend all being involved. One casualty in the first few hours of D-Day was Private James Mander of the 9th Battalion of the Parachute Regiment. Private Mander was aged just 19 when he was killed, but it was only after his death that the authorities realized this as he had joined up when only 16, claiming to be 19; the Army initially believed he was 23 at the time of his death in action in Normandy. James was the son of Mr John Mander of Wallsend (his mother had died before the war), but he had been brought up by his older sister, Miss Sarah Mander of 18 Oak Grove, Wallsend. He was the second son in the family to be killed, his older brother, Sergeant Reuben Matthew Mander (27), RAF, being killed as an air gunner near Malta in 1942. There were also two other brothers in the services: Signalman Thomas Mander (22), Royal Navy, and Corporal Harry Mander (26), RAF. Private Mander's family had the following inscription placed upon his headstone: 'Remembrance Like A Golden Chain Binds Us Till We Meet Again "At Rest"'.[17]

Another casualty on D-Day was Sub-Lieutenant Kenneth Keys, RNVR, of 7 Manor Road, Tynemouth. Sub-Lieutenant Keys was stationed at the combined operations training centre, HMS *Quebec*, at Inveraray in Scotland, but was at the forefront of the landings when he was killed in action. He was the only child of James and Evelyn Keys, and in October was posthumously mentioned in dispatches for his gallantry and devotion to duty. The citation stated that Sub-Lieutenant Keys had 'landed when the beach was still under heavy fire and until he was killed showed a fine example of courage and leadership'.[18]

Sub-Lieutenant Kenneth Keys, RNVR, was killed in action on D-Day. (Shields Daily News)

1944: THE BEGINNING OF THE END? 177

The fighting to break out of the beachhead was severe over following weeks and months. Amongst the local casualties was Corporal William Thompson McLean of the 22nd Dragoons, Royal Armoured Corps, who was killed on 7 August. The 22nd Dragoons had landed on D-Day ('A' Squadron and half of 'C' Squadron at Sword Beach, and 'B' Squadron and the other half of 'C' Squadron at Juno Beach), their Sherman Crab Flail Tanks proving useful in clearing mines and other objects on the beaches and the routes off them. This was obviously dangerous work which exposed the tank crews to the dangers of minefields but, as they had to drive at no faster than 1½ miles per hour when clearing mines, they were also very vulnerable to enemy fire. Corporal McLean (24) was a Wallsend man, the only son of Mr and Mrs H. McLean of 15 Vine Street, Wallsend.[19]

Corporal W.T. McLean, 22nd Dragoons, who was killed during fighting in Normandy in 1944. (Evening Chronicle)

Better news was received in the post by Councillor P.M. Laws and his wife at their home in Brighton Grove, Whitley Bay. The letter was from their son, Lieutenant Peter Malcolm Laws (25). Peter, a keen sportsman, had held the Dame Allan's School swimming cup for a period of six years and had obtained his colours for rugby at St Catherine's College, Cambridge, where he had studied and obtained a BA. Peter had joined the Army in May 1940 and had served in Africa with the Durham Light Infantry for the next three years. He had written to his parents from a hospital in Yorkshire, where he was recovering after being severely wounded. The letter was a typical one from son to parents, but in a postscript Peter added that he had just received a letter from his brigadier congratulating him on being awarded the MC.

Wing Commander Denys Gillam was still commanding 146 Wing during this period, and they saw a lot of action. This culminated in October in a daring raid on Dordrecht in Holland, where a high-level planning conference of German officers from the Fifteenth Army was taking place. Wing Commander Gillam led the raid, dropping a marker bomb and two 500lb bombs on the target building. Five Typhoons followed him on bombing runs and scored direct hits on the building, destroying it. The raid killed two generals, seventeen senior officers and 55 other officers from the Fifteenth Army HQ.

After more than a year, the Allied armies in the Italian campaign were still facing a determined and stubborn enemy. The German defenders were tenacious, with the fighting the most deadly infantry battle of any of the western campaigns. By July 1944, the Allies were pushing northwards from Rome, with battles to capture Florence and Ancona. The Allies were aware that the Germans had constructed a very strong defensive position in the northern Apennine Mountains, which they called the Gothic Line. Casualties amongst the infantry were extremely heavy, and in August Mr and Mrs Cole received a telegram at their home (19 The Avenue, Wallsend) informing them that their 21-year old son, Peter, had been killed in Italy. Driver Peter Cole, of the Royal Army Service Corps, had lost his life on 12 July, most probably dying of wounds as he is buried at Naples War Cemetery, which was the wartime site of several field hospitals.

Group Captain D.E. Gillam ended the war with the Air Force Cross, Distinguished Flying Cross (and bar) and Distinguished Service Order (with two bars). (Unknown)

The fighting in Italy raged on for the rest of 1944, with German resistance, poor weather and stretched lines of supply combining to both slow the advance and cause high numbers of casualties. September and October saw particularly heavy fighting as the British Eighth Army attempted to capture German positions on ridges and in towns. Hampered by heavy rain, which made crossing the many rivers in the area difficult or at times impossible, the fighting at one point was the deadliest since that around Monte Cassino, and at one point the Eighth Army was suffering 150 casualties every day. Part of the British forces in this battle was 46 Regiment, Reconnaissance Corps, Royal Armoured Corps. At the end of September, the regiment found itself facing the Fiumicino River and tasked with capturing the town of Montilgallo on the far side. An assault on 30 September failed to establish a bridgehead across the river, as the regiment came under intensive fire from machine guns and self-propelled guns. The offensive was held up for a week due to strong enemy resistance and heavy rain, which swelled the rivers and made fording them impossible. On 1 October, one of the casualties suffered by 46 Regiment was 24-year old Trooper Alex Sneddon. Trooper Sneddon was a Wallsend man, one of several from the town who were killed in the ferocious fighting in Italy.[20]

Back in Britain, as it became clear that enemy bombing raids were tailing off (even the threat of the V-Weapons being largely neutralized), ARP services in the Tynemouth and Wallsend area began to wind down. The Whitley Bay control centre ceased to be manned on a full-time basis on 15 November 1944 and even became the venue for local social events, dances and concerts every Thursday night, though it was reported that these were not well attended.[21]

Many of the local men killed during the war were serving with the RAF, and many of these were killed in the bombing of Germany by Bomber Command. However, it was not only flying on operations which cost lives; the training of airmen was a dangerous task, and many young men were killed in flying accidents during training before they even got to a squadron on active duty. Amongst these unfortunates was Sergeant William Burton Forsyth of 22 Buddle Street, Wallsend. Sergeant Forsyth (20) was an air gunner when he lost his life on 20 November. His parents received the news at their Wallsend home and were able to have his body brought home for burial. The inscription they had placed upon his Commonwealth War Graves Commission headstone was a poignant one: 'God Will Link The Broken Chain As One By One We Meet Again'.

Just five days later, another local man was killed serving with Bomber Command. Of the five groups that made up the command in November 1944, one was a Canadian group formed by and paid for by the Canadian government. However, the RCAF did not train men in the duties of flight engineer, in most cases borrowing British personnel to fill this role, whilst some other British (and other Allied) airmen found themselves flying in a Canadian squadron with a largely Canadian crew. Raw crews were often eased into operations by being sent on what were seen as easier operations, such as dropping mines in enemy waters, whilst crews nearing the end of their tour of thirty operations were also given such tasks if possible. On the night of 24/25 November, the Canadian 427 Squadron sent aircraft to drop mines in Danish waters. One of these aircraft, Halifax III (MZ304, ZL-H), took off from its base at Leeming in Yorkshire shortly after 1.00 am, but nothing more was heard until news came through that the aircraft had crashed into Spey Bay east of Buckie, Morayshire, at around 7.40 am, killing all seven men aboard. The flight engineer in the Halifax was Sergeant Matthew Rowntree (37) from North Shields. Sergeant Rowntree, a married man with two sons and a daughter, was brought back home for burial at Preston Cemetery.[22]

Notes
1. *The Shields Evening News*, 28 December 1944, p.6.
2. Sergeant Forster is commemorated on the Runnymede Memorial. The crew were: Sgt J.M. Smith (pilot); Sgt R.C. Betts (flight engineer); F/O A.L. Clogg, RCAF (navigator); F/O L.W. O'Neill, RCAF (bomb aimer); Sgt D.G. Forster (wireless operator); Sgt R.W. Chadwick (mid upper gunner); and Sgt N. Taylor (rear gunner).
3. Flight Sergeant Goulbourn is one of three crewmen buried at Briey. His pilot, Flight Lieutenant Day, suffered a very badly broken leg and was repatriated on 2 February 1945. The crew consisted of: F/L J.A. Day, DFC (pilot); Sgt E.J. Maggs (flight engineer); P/O R. Tandy (navigator); Sgt W.J. Hollis (bomb aimer); F/S J.W. Goulbourn (wireless operator); F/S J.M Woodburn (mid upper gunner); F/S S.I. Miller (rear gunner).
4. Flying Officer Pigg is buried at Abbeville Communal Cemetery Extension alongside his navigator, Pilot Officer William Joseph Wills. Flying Officer Pigg's mother, Edith Elsie Pigg, died aged just 53 in 1949. Flying Officer Pigg is mentioned on the family headstone, along with his parents and younger brother, in Preston Cemetery in his home town.
5. The all-NCO crew were: S. Hampson (pilot); S.L. Toon (flight engineer); F.G. Rees (navigator); R.A. Renwick (bomb aimer); P.F. Beard (wireless operator); T.A. Liddy (mid upper gunner); and S.A. Waterhouse (rear gunner). Sgt Waterhouse escaped by parachute and was taken prisoner.
6. The Halifax of Sergeant McFadden was the twenty-seventh British bomber to be shot down on this night from a total of ninety-six bombers lost on the raid, the highest number during the war. The raid was a complete failure, with many bombers misidentifying the target and bombing Schweinfurt instead or scattering their bombs in open countryside. More airmen were killed on this one night than in the whole of Fighter Command during the Battle of Britain. The crew of Halifax LW555 was: F/O C.E. O'Brien, RCAF (pilot); Sgt E.

Martin (flight engineer); F/O R.H. Carleton (navigator); F/O R.D. Van Fleet, RCAF (bomb aimer); Sgt A.L. Wangler (wireless operator); Sgt E. Bake (mid upper gunner); and Sgt T.C. McFadden (rear gunner).

7. *Shields Evening News*, 8 May 1944, p.4.
8. *Shields Evening News*, 9 May 1944, p.4.
9. *Shields Evening News*, 16 June 1944, p.3.
10. According to T. Dabb in 'Official Secrets', *Socialist Review*, vol. 185 (April 1995), p.3.
11. *Evening Chronicle*, 1 April 1944, p.4.
12. *Shields Daily News*, 3 April 1944, p.3.
13. *The Times*, 1 April 1944, p.4.
14. *Evening Chronicle*, 5 April 1944, p.4.
15. Bornstein & Richardson, *War and the International*, pp.12021.
16. Whilst HMS *Loch Shin* saw wartime service with the RN, she was later sold to the RNZN (Royal New Zealand Navy) and renamed HMNZS *Taupo*. Her sister ship, HMS *Loch Morlich*, did not see service with the RN as she was immediately transferred to the Royal Canadian Navy and saw action during the Battle of the Atlantic. At the end of the war it was sold to the RNZN and, renamed HMNZS *Tutira*, saw action during the Korean War. HMS *Rushen Castle* survived her service as a convoy escort and was transferred to the Air Ministry for service as a weather ship before being sold in 1977 and converted to a salvage vessel; she was scrapped in 1983. HMS *Shrewsbury Castle* was loaned to the Royal Norwegian Navy and renamed HNoMS *Tunsberg Castle*, but was mined on 12 December 1944 off the Norwegian coast and sank with the loss of five crewmen.
17. CWGC.
18. *Shields Daily News*, 6 October 1944, p.3.
19. Corporal McLean is buried at Hermanville War Cemetery in Normandy.
20. Trooper Sneddon is buried at Coriano Ridge War Cemetery near Rimini.
21. TWAS: MB/WB27/1 (T135/45). Whitley Bay Urban District Council (ARP Committee), final report, 1945.
22. The crew consisted of: F/L J.T. Hardy, RCAF (pilot); Sgt M. Rowntree, RAF (flight engineer); F/O S.G. Hall, RCAF (navigator); F/O J.R. Pollock, RCAF (bomb aimer); Sgt J.W.L. Patterson, RCAF (wireless operator); F/S H.J Cook, RCAF (mid upper gunner); and F/S J. Warburton, RCAF (rear gunner).

CHAPTER SEVEN

1945: Victories

The New Year's honours list saw the efforts of several North Shields seamen rewarded for their wartime service. The awards list was headed by an MBE for Lieutenant Donald Bewick Ward, RNVR, a DSC for Lieutenant Colin Frank Vine, RNR, and DSMs for Chief Engineman Peter W.M. Stark, RNR, Petty Officer Daniel Dixon Peterson, RNR, and Seaman Gunner William Crawford Black Dougal, RNR, whilst Able Seaman Stanley Judge was mentioned in dispatches.

Chief Engineman Stark lived at 142 Heaton Terrace and was at home on leave when the announcement of his DSM was made. Like many Shields men, he had found employment in the fishing industry and had signed on as a chief engineer on the trawlers before serving on minesweepers during the First World War. As a member of the RNR, he was called up shortly before the commencement of the Second World War and once again spent the war employed on minesweeping duties. Stark was a married man who had four grown-up sons serving in the forces and two daughters at home.

Seaman Gunner William Dougal (23) was another young man who had spent the war employed in the dangerous task of minesweeping. William had also been employed on the trawler fleet before the war, working aboard various trawlers owned by Messrs R. Irving & Sons. His family were well known locally in the industry, as his father, James Dougal (known as Jimmy), was a skipper of one of the trawlers owned by Messrs R. Hastie & Sons and was also serving in the RN. The family was originally from Eyemouth in Scotland but had moved down to North Shields when William was 9. William had been minesweeping since January 1942, and was married that year to a Lowestoft woman who had moved to North Shields after the marriage. His wife was not aware of her husband's award until she saw it in the newspaper.

Even in the final months of the European war, the role of the merchant seamen was one fraught with dangers as, although the battle was going against the U-boats, German submarines remained a threat. On 15 January 1945, the British steam tanker *Maja* was torpedoed by *U-1055* whilst sailing unaccompanied off Drogheda.[1] With the ship badly damaged, taking on water and developing a heavy list, Chief Engineer Sydney Goss Moffitt volunteered to go down to the pump room to pump out some of the cargo to right his ship, even though it was 30ft below deck and there was a very real danger of fire (the ship was carrying over 10,000 tons of gas, oil and petrol) or of him being trapped. Whilst he was below deck, the ship was hit by two more torpedoes and caught fire. Moffitt managed to extricate himself and get back on deck, but the ship sank with the loss of twenty-five of her sixty-five-man complement. The remaining crew were rescued by a Belgian trawler and landed at Holyhead.

Seaman Gunner William C.B. Dougal, RNR, was awarded the Distinguished Service Medal for years of minesweeping work. (Shields Evening News)

Amongst the Tynemouth men to be awarded medals during January was the familiar name of Denys Edgar Gillam. Following his exploits with his Typhoon wing, he was awarded a second bar to his DSO at the end of January before being promoted to the rank of group captain just a few weeks later.[2]

Although air raids seemed to be a thing of the past, the Tynemouth area was left with severe damage on the night of 18 January when an extremely strong and unexpected squall blew in from the north. With winds of hurricane strength, there was damage across the borough. Metal railings were blown down in many places, whilst some shop windows were blown in. In Tynemouth Front Street, several window panes were torn out, whilst elsewhere chimney pots were brought down. A large number of garage doors were also damaged and many trees were felled. In Preston Avenue, fallen trees had to be removed

The Maja, *sunk by a U-Boat in 1945.* (Public Domain)

by the police, whilst a large advertising hoarding was blown down in Waterville Road and had to be removed by the fire service as it was obstructing the road.

The official stand-down of the Home Guard was viewed by many of the guardsmen with some sadness. Although conscription into the Home Guard had been in place for some time, there were still a large proportion of volunteers and the local units had built up a great sense of comradeship. The end of the Home Guard was met with ambivalence as many were, no doubt, happy to escape the additional workload, whilst at the same time missing the comradeship, sense of belonging and feeling that they were contributing to the war effort. The 7th (Tynemouth) Battalion had fostered a particularly good spirit and held a well-attended stand-down dinner on Friday, 19 January at the Roselyn Hall, North Shields.

Lieutenant Colonel Stanley Holmes presided over the dinner, along with the Mayor of Tynemouth (Councillor T. Duff). There were many officers present, with guests from neighbouring Army units and a large number of the Home Guard's officers, including Colonel A.G. Tapp, Colonel R. Shrive, Major H. Graham (second-in-command of the 7th Battalion) and Major G. Sopwith (commanding officer of the Home Guard anti-aircraft battery).[3] There were also representatives from the Army Cadet Corps and Tynemouth Air Training Corps.

The Mayor, who was deputizing for the absent Viscount Allendale (who had been responsible for forming the Home Guard in Northumberland), proposed the toast to the battalion, and the evening passed with a fine meal and further toasts, interspersed with musical accompaniment from the Dunelm Singers.

The Mayor's speech at first concentrated on the leadership abilities of the officers of the Home Guard and the contribution that they had made for almost five years whilst also coping with their own jobs. He reserved especial praise for Major Randell and congratulated him on the award of the MBE (the Mayor had served under Major Randell for four years as orderly sergeant and then quartermaster sergeant), as well as Sergeant Johnson who had been awarded the BEM. He completed his toast by praising the fine relations which had existed between the local authorities and the Home Guard (reserving special praise for the relationship which had been built up between the Home Guard and the council's Invasion Committee) before thanking Lieutenant Colonel Holmes for his fine example and his leadership.

Responding to the Mayor's speech, Lieutenant Colonel Holmes began by thanking the Mayor for stepping in to replace Viscount Allendale at very short notice before relaying the thanks of the Viscount and assuring those present that the Viscount had always thought very highly of the 7th (Tynemouth) Battalion and held it 'in a very warm spot in his heart'. Many of the officers and men had, unusually (and perhaps uniquely), brought their wives to the dinner, and Lieutenant Colonel Holmes said he was pleased by this as it allowed him the privilege of thanking them for the sacrifices which they had made to enable their husbands to take part in the Home Guard. After thanking Major Graham and the rest of the officers, Lieutenant Colonel Holmes described how the unit 'had practically no trouble from the first day and our battalion has come to be recognised as one of the most efficient in the area'. He went on to say how his officers had never let him down, before thanking the officers from the regular forces who had assisted the battalion on numerous occasions (in particular Captain Hutchinson and the other officers of the Naval Station and Colonel Shrive). After this he expressed his gratitude to Miss Muriel Venus, who had been ever-present in the administration section. He said that the officers and men of the battalion wanted to let her know that they had all appreciated her unflinching commitment to the battalion, and that henceforth she would 'be known as "The Lady of the 7th"'.

After concluding his speech, Lieutenant Colonel Holmes presented Miss Venus with a silver cigarette case which had been engraved with the battalion crest, with an inscription that the case had been presented to Miss Venus by the colonel on behalf of the battalion 'as a mark of appreciation for devoted service which she rendered to the battalion'.

Major Graham then thanked four of the guests of the battalion (the Mayor, Colonel Shrive, Captain Campbell and Captain Hutchinson). Responding to this, Captain Hutchinson said that since he had taken over command of the naval base in 1940, he had always had a good relationship with the battalion and its commanding officer. He related how in the dangerous days of 1940 and 1941, when weapons were in short supply and the threat of invasion was high, he had found the weight of his responsibilities very heavy and the thought of probable invasion had preyed on his mind. However, he said that as he came to realize just how effective the 7th Battalion was becoming, he 'quickly lost his anxieties' as he saw that the increased efficiency of the unit meant that 'finally ... we had at our backs an efficient, keen, well-drilled and formidable protection'. He went on to say that he had always been impressed by the cheerful optimism and faith in themselves that he had found in the officers and men of the battalion, and concluded by saying that he saluted them on behalf of the visitors.

There then followed a second surprise presentation, Miss Venus handing Lieutenant Colonel Holmes a silver salver and a framed photograph of the officers of the battalion. During the presentation, Miss Venus thanked the battalion for her own gift. She added that she had been granted many privileges during her time with the Home Guard, but the honour of presenting the gifts to Colonel Holmes was the greatest of these. Acknowledging the gifts, Lieutenant Colonel Holmes said that he was deeply appreciative and highlighted the fact that all of the officers he had selected had been picked on merit, not because they were friends of his. He added that he particularly wished to thank Captain Campbell for his service as battalion adjutant and Captain Meadows for his efforts as battalion quartermaster.

The dinner ended with Major Randell giving what was described as a witty speech, thanking the wives of the officers and men of the

At the Home Guard stand-down dinner are the Mayor and Mayoress, Colonel Holmes and Mrs Holmes, Major H. Graham and Mrs Graham, Major Randall and Mrs Randall. (Shields Daily News)

Home Guard; the Lady Mayoress reciprocated, thanking the battalion for its hospitality and expressing their pride in the Home Guard.

We earlier saw how a 16-year-old NAAFI canteen assistant had been awarded the George Medal for his courage in helping to recover vital documents and code books from a sinking U-boat. Tommy Brown, of North Shields, was the youngest ever recipient of the award. Indeed, the inquiry into the incident had established that Tommy was actually only 15 when he joined HMS *Petard*, and, as the legal age of being able to go to sea with the NAAFI was 17, he was removed from the service and sent home to North Shields, from where he later joined the Royal Navy. By 1945, Tommy was a Leading Seaman aboard the light cruiser HMS *Belfast*, which was docked in the Tyne.[4] Tommy was on leave from *Belfast* and was sleeping in the kitchen of the family's Lily Gardens home. At about 2.30 am on 13 February, Tommy's mother was woken by a crackling sound and a shout of warning, and quickly realized that there was a fire in the property. Mrs Brown and eight of her children were able to escape, but there was no sign of Tommy or of the youngest child, 4-year-old Maureen. The fire service had been called, but neighbours had assembled and together with Police Constable Crawford made repeated attempts to enter the building, but were driven back by dense smoke. One of the neighbours, Mr Williamson, went back to his property and returned with his military respirator, and again entered the building. Feeling his way around in the dense smoke, Mr Williamson managed to find the unconscious form of Maureen in her bed and brought her outside. Neighbours attempted CPR on the child and she was taken by ambulance to nearby

Lily Gardens, the scene of the tragic fire in North Shields. (*Evening Chronicle*)

Leading Seaman Tommy Brown helped secure vital intelligence when just 15 but died in a house fire whilst on leave later in the war. (*Newcastle Journal*)

Tynemouth Infirmary, but was found to be dead on arrival. There was still no sign of Tommy, and the fire service could not enter the kitchen due to flames and smoke. Having broken the windows, the AFS successfully got the fire under control after an hour or so, and upon entering the kitchen they found the partially clothed and badly burned body of Tommy.

The reporting of Tommy's death highlights the depredation in which many working-class people were forced to live in Tynemouth Borough. Lily Gardens was a row of small houses in the Ridges Estate, and the fact that the Mrs Brown (her husband was a private in the army) was living there with nine of their ten (or possibly eleven) children hints at the overcrowding. This is confirmed when the family sleeping arrangements were revealed. Four of the girls were sleeping together in one room, the two youngest slept with their mother, the three boys slept in the back

Maureen Brown, the 4-year old sister of Tommy Brown, was also killed in the house fire. (*Evening Chronicle*)

room and Tommy slept in the kitchen. When they were initially evacuated, the family went to their downstairs neighbour's property. This was the residence of a Mrs E.J. Stonebanks, who lived there with her eight children.

These conditions were clearly not conducive to healthy living, and when a disaster such as a fire or bombing attack occurred, the overcrowding and cramped conditions could easily result in large numbers of casualties from individual families. Added to this was the fact that the Ridges Estate had actually been constructed to relieve slum conditions and overcrowding in North Shields; clearly this had not altogether worked as envisioned.

George Williamson of North Shields went into a burning building to rescue a child. (Evening Chronicle)

Many of the residents of the Ridges, however, resented some of the criticism that they felt they received from the local authority. A report undertaken by Tynemouth Borough Council said that out of 1,575 houses which had been inspected, only 758 were judged to be clean, whilst '817 were only in a fair state of cleanliness, and 6 needed constant visitation'. This provoked one resident to write to the letters page of the local newspaper to complain about what she saw as an injustice. The writer claimed that inspections of the houses had once been yearly, but this had been increased to every six months and then every three months, and that the inspector could enter the house at any time, with residents powerless to forbid him entry. The woman complained that most of the residents were mothers to large families, and were being victimized due to the fact that they had previously 'had the misfortune to have lived in slum property and are looked upon as unclean and ignorant'.

Arguing against the council's view, the woman stated that although the council seemed to think the houses on the Ridges were wonderful, most of the residents thought otherwise, and she went on to list the source of complaints in the construction of the houses. She lived in a downstairs flat and complained that any movement from the upstairs tenants could be overheard, resulting in a lack of privacy. The coal bunker was opposite the storage for coats, which meant that if a coal delivery had been made and she wasn't available to move the coats beforehand, they got filthy with coal dust. The larders in many of the houses were unfit for purpose because they had hot water pipes around the inside walls, which meant that they could not be used to properly store food. Finally, and most worryingly, the writer claimed that the drinking water on the estate was 'in a terrible state of uncleanliness' and that the council did not seem to be 'as keen to look for faults on their side as they are on ours'.[5]

We have already seen that there had been resentment between former trawlermen who, as members of the Royal Naval Reserve, were serving aboard minesweepers and similar vessels, and those who had remained in the fishing industry. The resentment centred around the belief amongst the RNR men that they were serving their country, whilst their erstwhile colleagues were serving themselves and making substantial profits due to the scarcity of fish and the increased demand. A meeting of the North Eastern Sea Fisheries Committee held at York in February sought to disprove this bone of contention by claiming that audits had shown that the average trawlerman earned less than £3 per week due to the government's price controls, which set the price of the landed catch. The committee went on to say that this was unacceptable and that some provision must be made to increase the pay of fishermen, given that they were taking extraordinary risks to land high-quality catches. This was a poor miscalculation, as an able seaman at the time was being paid approximately 6s. 6d. per fortnight! Thus, fishermen were making 60s. per week, or 120s. per fortnight, which means that those who stayed as trawlermen could expect wages which were over eighteen times greater than many of their former colleagues in the RNR. This does not take into account the examples of the black-market sale of fish by some trawlermen and the fact that the trawlermen continued to receive a portion of their catch (their 'fry') for their own use (many in fact sold it on).

Throughout the year, war weariness and the belief that the war, with Germany at least, was coming to its conclusion led to a significant downturn in some charitable donations. The Tynemouth Red Cross collection for March was down £50 compared to the previous month, which was one of the lowest totals on record.

With enemy raids now almost non-existent, there seems to have been some relaxation on the part of the authorities and the civilian population. This could have had severe repercussions, as was shown when a force of over seventy enemy night-fighters launched an intruder raid in the early hours of 4 March. Although a large number of returning British bombers were shot down, the raiders also strafed civilian areas and dropped a mixture of high explosive and anti-personnel bombs over the Tynemouth area. Thankfully, they caused no casualties and only minor property damage. The attempt was repeated the next night, with less success, but it seems that the lessons had not been learned, as many people later complained that the air-raid sirens had not sounded.[6]

With the large numbers of servicemen in the area, it was inevitable that drink would encourage some to take criminal actions. On 20 March, several members of the 3rd Maritime Battery, Royal Artillery, which was stationed in North Shields, had been drinking in the town. At approximately 10.30 pm, three gunners from the unit (named Lavender, Bell and Harmes) left the Unionist Club on Albion Road and walked down the street past the Albion Cinema. Whilst engaged in conversation, another member of the unit, Gunner O'Hagen (known to most as Paddy), came out of the club and butted into the conversation, making an abusive suggestion to Lavender. The two immediately began scuffling but were separated by the other two soldiers, who took them to opposite sides of the road. O'Hagen, however, broke free of Bell and rushed across the street to confront Lavender. The two witnesses later said that they could not see clearly what happened next as arms were raised, but they had seen no blows struck. Both witnesses reported that they thought that O'Hagen caught his foot on the kerb and, because he was drunk, lost his balance, falling so that his head hit a wall and knocked him unconscious. O'Hagen later died in hospital of pneumonia, brought about by a blow to the head. All agreed that O'Hagen had been drunk and had been spoiling for a fight, and that Lavender had taken no action but to ward off his attacker. This would seem to be a cut and dried case of self-defence, but Lavender gave a voluntary statement to the police in which he said that he struck O'Hagen twice before he had fallen, and this led to his arrest and appearance before the magistrates at North Shields on charges of manslaughter.

During the week of VE-Day, magistrates committed Lavender for trial at Northumberland Assizes, despite his solicitor arguing that no case existed and that a trial would be a waste of time and money. In June, Lavender had his case put before the assizes. As the only evidence against him was that of his own statement, his representative moved that this evidence be ignored in favour of that of the other two witnesses (arguing that Lavender had been in a highly emotional state at the time of this statement). Mr Justice Hallett agreed that a man certainly had a right to defend himself if attacked, but could not ignore the fact that the accused had admitted that he had struck the man who died, and had given no indication that this had been in self-defence. Finding Lavender guilty of manslaughter but with obviously mitigating circumstances, he sentenced him to just seven days imprisonment, which meant that with time spent on remand he was released immediately.

For many residents of the area, the strain of coping with a seventh year of the war was extreme, despite the growing belief that the conflict with Germany was nearing a successful conclusion. Escape from the strain of wartime life was essential, and recreational pursuits were keenly undertaken. The various dance halls and ballrooms of the area remained very popular, with large numbers attending regularly.

PLAZA Ballroom
Fully Licensed.   Tel. North Shields 1158.

7.30 p.m. — Every Wednesday — 10.30 p.m.
1/6   DANCE   1/6

7.30 p.m. — Every Thursday — 10.30 p.m.
OLD TIME AND MODERN
1/6   DANCE   1/6

7.30 p.m. — Every Saturday — 10.30 p.m.
2/6   DANCE   2/6

COME EARLY!!
After Nine O'clock We Cannot Guarantee Admission.
Music by Tommy Willis and his Boys

Advert for activities at The Plaza, Tynemouth. (Shields Daily News)

One of the most popular venues was the Plaza Ballroom, which was in the large seafront Gala Land building in Tynemouth. Throughout 1945, dances were held from 7.30–10.30 pm on a thrice-weekly basis. There were dances, accompanied by Thomas Willis and his Boys, held on a Wednesday and Saturday night, and an old time and modern dance on a Thursday. Prices were 1/6d. on a Wednesday and Thursday and 2/6d. on a Saturday, with customers advised to come early as the venue could not guarantee entrance after 9.00 pm.

Galaland also had an ice rink which catered for those who preferred a more unusual form of entertainment. Evening sessions at 7.00 pm were held on six days of the week (excluding Tuesday), whilst afternoon sessions at 2.30 pm were held on Wednesday, Saturday and Sunday, with admission fees of 6d. for ladies and 1s. for men on Monday to Saturday, and 1s. for ladies and 1/6d. for men on Sunday.

The cinema remained extremely popular with the majority of people in Tynemouth and Wallsend. There were large numbers of picture houses in the area, and people had a wide variety of films which they could see. In North Shields in one April week, for example, people could watch *Winged Victory*, which was the main feature at the

Cinemas and their attractions. (Shields Daily News)

Princes, or Roy Rogers (and Trigger of course) in *The Cowboy and the Senorita* (which was described as an exciting musical comedy western) at the Howard Cinema, *Two-Man Submarine* at the Boro, *Don't Take it to Heart* at the Rex or *Virginia City* at the Albion. In Whitley Bay, the New Coliseum was showing *Twilight Hour*, whilst the Lyric in Howdon was featuring Gene Tierney and Dana Andrews in *Laura*. As well as being entertained, people attending the cinema also caught up with the latest war news through the newsreels.

Sports were also still popular, with welfare and works football leagues being favourite forms of relaxation, whilst there was also the Shields and District Darts League, which was so popular that it had two divisions and fifty-five teams.

Although the screw was being turned on Germany, the men of the RAF continued to take the offensive to the Nazi forces. One of the targets was the enemy shipping which was using the seas around Scandinavia to ferry men and supplies. Based on Stornoway in the Outer Hebrides, several squadrons of RAF aircraft raided the areas around Scandinavia constantly and with great success, sinking many thousand tons of shipping. This task was a dangerous one, with the crews facing threats from enemy aircraft, anti-aircraft fire, the sometimes poor weather conditions and long flights. Shortly after midnight on 24 April, several Halifax bombers from 58 and 502 Squadrons were hunting the Kattegat (the sea between Denmark and Sweden) for the 5,433 ton German vessel *Tubingen*. The ship had been damaged by a 58 Squadron aircraft just five days previously, and was believed to be heading for Flensburg for repairs. One of the 58 Squadron aircraft involved on 24th was Halifax GRII (JP299), piloted by Flight Lieutenant A.T.C. Wilmot-Dear, DFC. His crew included Sergeant Allen Douglas Blakey, a 24-year-old native of Tynemouth. At least two German night-fighters were seen in the area in which the bombers were operating, and one of these, piloted by Oberleutnant Herbert Koch, encountered the Halifax of Flight Lieutenant Wilmot-Dear and his crew, attacking it at approximately 1.20 am. Just twenty minutes later, another 58 Squadron crew reported seeing two burning patches on the sea. It seems clear that Halifax JP299 had been shot down and either crashed into the sea or broken up in mid-air as a result of the night-fighter attack: all nine of the crew were killed.[7]

On 30 April, there was a potentially disastrous incident at Tynemouth Municipal High School when a blaze broke out in the roof of the chemistry room. There were more than 600 pupils in the school at the time, but at the sound of the fire alarm bell the youngsters, led by staff and prefects, filed out of the school in a calm and orderly manner. The prefects of the school's volunteer fire section attempted to fight the fire with hoses until the arrival of the National Fire Service. Brisk winds made the situation worse, and the fire service was forced to draft in units from neighbouring areas in order to prevent the fire from spreading to the rest of the building. Despite the large numbers of fire service units on the scene, the flames continued to spread and several areas of roof collapsed, whilst the firefighting efforts were also hampered by dense smoke.

As each new fire service tender arrived, they were cheered by the crowds of pupils, whilst large groups of onlookers also watched the growing fire, which continued into the night. By all accounts, the school-children were quite happy at the prospect of an impromptu holiday period. The announcement by the headmaster that school was suspended for the day was also met with cheers, as was the fact that no homework was set as many books had been lost. The headmaster rather optimistically told the students they would be expected back at school the next day.

By the afternoon there were twelve fire appliances at the scene, including units from North Shields, Whitley Bay, Blyth, Newcastle and Gateshead. The fire continued in many places and other classrooms had suffered severe damage from water, and it appeared very unlikely that the headmaster would see his wish to resume lessons the next day come true. By late evening much of the blaze had been brought under control (although parts continued to burn), but the damage to the roof was extremely severe, with that over the chemistry block being completely collapsed, whilst other areas of roofing were twisted by the severity of the fire.

The Bevin Boys scheme proved markedly unpopular in Tynemouth and much of Wallsend, where young men were far more eager to obtain work as apprentices in the shipyards. As we have seen, the scheme had provoked the Apprentices Strike in 1944. After the first attempts to direct labour into the mines, there was a rash of prosecutions of young men who refused to undertake work which they found extremely distasteful. The first prosecution in North Shields was of Richard Young (18) of 190 Bridge Road. Mr Young was employed locally as a firewood labourer, earning 35s. per week (30s. of which he gave to his mother) to help support the family, which consisted of his parents and six others. Mr Young had failed to appear at the Cramlington pit to which he had been allocated, arguing in an unsuccessful appeal that he feared he would not earn as much as he currently did. This was shown to be false, as he would in fact have been paid twice as much, but in court he argued that he would be forced to pay for lodgings and pay greater tax on these earnings. He continued that he did not like the idea of underground work and refused to go, and informed the bench that, if forced, he would rather go into the army. The magistrates appear to have been quite sympathetic and fined Mr Young £5, giving him ten weeks to find this amount.

The shipyards were extremely busy, the apprentices having their hands full merely keeping up with the orders. Tyneside shipyards had played a key role in the war effort, and had been responsible for the replacement of over two million tons of shipping from the approximately four million tons of shipping which had been lost. As we have seen, the majority of work in Tyneside yards was concerned with military contracts, but despite this, the yards still produced almost 600,000 tons of merchant shipping during the war. The total number of merchant vessels launched on the Tyne (many of them at Wallsend and North Shields) was seventy-four, but this was outmatched by the eighty-three naval vessels (over 250,000 tons in total) produced solely by Swan Hunter's during the course of the war.

Even in the final year of the war, Swan Hunter's continued to churn out naval vessels. They included the 18,000 ton Colossus Class aircraft carrier HMS *Vengeance*, which was (along with the rest of her class) designed as a disposable warship which would serve only during the war and was estimated to have an active service life of just three years. In the event, the ship did not see action but did sail to Hong Kong, where she became the venue for the surrender of the territory by the Japanese on 3 September. In 1952, *Vengeance* was loaned to the Royal Australian Navy for three years. Once back in Britain, the Royal Navy could find no use for *Vengeance* and she was sold in 1956 to the Brazilian Navy, undergoing a major refit at Rotterdam before being renamed the NAeL *Minas Gerais* and sailing for her new home in January 1961.⁸

Also constructed during the year were the Minotaur Class light cruiser HMS *Superb*, the destroyer HMS *Trafalgar*, cable ship HMS *Bullhead*, the tank landing ship LST *3020*, an oiler named *Olna*, coastal forces depot ship HMS *Derby Haven* and the Loch Class frigate HMS *Loch Cree*.⁹

Downstream of Swan Hunter's, the much smaller yard of Cleland's (Successors) Ltd continued to produce merchant vessels and Admiralty tugs. The yard had a history going back to 1872, but by the early Thirties was mostly employed in repair work and in 1934 had been taken over by the Craggs family, who also owned the Goole Shipbuilding & Repairing Co. Ltd. The war allowed an expansion of the yard, and by 1940 it had two shipbuilding berths and two slipways for repair work. During the course of the war, Cleland's built five coasters, thirteen tugs, a ferry and a barge, but also completed repairs on a great many damaged merchant vessels. This was vitally important

HMS Natal *(formerly HMS* Loch Cree*)*. (Public Domain)

work, and most of the yards along the Tyne also effected repairs on the many ships which suffered damage during the war.

Despite the higher wages being paid to workers in the shipyards, there were still those who engaged in petty theft. In late April, an 18-year-old apprentice caulker and his 15-year-old accomplice were tried for the theft of second-hand clothing and shoes from the Tynemouth Road store of Mr Thomas Wood, a rag collector. Mr Wood had locked up his store the previous afternoon, but on his return the next morning he found the padlock had been broken off and was missing, along with a quantity of clothing and shoes valued at £2. The apprentice, Sidney Thompson of Prudhoe Terrace, had been avoiding going into work, but said that he had begun stealing to make up his wages of £2 in order to deceive his widowed mother into believing he was attending the shipyards. To make matters worse, Thompson was also accused of (and admitted to) stealing woollen rags worth £4 from Mr Wood on a previous occasion, and it was revealed that since December 1940 Thompson had been before the magistrates six times for various offences, including breaking and entering, larceny and shop-breaking. In 1941, he had been sent to an approved school for over a year; upon being released in June 1943 he had found work at Swan Hunter's, but had been missing from work for several weeks. The head of the Netherton Approved School, where Thompson had been placed, spoke on his behalf, saying he had behaved well whilst there and that he thought placing Thompson in the army might be a good idea, telling the magistrates that he could arrange that within the month. The bench told Thompson that his record was very poor and that magistrates had been unduly lenient with him in the past, and sentenced him to one month in prison, expressing the hope that he would be placed in the army after that period. Thompson's young accomplice was referred to Wallsend Juvenile Court.

As a result of this case, two more youngsters were brought before the bench. Andrew Weirs (17), an apprentice fitter at Swan Hunter's, and a juvenile from Wallsend had received woollen rags worth 18s. stolen by Thompson and hidden in Northumberland Park. They had then attempted to sell these items to another second-hand dealer, but had been apprehended. Weirs also had a previous record, having been before the magistrates on four occasions. It was revealed that he was earning 28s. 6d. per week, and was also receiving 10s. per week pocket money from his father, who claimed that he wasn't a bad lad but had started keeping poor company and had been influenced by this. The magistrates fined Weirs 40s. and told his father to pay it from his pocket money.

For many of the families of those men who had been caught up in the fall of Singapore in 1942, news of their loved ones could take a great deal of time to reach them. Many of the men had been taken prisoner by the Japanese and found themselves in the hell of the Burma-Siam railway construction efforts, where approximately 13,000 PoWs died of malnutrition or disease, whilst others were executed by their captors (80,000-100,000 civilians also lost their lives). The North Shields family of Lance Sergeant Matthew Thompson (38) had been awaiting news of their son since 1942, having heard then that he had been taken prisoner, but in July 1945 they learned that he had succumbed to malnutrition in July 1943. Originally from Percy Main, Matthew had been a bricklayer for the Howdon firm of Weir & Sons but had been in the army for nineteen years. His parents still lived at 82 Linskill Street, North Shields.

Lance Sergeant M. Thompson died of malnutrition in a Japanese prison camp. (Shields Evening News)

Despite Tynemouth wardens having served in London during the V-weapon crisis, the people of the capital's boroughs where they had been stationed had not forgotten the efforts of the Tynemouth men and women. In July 1945, letters were published in the local press praising them and expressing sorrow that none of the Tynemouth contingent had been invited to the large parade for the ARP services which was held in London.

Another member of the local ARP wardens received an unexpected gift of a cheque in recognition of her services to the men of 3 Regiment, Maritime Royal Artillery, who had been stationed locally and were based at Kettlewell School in North Shields. Mrs E. Lee of 2 Hamilton Terrace, Tynemouth Road, North Shields, had a son serving abroad with the Durham Light Infantry. She took care of the men of the unit by doing their washing and sewing, as well as advising them on personal matters. She did this throughout the war, and in July the regiment held a meeting at which they expressed the wish to thank Mrs Lee for her generosity and kindness. Mrs Lee had joined the warden service six months before the war began (her husband was also a warden), and had been widely praised for her actions during the aftermath of the Wilkinson's shelter incident in 1941.

One of the features of the general election of July 1945 was the record number of women who became MPs. From almost ninety female candidates, twenty-three were elected (twenty-one of them were Labour candidates), including the Labour candidate for Tynemouth, Miss Grace M. Colman, who was elected with a majority of 3,079. The result was a huge shock locally, as Tynemouth had been a safe seat for the Conservative Party for many years, Sir Alexander West Russell having been MP for the constituency since 1922, with a 6,000 majority before the war. The result was announced shortly after 10.30 am, and was unexpectedly early. In her victory speech, Miss Colman thanked her opponents, but said that she could not thank the Conservative Party as she believed it had spread misinformation about the Labour Party during the campaign. Sir Alexander replied by congratulating Miss Colman, saying that he regretted the result not only for himself but also for outgoing Prime Minister Mr Churchill, 'whose services were now needed so urgently'.[10] Turn-out in the election was 77 per cent, whilst for local men and women serving away from Tynemouth the figure of returned ballots was 85 per cent.

The local Conservatives were notably dismayed, and had the misfortune to schedule a meeting at the Percy Hall on Military Road, North Shields, to discuss the reformation of the Borough of Tynemouth Conservative and Unionist Association for the very night that the election result had been announced. The keynote address was to be given by Sir Alexander Russell, whom it is assumed the Conservatives would have expected to still be their MP.

The local Labour Party was, unsurprisingly, in buoyant mood throughout July and August. A celebratory dance held at The Plaza on Tynemouth seafront on 27 August was well attended and, with musical accompaniment provided by Tommy Willis and his Band, went on until after midnight.

The shift to Labour was reflected across industrial Tyneside, with Labour candidates winning in Wallsend, South Shields, Jarrow and Houghton. In Wallsend, a sitting female MP, Irene Ward, lost her seat to Labour candidate Mr J. McKay, who secured a majority of over 10,000.

The wish to celebrate VJ-Day resulted in at least one young man ending up in court. James W. Beckworth-Smith (18) of 214 Brookland Terrace, New York, was employed as a driver for a West Allotment coal merchant (Frank Cook) and was accused of having stolen petrol and a lorry from the coal merchant's yard (which was locked up for the day) and having driven the lorry around the countryside before returning it to the yard. Beckworth-Smith had been seen by several witnesses driving the lorry with up to twenty other youths onboard, and he admitted having taken both the petrol and the lorry, but claimed that he was using the lorry to collect trees for a celebratory bonfire; he had no third-party insurance.

The bench heard that Beckworth-Smith was no stranger to the courts, having been placed on probation in March 1941 for several cases of housebreaking and stealing from gas meters, and then he had been sentenced to six strokes of the birch just two months later for housebreaking. In August 1941, he was again brought before the courts (this time at Hexham) for housebreaking, theft of money and the theft of a bicycle. This time he was sent to an approved school for almost two years.

After leaving the approved school, Beckworth-Smith found employment with Mr Cook and in July 1944 had been called up but was discharged as his services were no longer needed. Despite Beckworth-Smith's father informing the bench that his son had now gained employment in a local pit, the chairman, Mr Gladstone Walker, told him that the offence was a very serious one and fined him the sum of £4 and banned him from driving for a year.

The newly renamed mining engineering firm of Victor Products (Wallsend) Ltd was obviously a company of some importance to the war effort, and it had been felt in the early months of the war that this firm, along with many others in Wallsend, would be a priority target for the Luftwaffe. Although the Luftwaffe did not manage to put a single bomb on the premises throughout the war (the nearest miss was 200ft away), it became clear with the capture of documents as the Allies advanced through Europe that the Nazis had indeed been aware of the importance of the firm and had marked it out as a priority target. A German bombing manual found on a captured Belgian airfield included photographs and information on the company.

Victor Products (Wallsend) Ltd was in a very encouraging position at the end of the war, which allowed it to become a market leader both nationally and internationally. With a small London office opened to allow contact with export houses and foreign governments, overseas orders began to come in. In the final year of the war, for example, the company produced and exported fifty cycle drilling sets to India.

During the first week of May, it was clear that the Germans were on their last legs and that victory was now very close. Rumours of ceasefires and surrender spread like wildfire throughout the week, and on the night of 7 May more solid news leaked out of Germany's unconditional surrender. People began listening to their wireless sets in the hope of hearing the Prime Minister announce the news officially. Although people were obviously excited and in a joyous mood, the majority of Tynemouth residents accepted the news in a spirit of quiet jubilation. As the evening wore on, people became increasingly excited, but when the official news was broadcast there was a sense of 'disappointment and frustration' that the official celebrations would not start until the following day. The delay was not appreciated, as people had been keyed up to celebrate immediately upon hearing the news, and it led to confusion for many workers over whether or not they should turn in to work the next morning. This seems to have been reported in a rather pernickety way, as most workers would have surely known that the declaration of the days as an official national holiday meant that they would not be required. Nevertheless, local newspapers stated that some workers did turn up, only to be sent home again.

Despite this supposed disappointment, the time allowed meant that premises could be properly decorated. People set to work on this throughout the afternoon, evening and night of 7 May, and by midday on 8 May there were flags and bunting flying from hundreds of local buildings. At the Town Hall, the front of the building was lavishly decorated with streamers and bunting, whilst over the entrance was a large Union Jack flag in a circular plaque, accompanied by the crown and the flags of Great Britain, the USA and Russia.

Queues quickly formed at bakers and grocers shops throughout the borough as people bought provisions for the anticipated parties, with many running out of supplies. The grocers remained open until noon on VE-Day, but were closed the next day, whilst the butchers were closed for both days. Public transport ran to schedule, but on the second day of the holiday followed a reduced Sunday timetable, whilst the Post Office was closed on VE-Day but reopened the following morning.

At North Shields, much was made of 11-month-old Jean Fenwick, of 77 Coronation Street. Jean had been born the day after D-Day, with what was described as a V for Victory-shaped birthmark on her forehead. It was claimed that this mark had become more prominent in the run up to VE-Day, and her father, Petty Officer G. Fenwick, and his wife were particularly proud of this prophetic mark borne by their young daughter.

The Mayor of Tynemouth, Councillor T. Duff, wrote a short piece in the *Shields Daily News* giving thanks for the victory in Europe, but cautioning people that the celebrations must be short as British forces – and indeed men and women from Tynemouth – were still engaged in the war against Japan and needed every support that could be given. He then expressed the sympathy of the borough for those who had lost loved ones in the struggle against the Nazis. The Mayor went on to thank the armed forces and their commanders, the King and the Prime Minister, before expressing his thanks to the local civil defence, ARP, fire and police services, and finally for the 'workers in our factories, to those engaged in shipbuilding and ship repairing, and to all who have contributed in any way'.[11]

The *Shields Daily News* ran a banner headline on VE-Day and featured front page photographs of several commanders and prominent politicians (both British and Allied), of whom it claimed 'THEY HAVE WON BACK EUROPE'S FREEDOM'. Interestingly, given his controversial post-war lack of acknowledgement, the picture of Sir Arthur Harris was prominent in the line-up, accompanied by the caption 'His bombs paved the way'.

Several pages of the paper were given over to description of the war that Tynemouth had experienced. The newspaper gave extensive praise to the men and women who had served in the forces, the Merchant Navy, industry and the ARP and civil defence services. The report claimed that, at least in Tynemouth, people had been well aware of the approaching war, and that the nucleus of an effective ARP service had been formed well in advance. This contrasted with the experience of several other nearby areas, most notably Whitley Bay. After giving descriptions of several incidents and praising the generous nature of the people of the borough for donating so often to wartime charities, the article concluded by saying now that the war in Europe was over, Tynemouth Borough and its residents could 'honestly look back on its record with pride and satisfaction', but cautioned that there were still many sons of Tynemouth engaged against the Japanese.

On VE-Day itself, the Mayor gave an address from the steps of the Town Hall at 5.00 pm, whilst there were thanksgiving and memorial services held at all churches in the borough. A large open-air dance was also organized at Front Street in Tynemouth on 9 May from 8.00-11.00 pm, with music provided by the Jack Moor Band. The children of the borough must have been particularly pleased, as their holiday lasted a day longer because the Thursday following the VE-Day holidays was Ascension Day, so they would not return to school until 11 May.

Unfortunately, both days of the holiday were marred by bursts of rain but, despite this, nothing doused the ardour and enthusiasm of the revellers. The Mayor, after his speech outside the Town Hall, read the proclamation of victory and prayers of thanksgiving. This was attended by over 200 people, despite the pouring rain. In most places celebrations went on until the early hours, with the weather improving in the evening. On the second day, the well-attended open-air dance went ahead in conditions of sunshine and showers, with revellers spilling out onto other streets in Tynemouth. Bonfires were carried on from the day before (despite wartime laws forbidding them) and, once again, many effigies of Hitler (sometimes wrapped in a white flag) and, in at least one case, Lord Haw-Haw were burned upon them. Ship and works hooters were sounded throughout the day with deafening effect, although some complained that they could hardly hear the Prime

Minister on the radio because of them! The sunshine on the second day of the holiday had enticed large numbers of people to journey from Newcastle to the coast, and the Coast Road was busy with cyclists all day long as the joyous scenes of the first day of the holiday continued throughout the second. Many revellers once again did not stop until the early hours, with large numbers of people reportedly making their way home after 4.00 am. Despite this, the majority of workers turned up for work the next day, and the attendance at the local shipyards was seen as very encouraging. In many working-class neighbourhoods, people clubbed together and organized their own impromptu street parties to celebrate the German capitulation.

We have already seen how the controlled prices and scarcity of some varieties of fish had led to accusations of profiteering and a proliferating black market in the commodity. Whilst the VE-Day celebrations were taking place on 9 May, there were obviously some people who, despite the holiday, were still working. Equally, there were some who were working illicitly with an eye on making a profit. At around 8.30 am on that day, the Secretary of the Trawler Owners' Association, Mr A.E. Atkinson, was walking past the Quay Master's cabin at the entrance to North Shields Fish Quay when he noticed a man putting a box of fish and two empty boxes onto a trolley and wheeling them off. Stopping the man – fish porter William Robson (68) of 9 Dockwray Square, North Shields – he questioned him as to where he was taking the fish. Robson at first said that he was taking them for his employer, a fish merchant, but upon further questioning admitted that he had found the fish and was removing them himself. He asked Mr Atkinson to keep quiet about it and attempted to continue, but was prevented from doing so and the police were summoned. After being arrested, Robson again said that he had simply found the fish mixed in with the empty boxes. Appearing before Tynemouth magistrates the next day, he admitted stealing (but only by finding) the fish – 1¼ stone of plaice worth 18s. – and upon questioning from the bench admitted that he was intending to sell it. Robson had been before the bench some fifty-four times previously (mainly for drunkenness), and he had been acquitted of a similar charge the previous year when he had again claimed that he found the fish. The bench had little difficulty in reaching a guilty verdict, fining Robson 20s. and giving him one month in which to pay.

Despite the general happiness that pervaded the area during the week of the VE-Day celebrations, those who had lost loved ones must have viewed the parties with a strong sense of regret. Whilst the 10 May edition of the *Shields Daily News* reported on the celebrations on its front page, it also provided the name of a local man who had recently been confirmed as having lost his life with the Merchant Navy. Messroom steward John William Cawley (23) of 53 Briarwood Avenue, North Shields, had actually been killed whilst serving on the MV *British Reliance* in May 1944.[12] His death only being confirmed a year later, combined with the fact that his body was brought back to Tynemouth for burial, implies that his remains had washed ashore some time much later.

Just nine days after VJ-Day in August, Tynemouth and Wallsend councils were already well-advanced in their preparations for the post-war rebuilding programme which would be necessary. Many plans had been made by the authorities for new housing developments and construction, although materials could be hard to obtain. The local press blamed official muddle and inefficiency for the so-far slow progress. The *Shields Daily News* claimed that hundreds of thousands of skilled construction workers were being held in the armed forces, taking part in pointless drills and duties, whilst the best weather for construction was ebbing away. It also blamed official muddle for the poor supply of building materials, stressing that the building workers themselves were keen to get on with the job of reconstructing Britain.

For many, however, thoughts still remained with the war. Many men in the forces were still serving, and their families remained anxious over when they might be reunited. For those with relatives in the Far East, the opinions expressed in the press by some churchmen on the way the war with Japan had been ended must have aroused some anger and considerable contempt. Just days after the end of the war, a speech by the Bishop of Chelmsford, Dr Henry Wilson, was featured in the local press. In it he said that the dropping of atomic bombs on Japan was 'quite impossible' to justify, saying that the Allies had acted in the same manner as the Germans in indiscriminately slaughtering civilians, only 'to a degree a hundred times greater than did the Nazis'. This statement attracted great criticism from people in the area, especially those with relatives who had fought against the

Some of the crew of HMS Stalker *in the Far East.* (*Shields Daily News*)

A group of North and South Shields men at present serving in the Far East on H.M.S. Stalker. Front row (left to right): P.O. Wray, Bamboro Terrace, North Shields; Sub-Lieut. Marvell, Redburn View, North Shields; Sub-Lieut. Trotter, Wallsend; P.O. Sheader, Alice Street, South Shields; Ass. Cook Kimber, Linskill Street, North Shields. Back row (left to right): Fireman Blakey, Ord Avenue, Rosehill; Leading Photographer Wood, South Shields; A.B. Armstrong, Woodlea Crescent, North Shields; Fireman Stege, The Ridges, North Shields.

Japanese. For those with relatives who would have faced a bloody struggle to invade the mainland of Japan, the overwhelming feeling was that the Japanese had deserved everything they got and that the dropping of the bombs had saved a great many lives of Allied soldiers, sailors and airmen.

Although the blackout had been lifted, it was becoming clear to the council at Tynemouth that the seven years of blackout conditions had caused an 'enormous amount of damage' to street light fittings.[13] Shortages of available labour were impacting on the plans to improve the lighting in the borough, but for now the streetlights remained operating in summer conditions (i.e. one in every two lights were operating), but this was thought to be unsuitable with winter approaching.

The announcement of the Japanese surrender formally brought about the end of the war, and preparations for celebrations similar to those which had marked VE-Day were quickly begun. Unfortunately, the weather again intervened, a bitter wind and heavy rain washing out the majority of public celebrations. The planned open-air dance on Front Street in Tynemouth was a non-starter given the weather, and few people were about to hear the King's broadcast over the loudspeakers which lined the street. The busiest part of the street was outside the Carlton Cinema, where a small group was waiting for the late show under the canopy. The effort made to floodlight Tynemouth Castle went to waste, as there were few people willing to brave the awful weather. Most people celebrated in their own home. The largest crowds assembled to hear the Mayor of Tynemouth read a peace proclamation outside the Town Hall, and a crowd, the majority wearing raincoats and gumboots, did assemble at the Corporation tip at Billy Mill for the borough's VJ-Day bonfire. Fireworks played a large role in the evening's celebrations, with almost every street in Tynemouth, North Shields and Wallsend (as well as smaller communities such as Shiremoor and New York) setting off some sort of display.

Unfortunately, there was also a tragedy in the early hours of VJ-Day, when 11-year-old Mary Glass was killed on Shields quay. The

The Mayor of Tynemouth on VJ-Day. (Shields Evening News)

young girl had been in the company of her older sister and some others when she was shot in the back of the head and, despite the efforts of naval ratings, killed instantly. The shot had come from an armed vessel which was docked on the Tyne, and the police believed that a group of boys had got onto the ship and were messing around when they accidently discharged a weapon.

The next day brought no improvement in the weather, continuous rain again marring the celebrations. However, the people of Tynemouth were determined to celebrate, and the open-air dancing went ahead in Front Street. The revellers were also treated to a fancy-dress parade and a display of sword dancing. The Mayor addressed the crowds of celebrants, saying that now they had won the war it was up to them to win the peace and do everything they could to provide better housing for the people of the borough. Despite the celebrations in Tynemouth,

The thanksgiving parade in Tynemouth. (Shields Evening News)

the rest of the borough remained quiet, many people held their own house parties.

On Sunday, 19 August, Tynemouth held a thanksgiving parade to celebrate the victory over Japan and the end of the war. Hundreds of people lined the route despite the drizzle. Led by the Backworth Colliery Band, the parade consisted of representatives from all of the armed forces, the local council, cadets, boy scouts, sea rangers, girl guides and other youth groups. Oddly, the civil defence organizations were not a part of the parade, although several members did take part individually, along with members of the British Legion, WVS and other local groups.

After VE-Day and VJ-Day, it would seem that some fundraising efforts in Tynemouth Borough became less popular, the local press reporting with some concern that the last week in July had seen a fall of over 50 per cent in the amounts invested in the Tynemouth National Savings scheme (whereby people could invest in Savings Certificates, Defence Bonds or through Trustee and Post Office Saving Bank deposits). Even so, the amount for the week in question was still £16,928 (over £670,000 today) and the movement, which had begun in November 1939, had been overwhelmingly successful. Contributions to the scheme totalled £7,845,646 (almost £311 million today), an average of £138 13s. 3d. (almost £5,500) for every resident of the borough.

Despite the numbers of men and women from Tynemouth Borough who were serving abroad, the Tynemouth Welcome Home Fund was also struggling to make much headway by late August. At the end of the month, the total amount raised stood at only £828 10s. 4d. (less than £33,000 today). The donors came from across society, with local businesses, church organizations and ARP services at the forefront of the fund-raising effort.

As has been mentioned, the area had been a high priority target for the Luftwaffe due to the vital industries along the banks of the Tyne. Tynemouth and Wallsend suffered greater proportionately than areas such as Newcastle, as a result of both the concentration of heavy industry in the area and the inaccuracy of the Luftwaffe, which, even when targeting Newcastle, often dropped its bombs on Tynemouth and Wallsend as an easier target to reach than the slightly further inland and better defended Newcastle.

All of these factors resulted in Tynemouth Borough being one of the most heavily bombed areas in the North-East. Up until late October 1944, the area had endured 253 air-raid alerts and had been bombed on at least thirty-one separate occasions. Many of these alerts turned out to be false alarms, but they still had a morale and mental effect on the population, leading to sleepless and sleep-disturbed nights and increased levels of tension. Whilst the human tragedies suffered were horrible enough, the damage to property and the infrastructure of the area was severe. Tynemouth Borough suffered the loss of over 5 per cent of its rateable property value, and as a result of this the area received an allocation of an emergency supply of steel to be used for reconstruction purposes. Although the main targets of the Luftwaffe in the early period of the war were the industrial concerns in the area, the inaccuracy of their bombing meant that damage to these industries was actually fairly light. Whilst some industrial buildings needed to be replaced, there were few periods when production was seriously affected. The damage to the infrastructure of the area was far more severe. A survey of the catering facilities and schools in Tynemouth Borough showed that damage to these facilities alone would cost over £18,636 to repair (over £738,113 today).

Notes
1. The *U-1055* was declared missing presumed lost on 23 April 1945 and has never been found; all hands perished.
2. Group Captain Denys Edgar Gillam, DFC (and bar), DSO (and two bars), ended the war as Group Captain Ops of 84 Group and left the RAF in October 1945. He died in 1991.
3. Other officers present included: Majors W. Bentley, J.W. Randell, H.S. Hemsley, T. Coulson, J. Blakey and Carne, Captain Campbell and Captain R.B.C. Hutchinson.
4. There is some confusion over whether Tommy had joined the RN or remained as a member of the NAAFI, but the most reliable sources name him, by the time of his death, as a leading seaman, meaning he was a member of the RN.
5. *Shields Evening News*, 30 July 1945, p.2.
6. Just a fortnight later, the last known flights by manned enemy aircraft were made over Britain, with ten raiders causing minor damage over southern England.
7. The crew consisted of: F/L Arthur Thomas Charles Wilmot-Dear, DFC (pilot); F/L Walter Henry Hayden Hanks (a Canadian serving in the RAF); F/O Richard Bruce Livingstone (RAAF); W/O John Ian Murray; F/S George William Ramsay; Sgt Allen Douglas Blakey; F/S Ivor James Arthur Pidgen;

F/O Victor Godfrey Watling; and F/S Ronald Francis Watts. No bodies were ever found, and all are commemorated on the Runnymede Memorial to the missing. F/L Wilmot-Dear had earned his DFC just twelve days before his death by attacking and sinking the 5,273 T ship *Ostland*. Ironically, the *Tubingen* had already been attacked and sunk by a 502 Squadron Halifax an hour before JP299 was lost.

8. *HMS Vengeance* (*NAeL Minas Gerais*) became the longest serving aircraft carrier in history and was not decommissioned until 2001 and being broken up in 2004. A service life of 56 years, not too bad for a ship with an estimated life-span of three years!
9. HMS *Loch Cree* was immediately transferred to the South African Navy and renamed HMSAS *Natal*, and distinguished herself by sinking a U-boat (*U-714*) off St Abbs Head just hours after she was commissioned.
10. *Shields Daily News*, 26 July 1945, p.1.
11. *Shields Daily News*, 8 May 1945, p.3.
12. This seems rather odd, as the *British Reliance* had in fact been sunk in 1941. I am assuming that another replacement vessel had been given the same name.
13. *Shields Daily News*, 24 August 1945, p.5.

Conclusion

As the area and its residents adjusted to the return to peace after seven years of wartime conditions, there were many adjustments to be made. As we have seen, there was significant damage to property in the area and the local authorities quickly began to develop plans for the redevelopment of the area. This was to prove both costly and difficult, as materials and qualified workers were in short supply.

As well as damage to property, there was also substantial damage to some of the infrastructure of the area. Not all of this was down to that caused by the enemy. The streetlights in Tynemouth Borough, for example, were found to have been damaged by the enforced blackout of the previous years, and many had to be replaced along with the power supplies. Water mains had also suffered damage from bombs and from neglect during the war, and these proved costly to repair too.

For the industries on the Tyne, the pattern of the First World War was sadly repeated, as orders for naval ships which were on the books at numerous shipyards were cancelled and orders with armaments and engineering firms declined rapidly. Many of the firms in the area had been forced to adjust to the construction of war materiel, and now faced hefty bills in order to return to their original production patterns. Likewise, many of the men and women who had found employment in the industries during the war faced an uncertain peacetime future in which it was fully expected that the industries would once again face a precarious time in the aftermath of the war. Similarly, the return to peacetime conditions meant that the miners of the area also faced a return to the uncertainties of possible conflict with owners and a reduction in their power.

The area had seen several industrial strikes, which demonstrated that even at a time of national crisis many of the workers were unwilling to see their rights violated, and that they could organize themselves effectively despite opposition from bodies which, traditionally, would have supported them and given them some organizational structure.

Despite this, the industries of Tynemouth and Wallsend, especially the shipyards, mines and engineering works, had made a very substantial contribution to the war effort.

As the people of Tynemouth and Wallsend looked to an uncertain future, they could, however, reflect on the fact that they had indeed played a major role in the victory. Many young men and women had paid the ultimate price, losing their lives in the struggle (both at home and abroad), whilst others had worked longer and longer hours in labour-intensive jobs in order to provide vital materiel for the war effort. Those at home had suffered through the rigours of life in wartime Britain, coping with the blackout, the threat of enemy bombing, rationing and lack of leisure time and opportunities, but could proudly point to the fact that they had, in the words of the time, taken it.

Index

Air raids, 75–6, 99, 111–12, 131, 210–11
  anti-aircraft defences, 28, 30, 65–6, 68, 71, 76, 90
  casualties of, 54, 57–9, 63–4, 70, 93–4
    Anderson, Alice Sarah Jane, 57
    Armstrong, Denis Thomson, 99
    Baird (aka Morrison), Brian, 57
    Baird (aka Morrison), Mary, 57
    Brunton, Robert, 28
    Brunton, Richard Strake, 28
    Burns, Doris Elizabeth, 28
    Cavener, Edward, 59
    Cavener, Georgina Davy, 59
    Cavener, Minnie, 59
    Charlton, Eric, 66
    Charlton, Flora, 66
    Ewbank, Doris, 56
    Grant, Charles Edward, 64
    Matthews, William Henry, 59
    Morrison, Clara, 57
    police and civil defence workers, 54, 59, 64, 70, 93
    Scott, John Simpson, 66
    Scott, Margaret, 66
    Scott, Robert, 66
    Simpson, Hutchinson H., 64
    Sutton, Edward William, 56
    Thompson, Arthur John, 59
  Cullercoats, 28, 31–3, 53, 66, 70–1, 77–8, 99, 112, 115, 130, 141–2, 160
  Howdon, 30
    see also Townsley
  Monkseaton, 17, 28, 89–90, 98
    West Monkseaton High School, first aid post at, 9
  New York, 27–30, 64, 130
    Jackson's farm, bomb damage at, 28
    Murton school, 129, 130
    Robin Hood public house, 28
  North Shields, 28–30, 53–64, 66–7, 70, 111–12
    Callaghan, Joseph, 61
    Furse, Able Seaman William G., 29, 46
    gas works, fire at, 61
    Moor Park hospital, 29–30
    timber yards fire, 60
    Wilkinson shelter disaster, 68–70
  Percy Main, 66
  Shiremoor, 27, 66
  smoke generators, 49
  troops, use of, 60
  Tynemouth Borough, 26–32, 48–9, 53–67, 71, 92–3, 99, 191
  Wallsend, 26–7, 31, 53–4, 66–7, 92–4
    damage to shipyards and engineers, 30–1
  West Allotment, 66, 93
  Whitley Bay, 28, 68, 71
  'Z' rocket batteries, 53
    development of, 53
Air Raid Precautions Service, 22–5, 30, 48, 89–90, 91, 179, 199–200
  blackout;
    lifting of, 207
    relaxation of, 172–3
  gas and decontamination squads, 24, 57
  Grand Parade first aid post, bomb damage to, 31
  initial recruitment, 8–10

King, Patrick;
   award of George Medal, 26
   lack of enthusiasm for, 23
Lee, Ellen, 69, 199–200
NAAFI catering;
   appeal for female volunteers, 99
Preston hospital (first aid
   headquarters), 9–10
   severely damaged by bombing, 54–7
   rescue squads, 10–11, 57
      rumour mongers, reputation of, 73
   rest and feeding centres, 25–6, 65
      see also Women's Voluntary Service
Rex Cinema warden post, damaged by bombing, 64
Shotten, Stan, 24–5
sirens, 17
   training of, 22, 24–5
   Whitley Bay Control Room, 48
   winding down of, 179
youths;
   employment as messengers, 48, 91
   problems with, 48
Air Training Corps, 91, 115
Aliens, 44–5, 94–6
   attitudes towards, 20–1
   foreign seamen, 79–83, 93–6
   internment of, 20
Armstrong, George, life saving award, 76
   see also Mudd, John Cuthbert, life saving award
Army;
   casualties;
      Angus, Lt Keith, 136
      Cole, Dvr Peter, 178
      Mander, Pte James, 176
      McLean, Cpl William Thompson, 176, 181
      McMullen, Pte Patrick, 146–7
      Nicholson, Tpr James Norman, 172

      Sneddon, Tpr Alex, 178, 181
      Thompson, L/Sgt, 199
   prisoners of war, 199
      Wilson, Sgt William Langton, 142
Army Cadet Corps, 91
Atomic bomb, dropping of, 206–207
Auxiliary Fire Service (AFS), 10, 30
   Beaconsfield House station, bomb damage to, 31

Banks;
   curtailing of hours, 16–17
Battle of Britain, 41–2
Bevin boys scheme;
   opposition to, 195–6
   see also Industrial Unrest, apprentice strike
Black, Alderman T., 105
Boy Scouts, 134
Boys' Brigade, 91

Charities, 142, 150–1, 210
   Aid to Greece fund, 109–11
   Aid to Russia fund, 77
      paper salvage in aid of, 77
   donation of metal goods, 41
   Red Cross, 151, 190
   Russian Red Cross, Mayor's appeal fund, 77–8
   Salute the Soldier Week, 151–62
   Spitfire Fund, 41
   Tynemouth Tanks for Attack Campaign, 91
   Tynemouth Warships Week, 78–9
   Wings for Victory Week, 114–20, 121–2, 124–5
Charles Crofton & Co. Ltd., 2, 22, 134, 201–202
   female workers at, 88
   wartime production, 21–2
   Victor Products, renamed as, 170
Christ Church School, North Shields, 12
Christmas, 17–18

INDEX 217

Cinemas, 18, 64, 193–4
  Albion, the, 193
  Boro, the, 193
  Princes Theatre, 193
Colonial Rest House, North Shields, 93–6, 108
Crime;
  alcohol related, 191–2
    Dean, Albert Frank, naval rating, 145–6
    Dinsdale, Norman, 88–9
    drunk and disorderly, 45, 88–9
    Herbert, Ernest, 88–9
    Lucas, Pte Robert, 146
    Miller, Ronald, 88–9
    Thompson, Robert Mark, 146
    Usher, William, naval rating, 145–6
  blackout offences, 43–5, 79, 90
    Bennett, Lily, 90–1
    Goodinson, William, 79
    Klein, Florence, 43–4
    Macciochi, Thomasina, 90
    Mudditt, Henry, 44
    Yamada, Alice, 44
  house breaking, 198
  juveniles, and, 122–4
  manslaughter;
    Lavender, Gunner, 191–2
  murder;
    Karpathios, Spiros, 106–107
  theft, 42–3, 122–4, 128–9, 146, 198
    Beckworth-Smith, James W., 201
    James, Henry, 128–9
    Robson, William, 205
    Thompson, Sydney, 198
    Tunmore, Charles, 42–3
    Weirs, Andrew, 198–9
  vandalism;
    to air raid shelters, 111
  wartime laws, infractions of, 43
    Alsop, Special Constable Joseph R., 43
    Gonsales, John Longton, 89
    Holland, John Turnbull, 45–6
    Johansen, Einar A.W.E., 44
    Neilsen, Ebbe B., 44
    Persson, Osten, 89
    Stephenson, George Sidney, 131–2
    Weiss, Blanka, 44–5
    Young, Richard, 196
  wounding, 124
    Jonathan, Alfred Percy, 79–83
    Kennedy, James, 80–1

Dance halls;
  Gala Land, 193
  Plaza, the, 192
Duff, Cllr T., 204–205, 209
Dunkirk, 21

Empire Youth Rally, 91
Evacuation, 11–16
  destinations;
    Belford, 13–14
    Bellingham, 13–14
    Haltwhistle, 13
    Hexham, 13
    Morpeth, 13–14
    Norham, 13
    Rothbury, 13–14
    Tweedsmouth, 14
    Wooler, 13–14

Fishing industry, 1, 5–6, 32, 76, 89, 91–2, 126, 182, 190–2, 205
  G.R. Purdy Trawlers Ltd, 6
  Jarman, William Charles, 92
  McRuvie, Skipper David Pawse, 92
  Messrs R. Hastie & Sons, 5, 182
    Dougal, Skipper Jimmy, 182
  Messrs R. Irvin & Sons, 76, 92, 182
    Ben Screel, trawler, 92
  Rutherford Bros., 6
  T.B. Bilton & Sons Ltd., 89
  Trawler Owners' Association, 205
France, battle of;
  Metcalfe, Gnr Robert Noble, 21
Frater, Cllr G.I., 91

Gas masks, 16
  inspection of, 12, 142–3
Gee, Cllr Harry, 15–16, 24
General election, 194–5, 200–201
Girl Guides, 134

Hogg, Cllr J.W. 163
Holidays at Home, 98–9, 129–31, 170–1
Home Guard (previously Local Defence Volunteers), 96–7, 130–1, 143–5, 155–6, 170, 184–7
  ARP and, 30, 40–1
  Billy Mill observation post, 40–1
  formation of, 33, 36–40
  Gallilee, Mr W., 40
  Holmes, Col Stanley, 39, 43–4, 143, 184–7
  lack of equipment, 39–40, 72
  reasons for volunteering, 37
  stand-down of, 184–7
  training of, 40, 72–3, 98
  women and, 37–8, 97–8
    Whitley Bay & Monkseaton women's home defence, 98
  'Z' batteries, manning of by Home Guard, 97, 144–5
Howdon, 1–2

Industrial unrest, 71–2, 102–106, 154–5, 213–14
  apprentices strike, 163–70
    Davy, James William, 164, 169
    Haston, James Ritchie, 170
    Keen, Angel Rosalie, 170
    Lee, Lambert Heaton, 169–70
    Smith, T. Dan, 164, 169
    Tearse, Rawling, 169–70
  Communist Party and, 106–107, 164
  Independent Labour Party and, 164
  Parsons Steam Turbine Co., 102
  'Total Time' strike, 103–106
Industry, 1–6, 96, 204, 210
  coal, 1–4, 49, 134, 163–4, 201

  engineering, 1–4, 6, 31, 38, 102–103, 125, 213–14
    see also Charles Crofton & Co. Ltd.
  fishing see Fishing Industry
  shipbuilding see Shipbuilding
  strikes see Industrial Unrest
  timber, 1, 3–4, 54–6, 60–1

Lambert, Sir Arthur, 24
Laws, Cllr P.M., 177
Laws, Lt Peter Malcolm, wounded and awarded MC, 177
Licensed trade, 8

Mayo, Cllr Joseph, 104–105
Merchant Navy;
  Moffitt, Chief Engineer Sydney Goss, 183
  SS *Maja*, 183–4
  see also Tyne, River
Minto, G.U. 'Charlie' see Colonial Rest House
Mudd, John Cuthbert, life saving award, 76
  see also Armstrong, George, life saving award
Murray, Cllr G.C., 109

National Fire Service (NFS), 111, 195
  Dixon, William Henry Simmonds, death of, 111
New York village, 27
  New Year's dance at, 77
North Shields;
  Easter parade, 112
  economy of, 3–7
  Ridges estate;
    conditions at, 188–9
    resentment from residents, 189–90
Norway, fall of, 20

Parsons Steam Turbine Co., 102
Percy Main, 12

Post-war planning, 141, 206, 207, 211, 213–14
Tyne tunnel, 89
Preston cemetery, 21

Queen Victoria School, North Shields, 14

Rationing, 170
  petrol, 17, 98
  Tynemouth Food Control Committee;
    shop opening hours, and, 17–18
Richardson Dees School, Wallsend, 14
Royal Air Force, 16, 21
  Bomber Command, 120, 125–6, 137, 147–50, 179–80
  public support for, 120–1, 147
  casualties;
    Blakey, Sgt Allen Douglas, 194, 211
    Dron, Cpl C.P., 138–9
    Forster, Sgt Douglas George, 147–8, 180
    Forsyth, Sgt William Burton, 179
    Gibson, PO George Brian, 136–7
    Goulbourn, Sgt Jack William, 148–9, 180
    Goulden, Flt Sgt Thomas, 125
    Goulden, Sgt Donald, 125–6, 139
    Hobbis, Sqd Ldr Dudley Ormston, 137–8
    Mander, Sgt Reuben Matthew, 78, 107, 176
    McFadden, Sgt Terrence Christopher, 150, 180
    Pigg, FO Charles Harrison, 149, 180
    Purves, Flt Sgt Thomas Dowens, 162
    Renwick, Sgt Richard Alan, 149–50, 180
    Rowntree, Sgt Matthew, 180, 181
    Williamson, Sgt Arthur Fenwick, 137

Coastal Command, 125, 194
Fighter Command, 125
Gillam, Group Capt Denys Edgar, 21, 41–2, 47, 73, 76–7, 162, 177–8, 183, 211
Royal Fleet Auxiliary (RFA);
  RFA Ennerdale, 49, 52, 73
Royal Naval Reserve (RNR), 16
  Armstrong, Robert (Skipper), 19, 126–7, 140
  trawlermen, 1, 32
    resentment towards those who did not join, 190
  trawlers, use as minesweepers, 32
    Clay, AS Henry, 76, 107
    HMT *Clyne Castle*, 76
    HMT *Derby County*, 126, 128
    HMT *Ethel Taylor*, sinking of, 32
    HMT *Kingston Crystal*, 126–7
    HMT *Lilac*, 127–8
Royal Naval Volunteer Reserve (RNVR), 16
  casualties;
    Keys, Sub-Lt Kenneth, 176
    Ward, Lt Donald Bewick, awarded MBE, 182
Royal Navy (RN);
  Armstrong, Second Mate Ralph William, 101–102
  Brown, Tommy, 211
    death of, 108, 187–9
    recovery of enigma documents and award of George Cross, 100
  casualties;
    Gilpin, PO Ralph William, 84–5
  Dougal, Seaman Gnr William Crawford Black, awarded DSM, 182
  Judge, AS Stanley, mentioned in dispatches, 182
  Kitcat, Cdr Charles Arthur de Winton, 141–2
  losses;
    HMS *Cyrus*, 176

HMS *Patia*, 67
HMS *Somali*, 83–5
Peterson, PO Daniel Dixon,
    awarded DSM, 182
ships built on Tyne;
    HMS *Anson*, 85
    HMS *Bolebroke*, 85, 87
    HMS *Border*, 85, 87
    HMS *Bullfinch*, 33, 36
    HMS *Bullfrog*, 173–4
    HMS *Bullhead*, 197
    HMS *Calpe*, 49–50, 73
    HMS *Cyrus*, 175–6
    HMS *Derby Haven*, 197
    HMS *Edinburgh*, 7, 18
    HMS *Eridge*, 49, 53, 73
    HMS *Eskimo*, 84
    HMS *Exmoor*, 49–50, 73
    HMS *Farndale*, 49, 51, 73
    HMS *Gambia*, 85
    HMS *Grenville*, 133, 140
    HMS *Grove*, 85, 87, 108
    HMS *Hambledon*, 33–4
    HMS *Heythrop*, 49, 73
    HMS *Holderness*, 33, 35
    HMS *Hursley*, 49, 51
    HMS *Illustrious*, 73–4
    HMS *Janus*, 8, 18
    HMS *Kashmir*, 7
    HMS *Khartoum*, 7–8, 18
    HMS *Lamerton*, 49, 52, 73
    HMS *Loch Cree*, 197, 212
    HMS *Loch Morlich*, 173–4, 181
    HMS *Loch Shin*, 173, 181
    HMS *Manchester*, 73–4
    HMS *Mauritius*, 33–4
    HMS *Melbrake*, 85, 87, 108
    HMS *Mendip*, 33, 35, 47
    HMS *Meynell*, 33, 36, 47
    HMS *Modbury*, 85
    HMS *Newfoundland*, 86
    HMS *Petard*, 99–101, 108
    HMS *Portchester Castle*, 134, 140
    HMS *Quality*, 85–6
    HMS *Queensborough*, 85
    HMS *Rushen Castle*, 173, 175, 181
    HMS *Shrewsbury Castle*, 173, 181
    HMS *Somali*, 83–4
    HMS *St Margarets*, 173
    HMS *Superb*, 197
    HMS *Tartar*, 8, 18
    HMS *Trafalgar*, 197
    HMS *Tuscan*, 134
    HMS *Tyrian*, 133
    HMS *Vengeance*, 196–7, 212
    HMS *Vigilant*, 85
    HMS *Vindex*, 132, 140
    HMS *Virago*, 134
    LST *3019*, 173–4
    LST *3020*, 197
Ships, other;
    HMS *Stalker*, 207
    Stark, Chief Engineman Peter
        W.M., awarded DSM, 182
    Vine, Lt Colin Frank, awarded
        DSC, 182

Seaton Delaval, 26
Shiremoor, 26–7, 166, 208
    modern school, at, 27
    James Avenue, bomb damage at, 27
    Louisa Street, bomb damage at, 67
    Whitley Road, bomb damage at, 27
Shipbuilding, 83–5, 99–100, 127–8, 131–4, 162–3, 196–9
    see also Royal Navy; ships built on Tyne
    Cleland's (Successors) Ltd., 197–8
    Swan Hunters, 1–2, 7–8, 33–6, 47, 49–52, 73–4, 83–7, 131–4, 162–3, 173–4, 196–7
    Wallsend Slipway & Engineering Co., 49, 127–8
Slums, vi, 189–90

Territorial Army, 16, 21
Townsley family (Howdon);
    triplets, 31

Tyne, River;
  importance as a port, 31
  minelaying off, 31–2, 92–3
  ships sunk off;
    minesweeping trawler *Ethel Taylor*, 32
    MV *Jolly Girls*, 33
    SS *Brabo*, 83
    SS *British Officer*, 32–3, 46
    SS *Empire Knoll*, 49
    SS *Oslofjord*, 32–3, 46–7
    SS *Poznan*, 83
    tug *Hercules*, 32
Tynemouth Borough;
  economy of, vi–vii, 1
  hurricane at, 183–4
  municipal high school;
    fire at, 195
  New Year celebrations at, 75–6, 109, 141

VE-Day, 202, 206
  celebrations, 202–206
VJ-Day;
  celebrations, 207–10
  tragedy on, 208–209
Vickers Armstrong, 9

Walker, Mr Gladstone, 41
  contributions to charity, 77
Wallsend;
  economy of, vi–vii, 1–2, 7
Welch's confectionery factory;
  donations to charity, 78
Whitley Bay;
  medical services at, 22
  refusal of business owners to supply ARP members, 25
Women's Junior Air Corps, 91
Women's Voluntary Service (WVS), 25, 90